# ACTs420NOW

*For We Cannot Stop Speaking About
What We Have Seen and Heard*

# ACTs420NOW

*For We Cannot Stop Speaking About*
*What We Have Seen and Heard*

## marta e. greenman

REDEMPTION
PRESS

Published by Redemption Press, PO Box 427, Enumclaw, WA 98022. Toll Free (844) 2REDEEM (273-3336)

Redemption Press is honored to present this title in partnership with the author. The views expressed or implied in this work are those of the author. Redemption Press provides our imprint seal representing design excellence, creative content and high quality production.

All Scripture quotations, unless otherwise indicated, are taken from the *New American Standard Bible,* © 1960, 1962, 1963, 1968, 1971, 1972, 1973, 1975, 1977, 1995 by The Lockman Foundation. Used by permission.

Scripture quotations marked "NKJV" are taken from *The New King James Version* /Thomas Nelson Publishers, Nashville : Thomas Nelson Publishers., Copyright © 1982. Used by permission. All rights reserved.

Scripture quotations marked "ESV" are taken from *The Holy Bible: English Standard Version,* copyright © 2001, Wheaton: Good News Publishers. Used by permission. All rights reserved.

ISBN 13: 978-1-63232-566-2 (Print)
       978-1-63232-567-9 (ePub)
       978-1-63232-569-3 (Mobi)

Library of Congress Catalog Card Number: 2015945419

# CONTENTS

# ACKNOWLEDGMENTS

This Bible study is dedicated to the persecuted church from biblical history through today, of whom the world is not worthy. Thank you for your testimony of faith and what it has taught me. You are truly beloved by the Lord.

> *"When the Lamb broke the fifth seal, I saw underneath the altar the souls of those who had been slain because of the word of God, and because of the testimony which they had maintained; and they cried out with a loud voice, saying, 'How long, O Lord, holy and true, will You refrain from judging and avenging our blood on those who dwell on the earth?' And there was given to each of them a white robe; and they were told that they should rest for a little while longer, until the number of their fellow servants and their brethren who were to be killed even as they had been, would be completed also."*
> ### *Revelation 6:9-11*

I am always grateful and humbled by my Bible study-editing buddies. Your sacrifice for the work of the Lord is greatly noticed. Thank you Dianne, Gayle, Joy, Kathy, Mary, and Maureen. You are more precious than gold.

Becky and Kay, thank you for your dedication to Words of Grace & Truth. I could not do this without your faithful prayers before the throne.

Raschelle, thank you for your obedience to the Lord and your service to the ministry.

Marshall, you're always my hero. Thank you for your unconditional love and support.

Mama Lillie, not only have you influenced me but you are influencing the nations through your steadfast faith. thank you for your love and prayers.

To my Lord, Jesus Christ—Thank you for finding me worthy to be put into service.

**My Friend,**

Thank you for making God's Word a priority in your life. His Word is life changing. My prayer for you is that *ACTs420NOW* will transform your thinking in how you view your role in reaching the lost for Jesus Christ. I pray you see the time is now, and you play a critical role in God's plan to reach those who need Him. I pray your eyes are opened to the days we are living in, and understand time is short.

*ACTs420NOW* is a relevant Bible study for the times in which we are living. We will learn from the first-century church how to respond to unbelievers and to our culture. We will discover the first-century church was not alone in their trials and tribulations. We will see God-fearing believers who throughout time faced and overcame uncertainty because of their faith. You will come to understand we too, like those who have gone before us, will face difficult days. However, because you are equipping yourself with His Word and His strategies, you will overcome because of the Lamb and the word of His testimony in your life.

You will look at the lives of some great men and women who helped shape our Christian faith and great nation; men and women who gave their lives so we could enjoy the freedoms we have today. You will see how one life can make a difference. You will be left with piercing questions that will make you look inward and examine your own life.

I can't wait to hear how God has used this study in your life. Please contact us at info@wogt.org call or write and share how the Lord has spoken to you through *ACTs420NOW*.

Consumed by His Call,

—**Marta E. Greenman**
Founder
Words of Grace & Truth
P.O. Box 860223
Plano, TX 75086
469-854-3574
800-257-1626

*"For consider your calling, brethren, that there were not many wise according to the flesh, not many mighty, not many noble; but God has chosen the foolish things of the world to shame the wise, and God has chosen the weak things of the world to shame the things which are strong."*
**1 Corinthians 1:26-27**

# INTRODUCTION

D on't believe for a moment you are reading this by mere coincidence. God has handpicked you for this journey. He is entrusting His Word to you with the intention of transforming your life.

Every word written in *ACTs420NOW* has been prayed over, and you too have been in our prayers. There is no greater joy than discovering God's Word with God's people to discern God's message for today.

Get ready for God to open your eyes to His truth. The Bible might be an ancient book, but Jesus is the Word (**John1:1**) and He is the same yesterday, today, and forever (**Hebrews 13:8**). Therefore, every word found in the Bible is for today and for your life. Are you ready? The journey is well worth your time and effort!

## About Marta Greenman and Words of Grace & Truth (WOGT)—why we do what we do:

Many years ago, Marta read a book by Howard Hendricks, a professor from Dallas Theological seminary. The book, *Teaching to Change Lives: Seven Proven Ways to Make Your Teaching Come Alive*, gives an illustration that describes the passion behind the ministry of *Words of Grace & Truth (WOGT)*. Hendricks poses the question, "Why are we told not to feed the bears when we travel to a national park?" Because, over time, the bears will become dependent upon man to feed them and will not be able to find food on their own. When the weather becomes cold and humans stop coming to the parks for the winter season, the bears will starve and die.[1]

This illustration applies to Christians. Today, too many Christians are dependent on others (pastors, teachers, evangelists) to feed them spiritual truths, never learning how to feed themselves. Unfortunately, just like the bears, when we come to the winter of our lives we are starved, clueless as to how to dig deep into God's Word and receive life-sustaining spiritual food.

As one begins to study God's Word on a regular basis, God begins to transform one's heart and mind to meet His priorities, and not man's. This gives a person God's worldview, a biblical worldview—not that of the god of this world, Satan. As Marta likes to say, "Bible study is **not about information**, Bible study **is about transformation.**" We, as Christians, need to be transformed to become salt and light to those who need to know HIM.

*Words of Grace & Truth* is committed to using proven methods in their biblical material to teach believers how to study God's Word for themselves. Marta's heart beats like the heart of Paul when he commanded Timothy, "The things which you have heard from me in the presence of many witnesses, entrust these to faithful men who will be able to teach others also" (**2 Timothy 2:2**). Not only does Marta teach these methods in the written biblical material, she travels the world teaching others how to teach God's Word through *WOGT* material, equipping them to teach also.

## About *ACTs420NOW*:

In 2009, Marta attended a two-day seminar and listened to speakers from many nations like Israel, Iraq, and several African nations. The more Marta listened to their testimonies the more she was convinced the hardships of which these men and women spoke were headed to America. We, the American church, are ill-equipped for these days ahead. The next morning God awoke Marta in the early morning hours and gave her the seven Scriptures. These are the seven Scriptures outlined in this Bible study. These Scriptures will help equip believers for the uncertain environment we find ourselves in today.

It was still an additional few years before it became clear that these Scriptures were to evolve into a Bible study. Each principle/precept will build upon the previous week. Each week you will be challenged by God's Word and stretched to be obedient to what God calls each of us to do. God has something to teach each of us through *ACTs420NOW* and the first-century church. You don't want to miss this opportunity. Below are the seven Scriptures.

I. *Believe* there is salvation in none other than Jesus Christ (**Acts 4:12**).

II. *Pray* you will begin to speak the Word of God with boldness (**Acts 4:31**).

III. *Pray* the gospel is "unveiled" to a lost and dying America, and world (**2 Corinthians 4:3, 4**).

IV. *Humble yourself, pray, seek,* and *repent* to God for healing in our land (**2 Chronicles 7:14**).

V. *Persevere* by going and telling America and the world until our land is healed (**Isaiah 6:8-11**).

VI. *Love* your enemies and *pray* for those who persecute you (**Matthew 5:44-46**).

VII. *Never compromise* your faith, even unto death (**Philippians 1:20-21**).

## Each week

❖ You will find five lessons for each week of this study. Each lesson will take you approximately forty-five minutes to complete.

> **Note:** If you are new to studying God's Word, don't let this intimidate you! Just do your best. Even if you are only able to complete a portion of the study you will gain great wisdom from the Lord.

❖ Days 1-3 are considered a traditional Bible study method.

❖ Day 4 of each week will diverge from traditional Bible study and we will study two men: Martin Luther and William Tyndale. You will observe their lives and align them with Scripture to discover how God was working through these men in the 17th century.

❖ Day 5 of each week we will study the heritage of the United States of America. We will begin with the separatists/pilgrims in Britain in the 17th century and conclude with the American Revolution.

❖ Since Bible study is NOT about information but IS about transformation, you will be asked to apply every lesson to your life, your church, and your nation.

❖ You will be asked probing questions to trigger your mind to consider what is happening in your country today.

❖ Each week you will have a Bible study tip of the week. Pay close attention to these tips as they will help you in Bible study time in the future.

## What you will need and need to know:

❖ Bible—All biblical material referenced is from the New American Standard Bible (NASB) unless otherwise noted. Therefore, we like students to use this version of the Bible. The English Standard Version (ESV) is also compatible.

❖ Internet Bible—If you don't have an NASB or ESV version of the Bible, there are many Internet websites where you can find the verses, such as biblegateway.com or biblehub.com, among others. Spend a week trying both versions to decide which one best fits your needs, so you can make an intelligent purchase before you invest in a new Bible.

❖ Protection—One principle we know to be true is when people get serious about God's Word, the enemy of the world, Satan, gets serious about distracting them. You will be amazed at how many distractions will crop up when you sit down to study God's Word. Protect your time with the Lord. *Almost* everything can be put on hold until you finish your prayer and study time with the Lord.

❖ Perseverance—Make up your mind that you will finish this study, no matter what! If you want your life to change, you have to allow God to change your life. This can only be done through His Word and with a willing heart.

❖ It's too hard! Don't let anyone speak these words to you . . . even yourself. God brought you here for a reason. Don't focus on what you don't know or what someone else is learning from the study. Focus on what God shows you. We are all at different places spiritually. You wouldn't expect someone in kindergarten to be able to accomplish calculus; neither should one expect a new Bible study student to understand the *calculus* of God's Word as well as someone who has studied His Word daily for twenty years. God speaks to us individually. He brings young and old believers together so we can learn from one another.

# Bible Study Tips

❖ When studying a person in the Bible (a character study) try to find out as much as you can about that person. Making a list as you are studying a specific person will help you remember any important facts and give you insight.

❖ Finding out the original meaning of a Hebrew or Greek words will give additional insight into the meaning of Scriptures.

❖ When studying a subject in the Bible, try to look up every verse in the Bible related to the subject. This will give you God's perspective on the subject.

❖ When studying a book or chapter of the Bible, it is important to determine what kind of book it is. For instance, the book of Nehemiah is one of many history books in the Old Testament. Books can be more than one "type." For example, Daniel is both a book of history and prophecy. Many of the New Testament books are epistles or "letters." You would not study a history book in the same manner as an epistle. Many times epistles have exhortations, warnings, and instructions. You might want to make a list of what each teaches you. On the other hand, history books give an account of what took place. Watch for the flow of the events, focusing on the people, and plots.

❖ If/then statements are conditional clauses or statements. It is always important to look at what God says when He uses if/then clauses. These clauses can express implications, provide an explanation of a consequence, a result, or conclusion.

❖ Do not focus on what you don't understand right now. Instead, focus on the truths that *are* revealed to you today through His Word. Pray for the Lord to reveal more to you in His time.

❖ As you begin to study a book or individual in the Bible, it is important to understand as much as possible about the background of people and events. If you are studying a book of the Bible, try to learn about the history of the time the book was written. If you are studying a person, find out about his or her origin, what was happening during that time period, the culture, etc. Don't feel overwhelmed. God will give you additional insights each time you study a subject. Don't think you have to be an expert to begin.

❖ When you are studying a message addressed to a particular audience, try to learn everything you can about that audience. This will help you understand the message being communicated. Examples: think about who a specific message is to: a Jewish audience, a Gentile audience, a believer or unbeliever. Ask yourself, is the audience receptive or resistant to the message?

# Week 1 Overview

*For we cannot stop speaking about what we have seen and heard.*
**(Acts 4:20)**

Welcome to *ACTs420NOW*, my friend. We have been praying for God to work in a deep way through this study. The next eight weeks will equip, challenge, and grow you in your Christian life. The first week is pivotal in laying the foundation.

This week we will:

❖ Set the foundation for our study.
❖ Look at Jesus' command to the church.
❖ Look at the lives of Peter and John immediately after Jesus' ascension.

This week's applications include:

❖ Understanding first-century believers were people just like us.
❖ Understanding Christians need to speak out for our Christian faith and values.
❖ Understanding God has a plan and purpose for your life.
❖ Understanding the purpose of Bible study is to transform our lives.

This week's verse to memorize:

*"But Peter and John answered and said to them, 'Whether it is right in the sight of God to give heed to you rather than to God, you be the judge; for we cannot stop speaking about what we have seen and heard.'"*
***Acts 4:19-20***

# WEEK 1

For we cannot stop speaking about what we have seen and heard.
—Acts 4:20

## WEEK 1—DAY 1

"[F]or we cannot stop speaking about what we have seen and heard." Peter and John boldly spoke these words to the Sanhedrin about two thousand years ago. We find the words recorded in **Acts 4:20** penned by Luke the physician in the account of the first church. We will be exploring the following questions and more for the next eight weeks.

❖ To whom were they speaking?
❖ What were the circumstances behind these words?
❖ What was the result of their bold speech?
❖ What effect, if any, did Peter and John have on the culture of this time?

Ultimately, we want to address these application questions:
❖ What do these ancient words have to do with me, my church, and my nation?
❖ What action(s) will I take as a result?

Before we begin, in the space below, write a prayer to the Lord. Ask Him to give you wisdom, encouragement, and perseverance for this journey.

Let's get to know Peter and John and learn what they saw and heard.

1.  As you read the passage below, underline the word *John*, or any pronoun which refers to the name *John*. Circle the word *Andrew*, or any pronoun which refers to the name *Andrew*, as well as any reference to the *two disciples*. Lastly, put a box around the name *Peter* or any pronoun, which makes reference to his name.

³⁵ Again the next day John* was standing with two of his disciples, ³⁶ and he looked at Jesus as He walked, and said, "Behold, the Lamb of God!" ³⁷ The two disciples heard him speak, and they followed Jesus. ³⁸ And Jesus turned and saw them following, and said to them, "What do you seek?" They said to Him, "Rabbi (which translated means Teacher), where are You staying?" ³⁹ He said to them, "Come, and you will see." So they came and saw where He was staying; and they stayed with Him that day, for it was about the tenth hour. ⁴⁰ One of the two who heard John speak and followed Him, was Andrew, Simon Peter's brother. ⁴¹ He found first his own brother Simon and said to him, "We have found the Messiah" (which translated means Christ). ⁴² He brought him to Jesus. Jesus looked at him and said, "You are Simon the son of John; you shall be called Cephas" (which is translated Peter) **(John 1:35-42)**.

**Note:** This passage is referring to John the Baptist. In just a moment, we will learn about the John the apostle in **Acts 4:20.**

On the chart provided below, list what you read about each person.

| John the Baptist | Andrew | Peter |
|---|---|---|
| | | |

Andrew proclaimed to Peter that he had found the Messiah. The Hebrew word *māshīach* means *anointed. The term underlines the word Messiah, and the Greek derive.[derivative], Christ.... John 1:41 shows how the translation from 'Messiah' to 'Christ' came about. Ps. 45:6 spoke of the Messianic king as divine. The coming Messiah (Jesus Christ) would administer true justice, rule all men, and bring salvation.*[2]

Peter had seen the Messiah, the One who would bring *true* justice and salvation to all humanity. No wonder he could not stop speaking about what he had seen and heard!

2. Read **Matthew 4:17-25. Note:** The John referred to in this passage is the same John (the apostle) from Acts 4:20.

    a. What does this Scripture tell us that Jesus began to do (v.17)?

    b. Who were the first brothers called by Jesus?

18

c.  What did Jesus ask of Peter and Andrew?

d.  What was Peter's and Andrew's response?

e.  Who were the next two brothers called?

f.  What was James's and John's response?

g.  List what Jesus was doing when Peter, Andrew, James, and John began to follow Him.

Going about (v. 23)—(He went throughout (ESV))

❖

❖

❖

To where did news about Jesus spread (vv. 24-25)?

These men left their livelihoods, families, and comforts of the day to follow Jesus. As a result, they heard the words of His teaching and knew what was important to Him because they were with Him for His entire three-and-a-half-year ministry. They also saw the myriads of miracles Jesus performed.

Listed below is a summary of the miracles Jesus performed as recorded in the Bible. The chart below is taken from W.A. Criswell's *Believer's Study Bible*, I encourage you to take the time to read and discover the mighty works Jesus did while on earth.[3]

| Miracle | Matthew | Mark | Luke | John |
|---|---|---|---|---|
| 1. Cleansing a Leper | 8:2 | 1:40 | 5:12 | |
| 2. Healing a Centurion's Servant (of paralysis) | 8:5 | | 7:1 | |
| 3. Healing Peter's Mother-in-Law | 8:14 | 1:30 | 4:38 | |
| 4. Healing the Sick at Evening | 8:16 | 1:32 | 4:40 | |
| 5. Stilling the Storm | 8:23 | 4:35 | 8:22 | |
| 6. Demons Entering a Herd of Swine | 8:28 | 5:1 | 8:26 | |
| 7. Healing a Paralytic | 9:2 | 2:3 | 5:18 | |
| 8. Raising the Ruler's Daughter | 9:18,23 | 5:22,35 | 8:40,49 | |

| Miracle | Matthew | Mark | Luke | John |
|---|---|---|---|---|
| 9. Healing the Hemorrhaging Woman | 9:20 | 5:25 | 8:43 | |
| 10. Healing Two Blind Men | 9:27 | | | |
| 11. Curing a Demon-Possessed, Mute Man | 9:32 | | | |
| 12. Healing a Man's Withered Hand | 12:9 | 3:1 | 6:6 | |
| 13. Curing a Demon-Possessed, Blind and Mute Man | 12:22 | | 11:14 | |
| 14. Feeding the Five Thousand | 14:13 | 6:30 | 9:10 | 6:1 |
| 15. Walking on the Sea | 14:25 | 6:48 | | 6:19 |
| 16. Healing the Gentile Woman's Daughter | 15:21 | 7:24 | | |
| 17. Feeding the Four Thousand | 15:32 | 8:1 | | |
| 18. Healing the Epileptic Boy | 17:14 | 9:17 | 9:38 | |
| 19. Temple Tax in the Fish's Mouth | 17:24 | | | |
| 20. Healing Two Blind Men | 20:30 | 10:46 | 18:35 | |
| 21. Withering the Fig Tree | 21:18 | 11:12 | | |
| 22. Casting Out an Unclean Spirit | | 1:23 | 4:33 | |
| 23. Healing a Deaf-Mute | | 7:31 | | |
| 24. Healing a Blind Man at Bethsaida | | 8:22 | | |
| 25. Escape from the Hostile Multitude | | | 4:30 | |
| 26. Catch of Fish | | | 5:1 | |
| 27. Raising of a Widow's Son at Nain | | | 7:11 | |
| 28. Healing the Infirm, Bent Woman | | | 13:11 | |
| 29. Healing the Man with Dropsy | | | 14:1 | |
| 30. Cleansing the Ten Lepers | | | 17:11 | |
| 31. Restoring a Servant's Ear | | | 22:51 | |
| 32. Turning Water into Wine | | | | 2:1 |
| 33. Healing the Nobleman's Son (of fever) | | | | 4:46 |
| 34. Healing an Infirm Man at Bethesda | | | | 5:1 |
| 35. Healing the Man Born Blind | | | | 9:1 |
| 36. Raising of Lazarus | | | | 11:43 |
| 37. Second Catch of Fish | | | | 21:1 |

3.  Read **John 20:30-31.**

    a.  In whose presence did Jesus perform these signs?

    b.  What was John's purpose in writing down the many signs he saw Jesus perform?

    Result -

This John is the same man you find in **Acts 4:20** who was compelled by the Spirit of the Lord to pen the book of John. John courageously stood with Peter proclaiming, "Whether it is right in the sight of God to give heed to you rather than to God, you be the judge; for we cannot stop speaking about what we have seen and heard" (**Acts 4:19-20**).

Tomorrow we will continue looking at the lives of Peter and John. For now, let's close with some application questions and prayer. (If you have already completed the Bible study *Leaders, Nations, and God* you will be familiar with these questions.) Each day we will close with three questions. We will ask ourselves how best we can apply to our lives, our church, and our nation what we have studied in the current day's lesson. You may not always have an answer for all three of the questions, but be diligent to write what the Lord shows you each day. As we work through the study, you will find answering the questions becomes easier.

You may also want to use a simple system of L, C, and N in front of your answer(s) to help you remember. L stands for Life, C for Church, and N for Nation.

4.  What has God begun to show you through Peter and John for your life? Your church? Your nation?

5.  Write a closing prayer to the Lord. Ask Him for eyes to see, ears to hear and a heart to obey what you learn in this study.

*"And Jesus came up and spoke to them, saying, 'All authority has been given to Me in heaven and on earth. Go therefore and make disciples of all the nations, baptizing them in the name of the Father and the Son and the Holy Spirit, teaching them to observe all that I commanded you; and lo, I am with you always, even to the end of the age.'"*
***Matthew 28:18-20***

# WEEK 1—DAY 2

Yesterday we began to observe the lives of Peter and John. Today we will continue getting to know Peter and John and what they saw and heard. Before we begin, write your prayer to the Lord. Ask Him to give you insight into the personalities of these two men, and how this may apply to your life.

Many times, when we read about the lives of the people in the Bible, we don't realize they were people just like us with different personalities, strengths and weaknesses. God chose to love and use them despite their flaws. This is why we are exploring the character of Peter and John. Our lesson today is different from any other lesson in this study.

**Bible study tip of the week**—When studying a person in the Bible (a character study) try to find out as much as you can about the person. You will find it helpful, by making a list as you study, to remember any important facts and give you insight into the person.

1.  We will read Scripture with the specific intention of learning about Peter and John as well as what they saw and heard. Keep in mind our specific focus, as there are several Scriptures. Don't get caught up in trying to dissect the meaning of the Scriptures, rather focus on Peter and John. Using the chart below, read each Scripture listed, and in the space provided write what you learn about the two men. The first passage has been completed for you.

**Note:** You may or may not have answers for each space. In addition, most of the focus today will be on Peter. Tomorrow we will take a closer look at John.

| Scripture | Peter | John | What they saw and heard |
|-----------|-------|------|--------------------------|
| **Matthew** | | | |
| 14:22-33 | Peter walked on water!<br><br>Impulsive<br>Bold<br>Afraid<br>Leader<br>Knew who could rescue him<br>Double-minded<br>Little faith<br>Doubter<br>Believer! | Stayed in boat<br><br><br>Follower<br>Afraid<br>Believer | Saw:<br>Jesus' commitment to prayer<br>Jesus walk on water<br>Jesus calm their fears<br>Jesus calm the storm<br>How Jesus dealt with people when they failed |

| Scripture | Peter | John | What they saw and heard |
|---|---|---|---|
| **Matthew** | | | |
| **16:13-23** | | | |
| **18:21-22** | | | |
| **26:1-2** (Gives context) **26:30-35** (Prophecy) **26:69-75** (prophecy fulfilled) | | | |
| **26:36-46** **Remember:** This Scripture comes just after Peter said, "Even if I have to die with you, I will not deny you." | | | |

Peter and John were people just like you and me. Perhaps, as you were reading, something sounded familiarly like what your friend, spouse, or even you would do. The thought that God would use such flawed people is beyond comprehension. Yet, this is God's plan. I've heard it said that God doesn't have a plan B. He has one plan and that is to use His people, the Church, to fulfill His perfect plan called the Great Commission.

Have you been like Peter and John? Do you:

- ❖ Struggle with doubt?
- ❖ Stay in the boat?
- ❖ Get out of the boat?
- ❖ Become a stumbling block for the kingdom?
- ❖ Have a problem setting your priorities?
- ❖ Have a problem with forgiveness?
- ❖ Become prideful and too confident in your abilities?
- ❖ Betray the Lord?
- ❖ Sleep through life when you need to be on watch?

Regardless, whether you fit into all of these categories or even more, you can be assured like the prophet Jeremiah:

"Before I formed you in the womb I knew you, and before you were born I consecrated you;
I have appointed you a prophet to the nations."
**Jeremiah 1:5**

Before you were born, God appointed you for something. If you know what your appointment is, fill in the blank below.

Lord, I thank you that before I was ever formed you appointed me to:

_____

If you have yet to understand what your appointment is, you will have opportunity to pray for God to reveal this to you in your prayer time.

2. What has God begun to show you through the lives of Peter and John? How will you apply it to your life? Your church? Your nation?

3. Write a closing prayer to the Lord. Thank Him for what you are learning, and ask Him to open your eyes and heart to better understand His plan.

*"For the eyes of the LORD move to and fro throughout the earth that He may strongly support those whose heart is completely His."*
**2 Chronicles 16:9a**

# WEEK 1—DAY 3

As we looked at the lives of Peter and John yesterday, we worked on the questions, "Who were they?", and "What did they see and hear?" We discovered that Peter and John were among the first disciples called by the Lord. They walked with Him during His three-and-a-half-year ministry on earth. They had the privilege of hearing His teaching and witnessing Jesus' many miracles. **John 21:25** tells us, "There are also many other things which Jesus did, which if they were written in detail, I suppose that even the world itself would not contain the books which were written." Can you imagine the many sermons, teachings, and miracles about which we don't even know? One day, in heaven, I pray we will hear and comprehend the marvelous works our Lord did while walking this earth.

Let's begin by writing a prayer to the Lord. Ask Him to show you the many wonders He does every day in your life. Ask Him for spiritual eyes to see His mighty works, then a grateful heart to thank Him for His daily miracles.

1. We want to pick up where we left off yesterday. Just a reminder, we will read Scripture today with the specific intention of learning about Peter and John and what they saw and heard. Keep in mind our specific focus as there are several Scriptures. Don't get caught up in trying to dissect the meaning of the Scriptures, focus on Peter and John. Read each Scripture listed below, and complete the chart with what you learn about the two men.

   **Note:** You may or may not have answers for each space.

| Scripture | Peter | John | Jesus |
|---|---|---|---|
| John | | | |
| 13:21-30<br>**Note:** John often referred to himself as the one whom Jesus loved. | | | |

| Scripture | Peter | John | Jesus |
|---|---|---|---|
| John | | | |
| 19:24-27 | | | |
| 20:1-8 | | | |
| 21:7-8 | | | |
| 21:19-23 **Note:** you might want to read **John 21:15-18** for better context. | | | |

Just like yesterday, think about how you have been like Peter and John.

Do you:

- ❖ Think the Lord should tell you everything He is doing in others' lives?
- ❖ Behave impulsively?
- ❖ Become too fearful in your faith to accept the blessing the Lord has for your life?
- ❖ Believe your relationship with the Lord is superior to others'?
- ❖ Try to tell Jesus what to do with others, instead of focusing on yourself?

How wonderful to know the men Jesus chose were people just like you and me. I heard a comforting exhortation, "God doesn't call the equipped, He equips the called." I praise God that just as He equipped the disciples in biblical times, He equips you and me!

How did Peter and John grow into the godly, admired, courageous men we see them as today? In the coming weeks we will discover just how courageous Peter and John became during the formation of the early church. Let's take a look at the source of their courage. Let's rediscover this great truth.

2. Write **Acts 1:8** below.

 

 

 

   a. What were the disciples to receive?

   b. What were they to do?

   c. Where were they to witness?

 

The word *power* in **Acts 1:8** comes from the Greek word *dunamis* meaning *inherent power*.[4] Let's look at two Scriptures which will illustrate this inherent power.

3. Read **Mark 5:30** below.

   "Immediately Jesus, perceiving in Himself that the power proceeding from Him had gone forth, turned around in the crowd and said, 'Who touched My garments?'"

   a. Who had the inherent power?

b. What had happened to the power?

**Mark 5:24-34** gives us the account of Jesus healing a woman who merely touched His garment and was healed. At that moment, Jesus felt His power had connected to someone. The inherent power in Jesus healed a woman who had lived with illness for the previous twelve years. What healed this woman? Scripture tells us it was the woman's faith *and* Jesus' inherent power.

4. Read **Ephesians 1:18-19** below.

"I pray that the eyes of your heart may be enlightened, so that you will know what is the hope of His calling, what are the riches of the glory of His inheritance in the saints, and what is the surpassing greatness of His power toward us who believe. These are in accordance with the working of the strength of His might. ..."

a. What did Paul pray?

"_____ of your _____ may be enlightened . . . ."

b. What are the three things Paul wanted us to know?

❖

❖

❖

c. The power is directed toward whom?

Paul, the writer of this letter to the church in Ephesus, wanted them to know the greatness of Jesus' inherent power toward us who believe.

5. Let's return to **Acts 1:8** and take a fresh look.
   a. Who is to receive the inherent power?

   b. When does one receive the power?

   c. When one receives the power, what will he or she do?

The Greek word for *witness* is *mártus* meaning, *literally, one who remembers, one who has information or knowledge or joint-knowledge of anything; hence, one who can give information, bring to light, or confirm anything…. Peculiar to the NT [New Testament] is the designation as mártures (pl. witnesses) of those who announce the facts of the Gospel and tell its tidings…. Mártus is used as a designation of those who have suffered death in consequence of confessing Christ…. However, should not be understood as if their witness consisted in their suffering death but rather that their witnessing of Jesus became the cause of their death. The Lord Jesus in Rev. 1:5 is called the Witness, the Faithful One.*[5]

Before we begin to tie everything together, let's look at some additional Scriptures.

6.  Read **John 15:26-27.**

   a.  How is the Helper described?

   b.  Where does the Helper (the Spirit of truth) come from?

   c.  Who will testify about Jesus?

      Why?

   d.  Fill in the blanks with *your* name and reread the Scripture.

      When the Helper comes, whom I will send to_____ from the Father, that is the Spirit of

      truth who proceeds from the Father, He will testify about Me, and_____ will testify also,

      because_____ have [has] been with Me from the beginning.

      **Note:** The Helper, the Spirit of truth, has been with you since the moment of your salvation.

7.  Read **John 16:7-15**.

   What will the Helper (Spirit of truth) do when He comes?

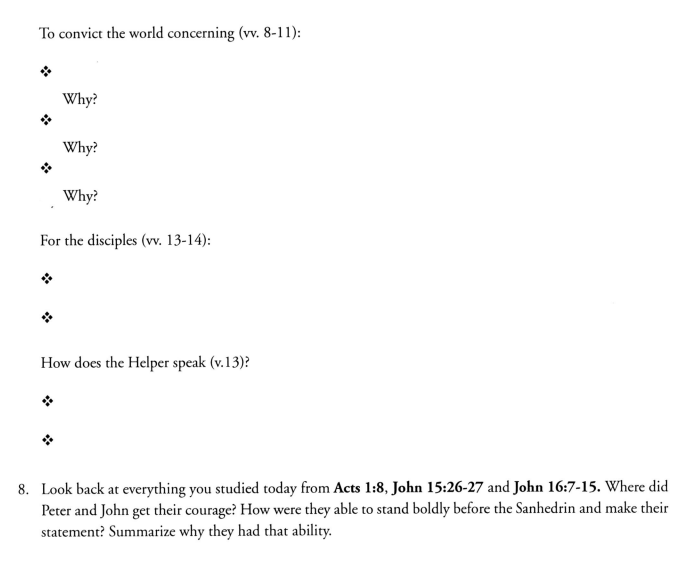

To convict the world concerning (vv. 8-11):

❖

   Why?

❖

   Why?

❖

   Why?

For the disciples (vv. 13-14):

❖

❖

How does the Helper speak (v.13)?

❖

❖

8.  Look back at everything you studied today from **Acts 1:8, John 15:26-27** and **John 16:7-15.** Where did Peter and John get their courage? How were they able to stand boldly before the Sanhedrin and make their statement? Summarize why they had that ability.

Peter and John were ordinary men who became extraordinary when the power of the Helper, the Spirit of truth, came upon them. The Helper gave them, from the Lord, the inherent power and the ability to speak truth. "Every good thing given and every perfect gift is from above, coming down from the Father of lights, with whom there is no variation or shifting shadow" **(James 1:17)**. The Helper is a good and perfect gift from God, and this Spirit of truth is living inside of you; if you are a believer in Jesus Christ, you have the same power as Peter and John.

We're learning a lot this week. We are setting the stage for the remainder of the study. Continue to meditate on what you are learning throughout your day. Let's close with our application questions and prayer.

9. How should what you studied today about the Helper, the Spirit of truth, impact your life, your church, and your nation?

10. Write a closing prayer to the Lord. Ask Him to continue to show you revelations about this week's lesson as you go about your day.

*"I will ask the Father, and He will give you another Helper, that He may be with you forever."*
**John 14:16**

# WEEK 1—DAY 4

This week we began to study the lives of Peter and John. The previous three days we have answered the questions:

❖ Who were they?
❖ What did they see and hear?

We have found Peter and John were amazingly human. They were people just like you and me with qualities we can relate to, as endearing or irritating as they may be. Yet, they were men chosen by God for His purpose and plan. "The first account I composed, Theophilus, about all Jesus began to do and teach, until the day when He was taken up to heaven, after He had, by the Holy Spirit, given orders to the apostles whom He had chosen" (**Acts 1:1-2**). My heart is encouraged that Jesus chose men like you and me, despite their failings and shortcomings. Begin today with your prayer to the Lord. Thank Him for calling you into service for His kingdom. Today, if you don't know what He has set you apart to do, ask Him to show you His purpose.

Each week on Day 4, we will look at a person in history whom God has set apart for His work. Ordinary people God chose, some familiar and some not. This person will relate to the subject we are studying each week. As I prayed for this study and asked the Lord to reveal these godly men or women to me, it was no surprise when the Lord gave me names like Martin Luther and William Tyndale. But it was a surprise when I heard His still, small voice whisper, "Tell *your* story the first week." My immediate response was, "No, Lord, they don't want to hear my story." Thankfully, my first response lasted only a few seconds, because if there is anything I have learned in my twenty-year-plus relationship with the Lord, telling the ruler of the universe *no* is futile. Once I got past the initial *no*, my next question was, "Why me Lord?" His answer was simple, "Because you're ordinary." How could I argue?

The day the Lord showed up in my life and said, "Follow Me," was more like Paul's experience on the Damascus Road rather than like Peter walking away from his chosen profession by dropping his fishing nets and following Christ. Although I was raised in the church, by the age of twenty-nine I was deep into the things of the world and living to please myself. Then, in one moment, "He brought me up out of the pit of destruction, out of the miry clay, and He set my feet upon a rock making my footsteps firm. He put a new song in my mouth, a song of praise to our God" (**Psalm 40:2-3a**). I praise God; through Him, our worst days can become the best days of our life.

To get to know me, and to illustrate just how ordinary I am, we will use stories from the Bible so that we can learn a little more about the disciples. In comparing these stories, you will also come to know my nature, the good and the bad.

1. Read **Matthew 15:1-16**.

There is so much in this passage, but we need to stay focused on our task; therefore, we will set aside dissecting the text and focus on what this Scripture tells us about the character of the disciples.

    a. What is the question the disciples asked Jesus in **Matthew 15:12**? Write it below.

I'm so encouraged when I read the words of these disciples. Like me, they were worried about what others thought of them. The disciples weren't as concerned about Jesus offending the Pharisees as they were about what the Pharisees would think of their being associated with Jesus, the One doing the offending! The disciples were worried about appearances, and what people would think. I have struggled in this area my entire life! Through the Lord, though, I have made great progress in transforming from a people-pleaser into a servant in whom the Lord is well pleased. Let's read a Scripture, which the Lord used to help me in my journey.

> "Stop regarding man, whose breath of life is in his nostrils; for why should he be esteemed?"
> **Isaiah 2:22**

When I began to consider how I might be perceived or judged by people, the Lord would (not so gently) remind me I only needed to pursue His opinion and not man's. He is the Creator of life and breath. I *must* be concerned about the opinion of our Creator, not the created.

Let's return to **Matthew 15** to see an additional characteristic about one of Jesus' disciples.

    b. What did Peter ask of Jesus in **Matthew 15:15**?

Sometimes I wish I were not like Peter in this area. Peter wanted to know the answers. He asked questions and wanted explanations. If there is one trait that is my best friend and worst enemy, this one tops the charts. Finding out all the answers has made me an exceptional student of the Bible. Digging in the Word has healed my wounded, troubled soul. Yet always needing to know doesn't always serve one well when one needs to be a bondservant of the Lord.

I've spent considerable time in various countries on short-term and extended missionary opportunities. One of the first rules I learned is if your "national" (a person you work with in the country) tells you, "Let's go now!" or "We need to change the agenda," you don't ask questions, you just obey. This can be very difficult for someone who has a need to know, but God has ways of showing you sometimes *not* asking is the appropriate response.

There is another characteristic in which *I am so Peter*. We looked at this Scripture a few days ago so we won't tarry. **Mathew 14:22-33** gives the account of Peter walking on the water with Jesus. In verse twenty-eight Peter tells Jesus, "Lord, if it is You, command me to come to You on the water." Yes, like Peter, I can be a bit impulsive. My husband will read this and say, "A bit?!" Ok, I can be very impulsive. Like the time I went on my first mission trip to Romania. In the five short weeks after I found out about the trip, God raised the money, moved mountains to acquire my passport, but the moment I was boarding the plane I realized I was afraid of flying! You would think someone going halfway around the world would think about this before boarding a plane. Not me, I spent almost all fourteen hours on the plane with my white-knuckled hands clinching the armrests. Like Peter when *I saw the wind*, I became frightened, very frightened. Thankfully, as with Peter, Jesus saved me.

God used this experience, multiple flights, and other circumstances to draw me closer to Him. He made me confront my doubts and fears, and in doing so, showed me His character and His nature. That made me like the disciples when Jesus rescued Peter, "And those who were in the boat worshiped Him, saying, 'You are certainly God's Son!'" (**Matthew 14:33**).

Now you know a little bit more about me, a recovering people-pleaser who is bold, impulsive, and won't stop asking questions. Yet I am one whom God rescued and set apart for His purpose.

2.  Who are you? What is your nature—good and bad? Make a list below of characteristics you have like those the disciples had in biblical times. Be honest, no one else has to see your list.

If you don't like what you see on your list, know this: first, and foremost, if you are a true believer in Jesus Christ, then you are a saint. There is an old expression, which says, *you're a saint or you ain't*. Paul described the church in Corinth as saints. He said, "To the church of God which is at Corinth, to those who have been sanctified in Christ Jesus, saints by calling" (**1 Corinthians 1:2a**). Paul's letters to the Corinthians were stern letters. The Corinthians needed the correction and healing of the Lord, yet Paul still called them saints. Let's take another look at Scripture we discovered yesterday. The apostle Paul wrote to the church in Ephesus:

> "I pray that the eyes of your heart may be enlightened, so that you will know what is the hope of His calling, what are the riches of the glory of His inheritance in the saints, and what is the surpassing greatness of His power toward us who believe" (**Ephesians 1:18-19**).

3.  Why did Paul pray for the eyes of their heart to be enlightened?

    ❖

    ❖

    ❖

The *Ryrie Study Bible* defines *the heart* in Scripture as *the very center and core of life*.[6] As saints, we have a calling, a rich inheritance, and His great power is provided to us to accomplish what the Lord called us to. If you are interested in the process of *how* the Lord sets you apart, my first Bible study, *Bound To Be Free*, is a great resource. The study can be challenging but worth the journey.

4.  Read **Ephesians 2:8-10**. Fill in the blanks below.

    You are saved by _____

    Through _____

    For _____ _____

    a.  How are we described (vs. 10)?

    b.  When were our good works prepared (vs. 10)?

    c.  What are we to do with our good works (vs. 10)?

When God thought of you, He had a purpose in mind. Long before you had fingers and toes, the Creator of the universe had a plan and purpose for your life. But if you're still thinking, "I'm too ordinary, too weak, not intelligent enough, etc., for the Lord to have prepared something for me to do," you are in good company. What does the Bible say?

5.  Read **1 Corinthians 1:26-31**.

    a.  When we look at our calling (our good works, which we are to do for the Lord) how are the people described?

        Not _____

        Not _____

        Not _____

    b.  Instead of the wise, mighty and noble, what has God chosen, and why?

    c.  What did Jesus become to us (v. 30)?

        ❖

        ❖

❖

❖

   d.  In whom are we to boast?

Are you beginning to see you are the perfect candidate the Lord would choose to use in service for Him? This Bible study is designed to equip you for the days ahead. The times in which we live are difficult and we must be equipped for the spiritual battle to which our Lord has called us. God has called you and set you apart for His service.

My prayer is, from today's lesson you see God calls ordinary people with strengths and weaknesses into His service. He did this in biblical times and He is still in the same business today.

As you work through this Bible study, don't treat the Bible as merely some ancient text you find interesting. Know every word is relevant to you today. He has given us His Word to train us for His purpose and if you are a believer in Jesus Christ this means you.

Let's close with our application questions and prayer.

6.  What has God begun to show you through the lives of Peter and John? How will you apply it to your life? Your church? Your nation?

7.  Write a closing prayer to the Lord.

*"Therefore I, the prisoner of the Lord, implore you to walk in a manner worthy of the calling with which you have been called, with all humility and gentleness, with patience, showing tolerance for one another in love, being diligent to preserve the unity of the Spirit in the bond of peace."*
**Ephesians 4:1-3**

# WEEK 1—DAY 5

As you discovered yesterday, on each day 4 of this Bible study we are focusing on people from our Christian heritage. Each Day 5 will take an additional twist in our study. If you have completed the *Leaders, Nations, and God* Bible study, you are familiar with what we will do. We are focusing our attention on the founding of the United States and our nation's heritage. Just as in *Leaders, Nations, and God*, we are exploring the questions, "Was America founded on Christian principles?" and "How does this apply to my life today?" However, before we begin we need to pray and ask the Lord for wisdom.

There are two schools of thought in the United States. One firmly attests that America was founded on Judeo-Christian values. The second proclaims that our forefathers were just merchants looking for wealth. Although both Pilgrims and merchants landed in the new world, which group shaped the heart of our country?

America is over 235 years old. What made the Pilgrims choose to come to this new world? What were the beliefs of the people who formed this country? How did these people affect our country's founding? Moreover, have we as a country stayed true to the beliefs of our founders? To answer these questions and others, we need to travel back to the close of the sixteenth century, almost 200 years before our Founding Fathers signed the Declaration of Independence.

On November 21, 1620, the Pilgrims landed in America. Webster defines *pilgrim* as *one who journeys in foreign lands*.[7] These men and women were part of the Puritan movement, which began in England. The group who felt they could not find the religious freedom they sought in England chose to become "pilgrims," travelers to the New World. Therefore, we must ask the basic question, "Who were the Puritans?" Sue Allen, a Puritan historian from Babworth, England, best answered this question in an interview with Kirk Cameron in the documentary *MONUMENTAL: In Search of America's National Treasure*. Read the following transcript from the film.

> Sue: For the first time, the Bible is printed in English and put into every church. Because until that point there were Bibles in English being smuggled into the country and they were deemed to be heretical. You could be burned [at the stake] for having an English Bible.
>
> Kurt: What was the fear of having English Bibles in the hands of the people?"
>
> Sue: What would happen if every Tom, Dick, and Harry got to read the Bible for themselves, and then started to study it for goodness sake, and realize that the church of the Bible, as Christ had deemed it should be, was not this church with Bishops and palaces, growing rich, when the parishioners were starving on the land.
>
> Kirk: People would then hold them accountable.

Sue: Precisely, and as soon as the Bible was in English that [being held accountable] started to happen.

Kirk: For the first time these people got Bibles in English that they could hold, and study in their own hands, in their own homes, with their children. This to them was worth more than anything else, even more than their own lives because this was God speaking to them.

Sue: And it got to a point that by 1593 there was an act against Puritans brought in and under that law, it became illegal to be a Puritan. Anyone that disagreed with Elizabeth's new church settlement got this name that you could spit out like a curse, PURITAN. The state, the queen, the monarch, used the clergy as their mouthpiece to control you.

Kirk: And because of that you had the government controlling the church, and the church controlling the people, and so that is where you have the tyranny and oppression that you can't get away from.

Sue: And the thought is coming to them 'If this church can't be purified maybe we should just separate ourselves away from all this unholiness.' That's where the word Separatists came from. And that's the dangerous step because you're stepping away from the church and you're denouncing the monarchy in the same breath.

Kirk: You're not just switching denominations as we would think of today.

Sue: This amounts to treason.

Kirk: By leaving the church? [Leaving the church amounts to treason.]

Sue: Yes.

Sue: They are fighting for their survival from that point, because they are going against the king. Its no matter [sic] just they are going against the church, and the king is the head of the church. It's treason.

Kirk: So there was my first clue. The Separatists were coming out from under the reign of Queen Elizabeth and into the rule of King James. And this guy was a tyrant king on steroids. He was the one who actually invented the phrase 'the Divine Right of Kings.' He bankrupted his nation. He tripled the debt and He considered himself to be a devout Christian while he was obsessed with hunting down and destroying the most devout people in his land. One of the things that fascinates [me] is knowing that once the Bible was translated into English and given to the common man that changed everything. Because they started thinking for themselves, they said this is what the word of God says; therefore church ought to be like what God says it should be not what the king says. And the king himself is a man who is under [the] authority of the King of Kings and he too must abide by the law of God.

Sue: Once they [Puritans] had come out and showed [sic] their true colors how Separatists had no choice but to leave the country or stay and be slaughtered.[8]

The Puritans' (Pilgrims') conflict started when they began to study God's Word and chose to live by what the Bible said instead of what man said. In their pursuit of God, they found the world and its leaders in conflict with their hearts' desire of placing God first in their lives. They were learning mature biblical lessons quickly; some at a very young age.

1. Read the following verses and in the spaces provided on the chart below make notes on how they relate to the lives of the Puritans and you.

| Scripture | Puritans | Myself |
|---|---|---|
| **Matthew 5:10-12** | | |
| **Matthew 5:44** | | |
| **John 15:18-21** | | |
| **2 Corinthians 4:5-10** | | |
| **2 Timothy 3:12** | | |

## Questions to Ponder

Does Sue Allen and Kirk Cameron's account of the Puritans (Pilgrims) differ from what you were taught in school? If so, how is it different?

Kirk Cameron mentioned the phrase "the divine right of kings". You may not be familiar with this term. Let's study it.

"The divine right of kings is a political and religious doctrine of royal and political legitimacy. It asserts that a monarch is subject to no earthly authority, deriving his right to rule directly from the will of God. The king is, thus, not subject to the will of his people, the aristocracy, or any other estate of the realm, including (in the view of some, especially in Protestant countries) the Church. According to this doctrine, since only God can judge an unjust king, the king can do no wrong. The doctrine implies that any attempt to depose the king or to restrict his powers runs contrary to the will of God and may constitute [a] sacrilegious act.

"The remoter origins of the theory are rooted in the medieval idea that God had bestowed earthly power on the king, just as God had given spiritual power and authority to the Church, centering on the Pope. The immediate author of the theory was Jean Bodin, who based it on the interpretation of Roman law. With the rise of nation-states and the Protestant Reformation, the theory of divine right justified the king's absolute authority in both political and spiritual matters. The theory came to the fore in England under the reign of James I of England (1603–1625, also James VI of Scotland 1567–1625). Louis XIV of France (1643–1715), though Catholic, strongly promoted the theory as well."[9]

As you are beginning to discover, the Puritans were in quite a predicament. Whom should they honor, their earthly king or their heavenly King? There might seem to be contradictory Scriptures in the Bible. Someone might quote **Romans 13:1**, "Every person is to be in subjection to the governing authorities. For there is no authority except from God, and those which exist are established by God." This verse seems to indicate that the Puritans would need to follow their earthly king. But suppose the earthly king (or government) contradicts the laws and precepts of the heavenly King? Let's take a look at what God's Word says.

2. Read the following verses. In the spaces provided on the chart below, make note of who is speaking, the circumstances, and what they said/did about whom to follow (earthly governing authorities or God).

| | Government Command/Order | Response of Follower(s) of God | Result |
|---|---|---|---|
| **Exodus 1:8-22** | | | |
| **Daniel 3:8-28** | | | |

| | Government Command/Order | Response of Follower(s) of God | Result |
|---|---|---|---|
| **Daniel 6:6-28** | | | |
| **Acts 5:28-29** (We will look at this text in greater detail in the coming weeks) | | | |

3. Read **Romans 13:1-5**.

**Remember:** Scripture does not contradict Scripture.

    a. Reflecting on what you have studied today, how would you answer the question, "Should the Puritans have obeyed the earthly king or the heavenly King, in regards to their religious freedoms?" Give a reason for your answer.

    b. Based on Scripture, when should someone obey God instead of earthly authorities?

These are tough questions in need of biblical answers. We certainly don't want to answer them based on our own opinions, but rather on the Word of God. You may have a clearer picture as we move through the study.

You have seen this week the tough decisions the Puritans had to make, just like Peter and John did. As believers we *too* will be called to make difficult decisions. A question we need to ask ourselves is, "How would I respond if I faced some of the same trials and tribulations?" The time to equip ourselves is not as we are going through the trial, but NOW, before the trial.

Anyone who follows football knows, "The key to a good offense is having a _____ _____." Of course, the key is a <u>good defense</u>! For the next seven weeks our focus is to establish a good defense. Below you will find seven key principles essential in the life of a Christian. We will study one principle each week and look at the life of someone from Christian history who has lived out this principle in his or her life. We will also stop and revisit our American heritage.

Each week the principle we learn will build upon the previous week. Think of building a house. You start with the foundation, then you add the walls, next the roof, then the windows and doors, and finally the detailed finish work begins. The house will not be sound until *all* aspects are finished, but you must have a firm foundation on which to build. This is a picture of what we will do together week by week. Below are the seven principles to live by so you like Peter and John, "cannot stop speaking what have seen and heard" (**Acts 4:20**).

I.   *Believe* there is salvation in none other than Jesus Christ (**Acts 4:12**).

II.  *Pray* you will begin to speak the Word of God with boldness (**Acts 4:31**).

III. *Pray* the gospel is "unveiled" to a lost and dying America, and world (**2 Corinthians 4:3,4**).

IV.  *Humble yourself, pray, seek,* and *repent* to God for healing in our land (**2 Chronicles 7:14**).

V.   *Persevere* by going and telling America and the world until our land is healed (**Isaiah 6:8-11**).

VI.  *Love* your enemies and *pray* for those who persecute you (**Matthew 5:44-46**).

VII. ***Never*** *compromise* your faith, even unto death (**Philippians 1:20-21**).


Let's close with our application questions and prayer.

4.  What has God begun to show you through the Puritans for your life? Your church? Your nation?




5.  Write a closing prayer to the Lord. Ask Him to keep the evil one from you over the next weeks so that you will be diligent and persevere in and through this study. Ask the Lord to give you a closeness and intimacy with Him you have never before experienced.




*"Therefore, since we have so great a cloud of witnesses surrounding us, let us also lay aside every encumbrance and the sin which so easily entangles us, and let us run with endurance the race that is set before us, fixing our eyes on Jesus, the author and perfecter of faith, who for the joy set before Him endured the cross, despising the shame, and has sat down at the right hand of the throne of God."*
***Hebrews 12:1-2***

# Week 2 Overview

*Believe there is salvation in none other than Jesus Christ.*
**(Acts 4:12)**

This week we will explore the importance of the foundational belief there is salvation in none other than Jesus Christ. Jesus said, "I am the way, and the truth, and the life, no man comes to the Father but by Me" (**John 14:6**). When people say there are other ways to go to heaven aside from Jesus Christ, what they are really saying is . . . "I am really not a true believer." This week should solidify and equip you in the foundational truth of **Acts 4:12**.

This week we will:

❖ Be equipped with God's Word about salvation in Christ alone.
❖ Investigate Peter and John's core passion, which says salvation is in Christ alone.
❖ Begin to look at Martin Luther, a sixteenth-century servant of the Lord.

This week's applications include:

❖ Grasping the importance of our foundational step.
❖ Arming ourselves with truth on this important subject so we may impart God's truth to a lost world.
❖ Beginning to develop a biblical worldview.

This week's verse to memorize:

*"And there is salvation in no one else; for there is no other name under heaven that has been given among men, by which we must be saved."*
***Acts 4:12***

**Foundational Step:** Believe there is salvation in none other than Jesus Christ (**Acts 4:12**).

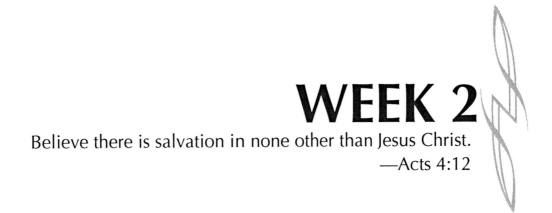

# WEEK 2

Believe there is salvation in none other than Jesus Christ.
—Acts 4:12

## WEEK 2—DAY 1

Last week we began to look at the lives of Peter and John. Were you surprised to find out they were people just like you and me? Yet we know God used them in powerful ways for the kingdom of our Lord. Throughout this study, we will continue to discover how God used unlikely people from the first church for His glory and how today He does the same. Before we dive into the details, begin by writing your prayer to the Lord. Ask for perseverance this week to continue in His Word, regardless of your schedule or circumstances. Ask Him to keep the evil one from you so you can clearly understand His Word.

Whether you are a bricklayer, a math teacher, or a makeup artist, you always want to begin with a solid foundation when you build anything. This is what we need to do; then we will build upon that firm foundation. Each week as we move through this study, we will focus on one truth or application for our lives in the building process. Our foundation is:

*Believe there is salvation in none other than Jesus Christ.*

For most of you walking through *ACTs420NOW*, this week will serve more to equip you rather than convince you of this foundational truth, but we need to assess how this fundamental tenet should shape our lives. George Barna, of The Barna Group, wrote in *A Biblical Worldview Has a Radical Effect on a Person's Life*, "Only four percent of adults have a biblical worldview as the basis of their decision-making." Stop! Read that sentence again—four percent! Barna continues,

"If Jesus Christ came to this planet as a model of how we ought to live, then our goal should be to act like Jesus. Sadly, few people consistently demonstrate the love, obedience, and priorities of Jesus. The primary reason that people do not act like Jesus is because they do not think like Jesus. Behavior stems from what we think—our attitudes, beliefs, values, and opinions. Although most people own a Bible and know some of its content, our research found that most Americans have little idea how to integrate core biblical principles to form a unified and meaningful response to the challenges and opportunities of life. We're often more concerned with survival amidst chaos than with experiencing truth and significance."[10]

My friends, we need to *know* Jesus, we need to *think* like Jesus, before we will *act* like Jesus. We must allow Him to mold our lives and our decision-making processes. The result of allowing our Lord to mold our lives is a church more conformed to His image. The result of our church being more conformed to His image is a nation more obedient to Christ. An obedient nation brings glory to God. Therefore, if we want to change a nation, change begins with the individual—and *that* change begins with you.

1.  Let's do a quick exercise. Don't spend time calculating the answers to the questions below. Simply estimate quickly in your head the answer and jot it down. The point of the exercise is not the accuracy of the numbers, but a general observation of our personal habits. You may want to write your answers in pencil or on a different piece of paper.

| Question | Yourself | A child living in your home (if applicable) |
|---|---|---|
| a. How many hours a week do you spend at your job (especially homemakers—you work more hours than most)? | | |
| b. How many hours do you spend on recreation (this includes television, reading, sports, etc.)? | | |
| c. How many hours do you spend in the car—commuting, driving to activities, or running errands? | | |
| d. Total hours | | |
| e. How many hours a week do you spend in a church worship service, personal devotional time, family devotional time, and related activities? | | |

If you don't like the answers you see, one simple way to increase your opportunities with the Lord is to convert your driving time into a worship time or a biblical learning session through the media you listen to in your car. Christian radio stations provide music that draws your heart near to Him. The Bible is available on CD, and there are teaching and training audio lessons available in many formats.

Proverbs tells us, "For as he thinks within himself, so he is" (**Proverbs 23:7a**). If we want a nation more conformed to His image, we need to begin to think more about Him than we think about the world in which we are engaged. Remember, changing a nation begins with one person—you.

Throughout our discovery journey, our companions will be from the early church. Moving forward, each week we will begin in Acts and expand our study of the first church. In **Acts 4** Jesus had already died, risen and ascended to sit at the right hand of the Father. The Holy Spirit had come and Jesus' disciples became His witnesses to all who would listen.

**Acts 3** tells us of Peter and John going to the temple to pray. On their way, a lame man begged alms and spoke to them. Instead of handing the man money, Peter, by the power of Jesus, healed the lame man. The man began leaping and praising God. Everyone stood in amazement because the crowd recognized this man as the one who daily begged alms in front of the temple gate. Peter replied to the people and questioned their amazement, asking, "Why do you marvel at this, and why do you gaze?" (**Acts 3:12**) This opened the door for Peter to explain to the crowd the power behind the man's healing. Next week we will examine the bold gospel presentation Peter made following this miracle.

2. **Read Acts 4:1-4** then answer the following questions. (The "they" in verse one is a reference to Peter and John.)

   a. Who walked up as Peter was speaking to the people? (see v. 1)

      ❖

      ❖

      ❖

   b. Why were the priests, captain, and Sadducees disturbed? What were Peter and John teaching?

   c. What happened to Peter and John?

   d. Who threw them in jail?

   e. Despite the circumstances, what happened because of their proclamation of the gospel?

Many who heard—Believed. Note: the Bible tells us the number of *men* who heard was about five thousand. How many women and children believed? What might the actual number of believers have been? Today, we have evangelistic events in large stadiums. If you haven't been to one of these events, you have probably heard of one or have seen accounts of large revivals on television. Often at the end of the program thousands make professions of faith. These gatherings are planned for months, sometimes years. Contemplate Peter's and John's message spreading spontaneously, like wildfires, without microphones, committees, or stadium seating. When I read of events like these in the Bible, they seem surreal, incapable of happening, but God's Word is true; therefore, we must grapple with this reality. This was the first proclamation of the gospel recorded after Pentecost. It caused quite a stir. Disregarding Peter's and John's arrest, we would call the event today a phenomenal success.

3. Rest assured, we will talk about Peter's and John's arrest, but for now read **Acts 4:5-7**.

   a. List those who were gathered in Jerusalem (vv. 5-6).

      ❖

      ❖

      ❖ Caiaphas, John, and Alexander, who were all of _____ descent.

   b. What question did these men ask Peter and John (v. 7)?

   **Remember:** *this* is the healing of the lame man.

**Bible study tip of the week**—Finding out the original meaning of a Hebrew or Greek word will give additional insight into the meaning of the Scriptures.

The word *power* in **Acts 4:7** comes from the Greek word *dúnamis meaning power. Dúnamis is derived from dúna, which has the basic meaning of being able or capable. Dúnamis <u>can</u> denote miraculous power. The mighty power of signs and wonders means the power of working miracles.*[11] This is the same Greek word Peter used in **Acts 3:11**, "While he [the lame man] was clinging to Peter and John, all the people ran together to them at the so-called portico of Solomon, full of amazement [dúnamis]."

4. Read **Acts 3:12**.

   a. Why were the people gazing at Peter and John?

   b. From **Matthew 21:23-24** below, who else had been asked a similar question regarding authority?

   "When He entered the temple, the chief priests and the elders of the people came to Him while He was teaching, and said, 'By what authority are You doing these things, and who gave You this authority?' Jesus said to them, 'I will also ask you one thing, which if you tell Me, I will also tell you by what authority I do these things.'" (**Matthew 21:23-24**).

   c. What insights do these Scriptures give you about the motivation for the high priests' question in **Acts 4:7**, "By what power, or in what name, have you done this [healed the lame man]?"

Peter and John were in quite a predicament. In essence, they were arrested because they healed a man and proclaimed Jesus, who rose from the dead, to be the source of the healing. Before we take a deeper look at who arrested them, let's see how Peter and John responded.

5. Read **Acts 4:8-12**.

   a. To whom did Peter and John give credit for healing the lame man?

   b. As Peter proclaimed Jesus as the healer, who did he blame for Jesus' crucifixion?

Can you see the predicament in which Peter and John found themselves? The group of men before whom Peter and John stood and declared Jesus responsible for healing the lame man were the same men who arrested and questioned Peter and John. They were also the same men the two apostles blamed for Jesus' crucifixion.

Central to the Jewish faith since the time of Moses was an expected Messiah. Peter continued his discourse on Jesus by quoting **Psalm 118:22**, confirming his belief the prophecy was fulfilled. Peter and John knew Jesus was the Messiah spoken about to Israel for two thousand years. Jesus was in fact the cornerstone of the faith,—the cornerstone which would be rejected.

   c. What was Peter's final declaration about Jesus in **Acts 4:12**? Fill in the blanks below.

      There is _____ in no one else; for there is no other name under heaven that

      has been given among men, by which we _____ _____ _____.

This is quite a declaration from Peter! He and John believed salvation was from Jesus Christ alone. Today many people, even those who attend church, say there are many roads to heaven. Read an excerpt from an article entitled, "Americans: My Faith Isn't the Only Way to Heaven."

   "America remains a nation of believers, but a new survey finds most Americans don't feel their religion is the only way to eternal life—even if their faith tradition teaches otherwise.

   The findings, revealed Monday in a survey of 35,000 adults, can either be taken as a positive sign of growing religious tolerance, or disturbing evidence that Americans dismiss or don't know fundamental teachings of their own faiths.

   Among the more startling numbers in the survey, conducted last year by the Pew Forum on Religion and Public Life: 57 percent of evangelical church attenders said they believe many religions can lead to eternal life, in conflict with traditional evangelical teaching."[12]

6. Read **John 14:6**.

   "Jesus said to him, 'I am the way, and the truth, and the life; no one comes to the Father but through Me.'"

   a. Does Scripture give any indication as to alternative ways to God other than Jesus?

   b. What do you say? God's Word clearly says Jesus is the source of salvation and the only road to heaven. Although the Bible is clear, the choice is yours. Who do you say Jesus is?

c. Are you willing, like Peter and John, to proclaim Jesus as Savior and Lord even when you are in a difficult situation? Write your thoughts below.

Not only did Peter claim salvation is obtained through Christ alone, but salvation comes through Jesus, the one these leaders rejected and killed. Who were those leaders? They obviously had the authority to place Peter and John in jail. These men were known as the Sanhedrin.

Moses originally appointed seventy elders as spiritual and community leaders. This is believed to be the origin of the Sanhedrin. Ezra is presumed to have reorganized this body after the exile. In Ezra's time, the Persians gave authority to this Jewish body in local affairs. Later, the Greeks permitted a body known as the *gerousia* ("senate"), which was made up of elders, to represent the nation. This body has wide powers under the Romans, with the exception of a short period under Gabinius. The term used for the district councils was subsequently adopted for the more powerful *gerousia* at Jerusalem, and by the close of the first century BC this council was known as the *synedrion*.

By the time of **Acts 4**, under the Roman Empire, "the powers of the *Sanhedrin* were extensive; the internal government of the country lay in its hands." They had shifted from helping Moses with disputes among the people to becoming Israel's judge and jury under the authority of the Roman government. In the days of Peter and John, the Sanhedrin consisted of priests, scribes, and the elders of Israel who were led by the high priest.[13] Although the text does not use the word *Sanhedrin*, **Acts 4** gives us every indication these leaders had judicial authority. These men could make life or death decisions. In the earthly realm, they had this power over the lives of Peter and John, just as they had had it over Jesus. How could these *religious* leaders have power to put people in jail? This may be a difficult concept to grasp for those of us born and raised in the United States, yet this was reality in the first century for the Jewish people in Jerusalem.

---

### Questions to Ponder

Do you see our society or government trying to suppress Christian values?
If so, why do you believe this to be happening?

---

Richard Wurmbrand, founder of **Voice of the Martyrs** in Bartlesville Oklahoma, was born in Bucharest, Romania. He spent fourteen years imprisoned in Europe for his views against communism. His first arrest was in 1948 and after he served eight-and–a-half years in prison, he was released. Like Peter and John, he was told not to preach again in the name of Jesus. In 1959 he was rearrested and sentenced to twenty-five years in prison for speaking from the pulpit "ideas contrary to Communist doctrine. Due to increased political pressure from Western countries, Richard was granted another amnesty and released in 1964. In December 1965, the

Norwegian Mission to the Jews and the Hebrew Christian Alliance paid $10,000 in ransom to the Communist government to allow the Wurmbrand family to leave Romania."[14] Within a year, the Wurmbrands were in the United States. Richard never intended to stay, but God had different plans. Richard's knowledge of the Communist system was extensive. He wrote over twenty books in which he openly spoke of the philosophy and schemes of the Communist party and its leaders. He wrote:

*Vetchernaia Moskva*, a Communist newspaper, let pass a Freudian slip of the pen:

> *We do not fight against believers and not even against clergymen. We fight against God to snatch believers from Him.*[15]

A "fight against God to snatch believers from Him" is the only logical explanation for the Communist fight against religion. . . . It was not a fight against false belief in a nonexistent God that preoccupied him [Marx]. He [Marx] believed that God does exist and wanted to see this Absolute Spirit decompose, like many prisoners of the Communists who were made to rot in jail. . . . Marx wrote in *"The Communist Manifesto"* that his aim was the abolition not only of all religions, but also of all morals, which would make everything permissible. . . . Inscribed on a poster [in Paris in 1968], "It is forbidden to forbid," which is the natural consequence of "Nothing is true, and everything is permissible."[16]

**Romans 1:18-20** teaches:

"For the wrath of God is revealed from heaven against all ungodliness and unrighteousness of men who suppress the truth in unrighteousness, because that which is known about God is evident within them; for God made it evident to them. For since the creation of the world His invisible attributes, His eternal power and divine nature, have been clearly seen, being understood through what has been made, so that they are without excuse."

In **John 8** Jesus was speaking with the Pharisees and told them "I am He," indicating that He was the long-awaited Messiah, the Pharisees wanted to kill Jesus and began to look for ways to accomplish this. **Note:** Although the Sanhedrin had extensive powers at the time of Christ, under Roman law the Sanhedrin could not put someone to death. Therefore they had to manipulate and falsify Jesus' words and actions to accomplish their goal of killing Jesus. We will look at the Sanhedrin's tactics as we move throughout this study.

The Sanhedrin was trying to prevent Jesus from speaking truth. Below are the words Jesus spoke to those whose mission was suppression.

"You [Pharisees] are of your father the devil, and you want to do the desires of your father. He was a murderer from the beginning, and does not stand in the truth because there is no truth in him. Whenever he speaks a lie, he speaks from his own nature, for he is a liar and the father of lies" **(John 8:44).**

Can you see, ultimately, the earthly source of suppressing Christianity is not the *true* perpetrator? The Sanhedrin, a community, society, or government might be dismissive, show contempt, or even try to restrict your free expression of the gospel. They don't want the light exposed and are suppressing the truth within them.

Suppression of truth has been a tactic of Satan's from the beginning. You must decide today whose agenda you will promote.

Before we close, read one last exhortation from our Lord.

> "So do not fear; you are more valuable than many sparrows. Therefore everyone who confesses Me before men, I will also confess him before My Father who is in heaven. But whoever denies Me before men, I will also deny him before My Father who is in heaven" **Matthew 10:31-33**.

Tomorrow we will see how the Sanhedrin reacted to Peter and John and how they wanted to silence the apostles' witness. For now, think about what the Lord has shown you today.

7. What has God shown you that you need to apply to your life? Your church? Your nation?

We will continue our study in **Acts 4** tomorrow. Close with your prayer to the Lord. Ask Him for wisdom for this study and the troubled times in which we live.

*"But Peter and John answered and said to them, 'Whether it is right in the sight of God to give heed to you rather than to God, you be the judge; for we cannot stop speaking about what we have seen and heard.'"*
*Acts 4:19-20*

# WEEK 2—DAY 2

Yesterday we discussed our foundational truth—***Believe there is salvation in none other than Jesus Christ.*** This is the foundation of the Christian faith; without this belief cemented firmly in the recesses of our souls the subsequent steps are impossible to comprehend. As a seasoned believer, you might have a tendency to skip or skim through this fundamental principle because you are well acquainted with this truth. However, valiant warrior, this week will better equip you for the battles ahead. Therefore, press on . . . press on, my friend.

As always, we want to begin our study with a time of prayer before the Lord. Ask Him to implant His Word in your heart. His Word is truth. His Word is wisdom. Ask for fresh insights about the fundamental principle of salvation in Jesus Christ alone.

We begin with a review of Day 1. These points will help refresh your memory.

- ❖ Peter and John healed the lame man at the temple.
- ❖ The people were amazed and thought the power (*dúnamis*) was from Peter and John.
- ❖ Peter proclaimed the power (*dúnamis*) was from Christ.
- ❖ Peter began to preach salvation is *in Christ alone* to the people at the temple.
- ❖ The priest, temple guard, and Sadducees were disturbed by Peter and John and put them in jail.
- ❖ Peter and John were brought before the high priest.
- ❖ The high priest asked by what power (*dúnamis*) Peter and John healed the lame man.
- ❖ Peter proclaimed Christ as healer and stated salvation is in none other than Christ.

What did the Sanhedrin think of Peter's and John's proclamation? How did the Sanhedrin respond? This is where we will begin today.

1. Read **Acts 4:13-14**.

    a. What did the Sanhedrin observe about Peter and John?


    b. What did the Sanhedrin understand about Peter and John?

        ❖

        ❖


    c. What did the Sanhedrin recognize about Peter and John?

d. Who accompanied Peter and John?

e. How did the Sanhedrin respond?

Peter and John left the Sanhedrin speechless! Don't you enjoy God's sense of humor sometimes? Let's expand on these Scriptures for just a moment. Below are key English words used in the text and their Greek meanings.

**Confidence**–*parrēsia: the act of speaking, freedom or frankness in speaking. New Testament meaning–freedom in speaking all that one thinks or pleases.*[17]

**Uneducated**–*agrámmotos: unlearned, illiterate [I am sure you can recognize the English word grammar from this Greek root word.] The a at the beginning of the word denotes without. Therefore, it translates without grammar.*[18]

**Untrained**–*idiē 'tēs: A common man as opposed either to a man of rank or education.*[19]

**Recognize**–*epiginō 'skō: To know fully, to be fully acquainted with.*[20]

f. Imagine what the Sanhedrin might have said to one another after Peter's and John's speech. Write below what you think they might have said.

"Now as they observed the confidence of Peter and John and understood that they were uneducated and untrained men, they were amazed, and began to recognize them as having been with Jesus" **(Acts 4:13).**

---

### Questions to Ponder

When the words of **Acts 4:13** jump off the page we often feel the weight of God's conviction. Thus, we need to ask the hard questions:

❖ Do people marvel at me because they can see I have been with Jesus?
❖ Do people observe my confidence in my relationship with Him?
❖ Do I speak boldly about Jesus, despite my lack/abundance of education or training?
❖ Do I speak the truth despite a possible unpleasant outcome?

Write your thoughts about these questions below.

---

2. Read **Acts 4:15-18**, then answer the questions below.

    a. The high priest, Annas, sent Peter and John out of the Council so the Council could talk amongst themselves. What question did the Sanhedrin pose?

    b. What could the Sanhedrin not deny?

    c. What was the goal of the Sanhedrin (v. 17)?

    d. When the Sanhedrin summoned Peter and John, what did they command (v.18)?

Peter and John were experiencing firsthand the same treatment Jesus had received from the Sanhedrin just before Jesus went to the cross.

An unfortunate reality is, efforts to stop the spread of the gospel places restrictions on people speaking or teaching in the name of Jesus and are tactics not limited to biblical times. Satan continues to use restrictions effectively. Richard Wurmbrand, in *Tortured for Christ*, spoke about this very tactic:

> The year 1956 arrived. I had been in prison eight-and-a-half years. I had lost much weight, gained ugly scars, been brutally beaten and kicked, derided, starved, pressured, questioned ad nauseum, threatened, and neglected. None of this had produced the results my captors were seeking. So, in discouragement—and amid protests over my imprisonment—they turned me loose. I was allowed to return to my old position as pastor for just one week. I preached two sermons. Then they called me in and told me that I could not preach anymore, nor engage in any further religious activity.[21]

3. Do you see this tactic of specifically suppressing the gospel used today? Write your thoughts below.

Let's return to Acts and find out how Peter and John responded to the Sanhedrin who were prohibiting them to speak about Jesus.

4. Read **Acts 4:19-20**. Fill in the blanks below.

"Whether it is _____ in the sight of God to give heed to _____ rather than

to _____, you be the _____; for _____ _____

_____ speaking what we have _____ and _____."

"We [Peter and John] cannot stop speaking what we have seen and heard." **Acts 4:20** is the heart of this Bible study. We should be as passionate as Peter and John about proclaiming the gospel message for the same reasons they were passionate. We should not be able to keep ourselves from speaking about the miracles we have seen Christ do in and through our lives. Along with speaking of those miracles we can speak of what we have heard Christ has done in the lives of others around us. You may think, "I have not seen any miracles." Isn't salvation from hell's pit a miracle? At the moment of salvation you were transformed from a child of darkness into a child of light. The angels in heaven rejoiced and your destiny was sealed! In one moment, you went from eternal damnation to eternal life. What greater miracle can there be?

Salvation in Christ was the core of Peter's and John's passion. Their belief was so imbedded in the recesses of their souls they were willing to boldly proclaim Christ's name, no matter what the cost.

We can speak boldly like Peter and John about what we have seen and heard when we have an unwavering assurance and belief in Jesus Christ as the source of salvation. This is where we will spend the remainder of our time together this week. Let's look at other Scriptures that correspond with this week's foundational truth—**Believe there is salvation in none other than Jesus Christ.**

The book of Hebrews is about Jesus being *greater than*: greater than the angels—greater than Moses—greater than the priests of old. Therefore, Hebrews is a *great* place to launch our discovery process.

5. **Hebrews 5:9** says, "And having been made perfect, He [Jesus] became to all those who obey Him the source of eternal salvation."

    Jesus is the source of what to those who obey Him?




This was an important proclamation to the Jewish audience who received this epistle. The Jews were steeped in tradition like a good tea steeped in hot water. After the water is infused with the tea you can't separate the two. The Jews so identified themselves with tradition, if you were to remove their customs it would be like removing Jewishness itself.

In the Old Testament, God chose to visit many of the patriarchs through angels; as a result, the Jews' reverence and awe of angels bordered on worship. Moses was their deliverer from physical bondage; they revered him as much as they revered angels. They revered the Law, handwritten by the finger of God, which Moses had brought down from the mountain. They believed the Law was their source of salvation, instead of the One who gave the Law, our Lord Himself. The Jews who received the letter we know today as the book of Hebrews did believe in Jesus, yet they continued to try to "add" to the salvation message; they continued to make other traditions equal to Jesus. The writer of Hebrews, like a good lawyer, took each Jewish ordinance and compared it to Jesus. The conclusion is there is nothing under the earth, on the earth, or above the earth, which is greater than Jesus. Salvation is through Christ alone. The writer took everything the Jews held so dear, cast a shadow upon the traditions of old, and pointed the people to Jesus. Jesus, the One who deserves worship, is the source of eternal salvation.

What do we hold on to, my friend? Are there traditions, people, or things, which keep us from devoting our worship to the only One who is worthy? Jesus is the only One who is *better than* any tradition. Just as with the Jews, anything which seeps into your belief system, attitudes or behavior and becomes important in and of itself, needs to be removed from the kingship seat. Traditions, when you hold them greater than Jesus, turn from good to destruction. If the tradition is being held with equal or higher regard than your relationship with Christ, the tradition needs to be put in its place!

It's time to do some soul-searching. We need to self-assess by reviewing the list below regarding customs, people and cultures. The list could be endless so we will keep it to a minimum. There will also be room at the end to write down anything God may show you personally.

6.  As you read the items in each category, ask the Lord to convict you if there is anything you have made more important than your relationship with Christ.

| Church Custom: | People: | Today's Culture: |
| --- | --- | --- |
| Baptism | Pastor | Job |
| | Bible study teacher | Politics |
| Style of worship | Spouse | Money |
| Denominational differences | Children | Success |
| | | Power or position |
| Love of the brethren | Friend | Education |
| Church attendance | Governmental leader | Popularity |

Is the Lord speaking to you about some things in your life, even something not listed above? Write your thoughts below.

Jesus needs to be our sufficiency. He is the One who will carry us through when we lose our job and the money is gone. He is the One who is there when we are old and gray and our mind is gone. He is our peace when our loved ones die or our friends betray us. He is our healer when we are diagnosed with a deadly disease. He is there to pick up the pieces when our world is falling apart, and He can restore what man cannot. My friend let nothing come before Christ. We owe it all to Him because He paid it all for us.

7.  You've work hard today; let's close with our application questions. What has God shown you today, which you can apply to your life? Your church? Your nation?

8. Close today with your prayer of praise to the Lord, for He is worthy of praise. Thank Him for so great a salvation. Salvation is undeserved by man but graciously given by the only One capable of paying for sin. Praise Him, thank Him, and worship Him!

*"Then I looked, and I heard the voice of many angels around the throne*
*and the living creatures and the elders; and the number of them was*
*myriads of myriads, and thousands of thousands, saying with a loud voice,*
*'Worthy is the Lamb that was slain to receive power and riches and wisdom*
*and might and honor and glory and blessing.'"*
**Revelation 5:11-12**

# WEEK 2—DAY 3

Peter and John proclaimed to the Sanhedrin in **Acts 4:12**, "And there is salvation in no one else; for there is no other name under heaven that has been given among men, by which we must be saved." As we continue to study this fundamental belief, begin today with a prayer to our Lord. Ask Him to enlighten you to this foundational tenet.

Yesterday we closed with **Hebrews 5:9**, "And having been made perfect, He became to all those who obey Him the source of eternal salvation." We spoke about the theme in Hebrews stating Jesus is *greater than*. If Christ is to be *greater than* in our lives, what are some attributes we must look for as we look within and inspect our hearts? Let's look at **1 John** for some clues to our question, "What attributes of Jesus do we as believers need to possess?"

1.  Read **1 John 4:11-17** and answer the following questions.

    a.  Of what are we to bear witness (v. 14)?

    b.  What do we learn about those who confess Jesus as the Son of God (v. 15)?

A key word in **1 John 4:11-17** is *abide*. This word comes from the Greek word *ménō* meaning, *to remain in something, being steadfast, persevering in.*[22] Abiding in Christ is in the DNA of a believer. What does it mean to abide in Christ? Let's observe what **1 John** teaches about a believer's DNA in Christ.

    c.  **1 John 4:13** tells us, "By this we know that we abide in Him and He in us . . . " Write the message from **1 John 4:13-16**.

      ❖ He has given us _____ _____ (v. 13).

      ❖ We bear witness that the Son is the _____ of the world (v. 14).

      ❖ We _____ Jesus is the Son of God (v. 15).

      ❖ We have come to _____ and have _____ the _____ which God has for us (v. 16).

      ❖ One who abides in _____ abides in _____ and God abides in _____ (v. 16).

d.  What a description of one who abides in Christ! Now review the sentences and make them personal. Replace the pronouns, where appropriate, with your name.

Some DNA characteristics may seem obvious, but note **1 John 4:16**, ". . . the one who abides in <u>love</u> abides in God" [emphasis mine]. Abiding in love may seem like a simple task until you start delving into what John is trying to teach us. The Greeks had several meanings for the word *love*. In most of the New Testament, including this text, the Greek word for love is *agápē*, *"It involves God doing what He knows is best for man and not necessarily what man desires. God gives man what he needs, not what man wants."*[23] *Agápē* is used in each reference to *love* in **1 John 4:11-17**.

e.  Returning to our text in **1 John 4:11** fill in the blanks.

"Beloved, if God so loved _____, we also ought to _____ one _____."

**If** we believe there is salvation in none other than Jesus Christ . . .

*and*

**If** we believe Jesus is greater than . . .

**Then** we will love, *agápē,* others.

We are to do what is best for others, regardless of whether or not they think it is best for them. Often this can put us in quite a dilemma.

The concept of loving someone enough to do what is best for him or her can be illustrated by the parent/child relationship. When a child is a toddler, parents often go to great lengths to childproof their home. They mount cabinet and drawer locks in the kitchen and bathrooms so little hands can't obtain and ingest harmful ingredients. Parents may install plastic plug covers for the electrical sockets to prevent children from getting nasty shocks. The child may be curious and consistently try to acquire what is hidden and unobtainable. Some children may throw temper tantrums, yet the parent, out of love, gives the child protection—what he or she needs instead of what he or she wants.

This illustration is similar to what Christ does in our lives. Humanity is the Lord's greatest creation. His fondest desire is for our salvation. That is why He died to be our Savior. Once we become believers in Him, He continues to sanctify us until we are face to face with Him. By the way, my first Bible study *Bound To Be Free* teaches about the sanctification process. Let's equip ourselves with Scriptures to solidify the concept of *agápē*.

2.  a.  Read **1 Timothy 2:3-4** below.

"This is good and acceptable in the sight of God our Savior, who desires all men to be saved and to come to the knowledge of the truth."

b. What is God's desire for all men?

&#10087;

&#10087;

3. a. Read **2 Peter 3:9-10** below.

"The Lord is not slow about His promise, as some count slowness, but is patient toward you, not wishing for any to perish but for all to come to repentance. But the day of the Lord will come like a thief, in which the heavens will pass away with a roar and the elements will be destroyed with intense heat, and the earth and its works will be burned up."

b. What is the "promise" (v. 10)?

c. Why is the Lord slow in returning (v. 9)?

d. Looping back to **1 John 4:10-11**, verse 10 tells us, "this is love . . ." Who loved whom first?

e. Because God loved us, what is our responsibility?

f. How did God demonstrate His love (v. 10)?

What a fancy word, *propitiation*. *Merriam-Webster Dictionary* defines propitiate as, *to gain or regain the favor or goodwill of; appease.*[24]

The Greek word for *propitiation* is *hilasmós,* referring *to Christ as the one who not only propitiates but offers himself as the propitiatory sacrifice. He is both the sacrifice and the officiating High Priest.*[25]

One of the best-known verses in the Bible gives us a picture of God's *agápē* love, and also helps us illustrate the definition, this verse is **John 3:16**. "For God so loved the world that He gave His only begotten Son . . ." God's *agápē* love was demonstrated by giving Christ as the sacrifice so man could regain favor (propitiate) with God. Only through Christ is man able to regain favor with God; therefore, we must **believe there is salvation in none other than Jesus Christ.**

Let's turn our attention to the key word *believe*. Christ's sacrifice on the cross is essential to salvation. Just as essential is man's need to believe; yet both are crucial for salvation which gives eternal life. What does truly believing in Jesus mean? **James 2:19**, says, "You believe that God is one. You do well; the demons also believe, and shudder." If even the demons believe, what does a true belief produce?

To begin this discussion let's look at the original definition for the word, *believe*. The Greek word *pisteúó* means, "*to believe, also to be persuaded of, and hence, to place confidence in, to trust, signifies, in this sense of the word, reliance upon, not mere credence.*"[26] This belief is not mere knowledge but belief, which empowers you to trust and have confidence in Christ, which moves you into action. Let's look at some examples from God's Word to explain this daring statement.

Most people are familiar with the story of the woman at the well in **John 4:23-26**. Jesus had an encounter with this Samaritan woman and brought out the facts of this woman's life. She had been married five times and was currently living with a man who was not her husband. Jesus then began a discussion about worship saying, ". . . true worshipers shall worship the Father in spirit and truth." The woman replied, "I know that Messiah is coming (He who is called Christ) [Christ is the Greek word for Messiah]; when that One comes, He will declare all things to us." Jesus' response to this Samaritan woman was, "I who speak to you, am He" **(John 4:23-26, comment added).** This is where we begin our investigation, researching the woman's response to Jesus' proclamation of His Messiahship.

4.  Read **John 4:28-30, 39-41**.

    a.  Do the Samaritan woman's actions display a belief *(pisteúó)* that persuaded her to trust Christ, the Messiah?


    b.  Because of the Samaritan woman's belief, what action(s) did she take (v. 39)?



    c.  The Samaritan woman's action was to testify. What was the result of her belief and action?



5.  Read **John 4:42**.

    What did the people tell the Samaritan woman?

These verses show the natural progression of the belief process.

The Samaritan woman believed.
→ The Samaritan woman testified to others.
→ The others believed because of the Samaritan woman's testimony.
→ The others' belief became their own because of their experience with the Lord.

When Paul wrote to the church at Colossae, he confirmed to them that after they believed they were continually bearing fruit (**Colossians 1:6**). Paul told the church he was praying for them that they "may be filled with the knowledge of His will in all spiritual wisdom and understanding" (**Colossians 1:9**).

6. Read **Colossians 1:10-11**. These Scriptures give us the reasons why Paul was praying for the church. List them below.
   ❖
   ❖
   ❖
   ❖

Let's recap the words or actions of Peter and John, the Samaritan woman, and Paul.

| Peter and John | Samaritan Woman | Paul |
|---|---|---|
| **Acts 4:20**<br><br>"…we [Paul & John] cannot stop speaking what we have seen and heard." | **John 4:28-30**<br><br>❖ Woman left waterpot, went to city and said to the men:<br>❖ "Come see a man who told me all the things that I have done; this is not the Christ, is it?"<br><br>**John 4:39-42**<br>❖ Samaritans believed in Him because of the word of the woman who testified.<br>❖ Samaritans said—"It is no longer because of what you said that we believe, for we have heard for ourselves and know this One is indeed the Savior of the world." | **Colossians 1:10-11**<br><br>Paul prayed for the church.<br><br>**Why?**<br>❖ Walk in a manner worthy of the Lord.<br>❖ Please the Lord in all respects.<br>❖ Bear fruit in every good work.<br>❖ Increase in the knowledge of God. |

b. How does the statement on page 62 "Belief is not mere knowledge but belief which empowers you to trust and have confidence in Christ, which moves you into action" apply to each of these situations? Write your answer in the appropriate column of the chart below.

| Peter and John | Samaritan Woman | Paul |
| --- | --- | --- |
|  |  |  |

c. One of my favorite Scriptures, which talks about a belief that propels you into action, is **Daniel 11:32b.** Write it out below.

This Scripture comes from one of the most fascinating books in the Old Testament. Daniel, a prophet of the Lord, received visions of future events dealing with the Jewish people. These dreams were so accurate biblical skeptics try to claim the book of Daniel was written AFTER the events occurred. Skeptics cannot conceive of a God who is Sovereign and knows the end from the beginning. Yet we know He is the Alpha and Omega; not only does He know the end from the beginning, He created the end from the beginning.

Daniel was captured and taken to Babylon by King Nebuchadnezzar in 605 BC when he was about fifteen years old. Daniel 11:1 opens in the first year of Darius the Mede, which history tells us is sixty-six years later in 539 BC This makes Daniel eighty-one years old.

**Daniel 10** prophesies the fall of the Persian Empire to the prince of Greece. We know today this prince was Alexander the Great. **Daniel 11:4 comment added** tells us, "But as soon as he [Alexander the Great] has arisen, his kingdom will be broken up and parceled out toward the four points of the compass, though not to his own descendants…for his sovereignty will be uprooted and given to others besides them." **Daniel 11:5-35** focuses on the kingdoms of the north and south, (which would be parceled out at the death of Alexander the Great). The kings of the south refer to the Ptolemaic kingdom of Egypt and the kings of the north refer to the Seleucus/Antiochus empire. This territory includes modern-day countries like Iran, Iraq, parts of Turkey, and Syria.[27] **Daniel 11:21-35** speaks of Antiochus IV Epiphanes, King of the North. Antiochus is described as a despicable person arising in a time of tranquility and seizing the kingdom by intrigue. He makes an alliance but his true intent is deception. He gains power devises schemes, and confiscates riches. Then a king from the south [Ptolemy VI Philometor] will mobilize for war. **Daniel 11:27** teaches, "As for both kings, their hearts will be intent on evil, and they will speak lies to each other at the same table ...” Philometor is defeated by Rome and Antiochus returns to Jerusalem where he plunders the temple and massacres any Jews opposed to him.

The Jews know this time in history as the Maccabean revolt. *The Bible Knowledge Commentary: An Exposition of the Scriptures* by J. F. Walvoord, and R. B. Zuck, gives us this enlightening commentary:

> “Antiochus took out his frustration on the Jews, the city of Jerusalem, and their temple. He vented his fury against the holy covenant, the entire Mosaic system, favoring any renegade Jews who turned to help him. He desecrated the temple and abolished the daily sacrifice. Antiochus sent his general Apollonius with 22,000 soldiers into Jerusalem on what was purported to be a peace mission. But they attacked Jerusalem on the Sabbath, killed many people, took many women and children as slaves, and plundered and burned the city.
>
> In seeking to exterminate Judaism and to Hellenize the Jews, he forbade the Jews to follow their religious practices (including their festivals and circumcision), and commanded that copies of the Law be burned. Then he set up the abomination that causes desolation. In this culminating act he erected on December 16, 167 BC an altar to Zeus on the altar of burnt offering outside the temple, and had a pig offered on the altar. The Jews were compelled to offer a pig on the 25th of each month to celebrate Antiochus Epiphanes’ birthday. Antiochus promised apostate Jews (those who ... violated the covenant; cf. v. 30) great reward if they would set aside the God of Israel and worship Zeus, the god of Greece. Many in Israel were persuaded by his promises (flattery) and worshiped the false god. However, a small remnant remained faithful to God, refusing to engage in those abominable practices. Antiochus IV died insane in Persia in 163 BC.
>
> This has in view the rise of the Maccabean revolt. Mattathias, a priest, was the father of five sons. (One of them, Judas, became well known for refurbishing and restoring the temple in late 164 BC. He was called Judas Maccabeus, “the Hammerer.”) In 166, Mattathias refused to submit to this false religious system. He and his sons fled from Jerusalem to the mountains and began the Maccabean revolt. At first only a few Jews joined them. But as their movement became popular, many joined them, some out of sincere motives and some from false motives. The suffering that the faithful endured served to refine and purify them.”[28]

Knowing the events about which Daniel prophesied about gives new insight into the phrase, “but the people who know their God will display strength and take action”! As you can see ***“Believing there is salvation in none other than Jesus Christ”*** is not a passive belief. This belief empowers you to take action. We have seen this to be true for the Samaritan woman through her testimony, Paul through his prayers, Peter and John through their confidence to continue speaking about what they had seen and heard, and our fearless Maccabeans who could not allow God’s temple to be defiled.

You’ve worked hard today. Let’s close with our transformation questions.

7. What has our Lord been showing you today? Write what you gleaned from today's lesson and desire to apply to your life? Your church? Your nation?

8. Write your closing prayer to Him.

*". . . but the people who know their God will display strength and take action."*
**Daniel 11:32b**

# WEEK 2—DAY 4

This week we learned a Christian's belief is not merely knowledge, but knowledge which empowers one to have faith, trust and confidence in Christ, thereby moving one to action. We studied Peter and John who were commanded by the Sanhedrin not to speak or teach in the name of Jesus. But their belief gave them courage to say, "Whether it is right in the sight of God to give heed to you rather than to God you be the judge; for we cannot stop speaking about what we have seen and heard" (**Acts 4:19-20**). We examined how the Samaritan woman's belief compelled her to testify to others what she had seen and heard. The result of her actions led many to know Jesus as Messiah (which, translated, means *Christ*). We saw how Paul's belief led him to pray for others so they could follow Paul's example, walk in a manner worthy of our Lord and bear fruit. Finally, we looked at the Maccabean revolt, foretold by the prophet Daniel 350-400 years before those events took place.

Jesus describes belief as truth which empowers us to trust, and moves us to action. Let's see what Jesus says.

1. Read **Matthew 12:33-34**.

   a.  How is a tree known?


   b.  What is spoken out of one's mouth (v. 34)?



Our prayer focus today is to ask our Lord to give us confidence like the great heroes mentioned earlier. This will drive us to action so that we will bear fruit, which is evidence of our belief. Jesus also said, in **Luke 6:45**, "The good man out of the good treasure of his heart brings forth what is good; and the evil man out of the evil treasure brings forth what is evil; for his mouth speaks from that which fills his heart" (emphasis added). These verses demonstrate how our lives will be the evidence of what we believe. Write your prayer.




**Remember:** Today is Day 4 of our study and we are stepping away from the traditional Bible study method. We are studying our Christian heritage and the men and women whose strong belief propelled them into action. These great men and women of God did extraordinary acts because of their faith in our Lord Jesus Christ. We will begin our journey with Martin Luther. As I read Martin Luther's biography, my first thought about him was how ordinary he was. Yes, Luther was an ordinary man with extraordinary faith. God's specialty is taking sold-out believers, people like you and me, and doing extraordinary works through them to point people to Himself. **James 5:17** talks about an ordinary man with a nature just like ours. What did this ordinary man accomplish because of his belief?

2. Read **James 5:17-18**.

    a.  What was Elijah able to bring about through prayer?

    b.  What happened the second time Elijah prayed?

God used Elijah, an ordinary man in biblical times. Throughout history He has continued to work through ordinary people, and He continues His work through ordinary people today. Martin Luther was just such an ordinary man. It has been said of Luther, "It's no exaggeration to say that almost every branch of modern Protestant Christianity owes some portion of its spiritual heritage to Martin Luther, a man of radical faith."[29] Let's consider the life of Martin Luther to see how God worked through the ordinary man we know today as "The Great Reformer."

Martin Luther was born in 1483 to Hans and Margaret, devout Catholics, who raised their children as devout Catholics. "His parents taught him the value of good works, taught him the reliance on the priesthood and deep faith in church. His father walked uprightly and lived in honor, carrying the doctrines of Catholicism close to his heart."[30] This was the heritage Hans and Margaret passed down to Martin and his brothers and sisters.

Martin's parents struggled to rise above poverty and to make life better for their children. Hans worked as a miner in Eisleben, Saxony (later called Germany), but soon moved to Mansfield in hopes of leasing a mine. Hans wanted to ensure a prosperous future for his children; therefore his aspiration was for Martin to become a lawyer. This would give his oldest son financial security and an elevated standing in the community. At the age of thirteen, Hans sent Martin to the neighboring town of Magdeburg to continue his education. From that time on, Martin never lived with his parents more than summers or Christmas breaks. Although the Luthers' had made great strides in overcoming poverty, Martin still had to beg for his food in Magdeburg because his father could only provide enough money for his school tuition. The practice of begging was common for these young boys, but Martin found the times particularly difficult. He longed for the more comfortable days with his family, yet he relished the days in school because of his hunger for learning. Others noticed his enthusiasm for learning and Martin became known as a gifted student. In the end, Martin's passion for knowledge eventually overcame his longing for the comforts of home.

As Martin grew older, thoughts of entering the priesthood would often surface. He would quietly shove them back in the recesses of his mind, as Martin had never defied his father's wishes, and his father was determined Martin would be a lawyer. John Braun, an older friend of Martin's, spoke of the many struggles he had before entering the priesthood. During one of these conversations, John told Martin when he made his final decision to answer the holy calling, a deep peace overtook him. Braun's account continued to resonate with Luther and fueled his own dilemma.

Despite Martin's inner battle, he could not defy his father, so he conformed by entering law school at the age of twenty-two. Soon afterward, while traveling from home after a visit, a bolt of lightning knocked him off his horse. Immediately, Martin contemplated standing before God and confessing he had followed his earthly father's wishes rather than his Heavenly Father's desires. So disturbed by this image, Martin, upon arrival back at school, promptly resigned and entered the priesthood. Hans refused to give permission, refused to see or speak to Martin, and many years passed before he finally acknowledged the decision.

Martin's struggle was not different from many of the faithful men and women of the Bible. Remember Peter who unashamedly stood before the Sanhedrin and proclaimed, "We cannot stop speaking about what we have seen and heard" (**Acts 4:20**). Just two months before Peter's great proclamation, we saw a very different, very timid Peter. Let's look at this encounter.

3. Read **Luke 22:31-34**.

    a. This event was immediately before Jesus was crucified. What did Jesus tell Peter in **Luke 22:34**?

    b. What had Peter just told Jesus (v. 33)?

4. Let's read the outcome of Jesus' prophecy in **Luke 22:60-62**. Contemplate with me for a moment the words, "And the Lord turned and looked at Peter. And Peter remembered . . . ." What might Peter have been thinking and feeling at this time?

Peter had indeed denied Jesus three times. How could this be? Peter had spent almost every day of the previous three-and-a-half years with Jesus. How did Peter change from being a denying friend into a bold witness in just two months?

5. Read **Mark 16:1-7**.

    a. What did the angel tell Mary Magdalene (v. 7)?

**Note:** We know Jesus is the young man in white from **John 20:11-21**. If you have a moment you may want to read these corresponding Scriptures.

    b. Let's contemplate the words from Mark. He heard Mary say something like, "I just spoke to an angel! And he told me to go and tell the disciples and Peter, 'Jesus is going to Galilee, there you will see Him, just as He said you would! Jesus is alive. He's alive!'" What do you think Peter might have thought/felt? He had denied Jesus before His crucifixion, yet Jesus still called for him. Write your thoughts below.

What happened? Jesus happened! He died, rose from the dead, and conquered death. Jesus also sought out Peter after his embarrassing betrayal. Jesus met Peter at his point of need, and let him know that despite his past he still had a future with Jesus. Don't we need to hear the same message? The world may be saying you're finished, but as long as you still have breath in your body our Lord still has a purpose for you on this earth. Peter had a radical experience with a radical God. This was the answer for Peter's timidity and doubt, and this was the answer for Luther.

Are we any different than Martin Luther or Peter? In the late 90s I went on staff with a church-planting organization. The marketing manager wanted to put my talents in marketing/advertising and sales to use for *kingdom purposes*. After a very long conversation in which I all but accepted that position, I woke up the next morning to spend time in God's Word. That day my Lord spoke to me in a non-audible voice but it was as loud as thunder. I heard, "Stop trying to please your earthly father and start trying to please your heavenly Father, and I [Lord] will do great and mighty things in and through your life." The message was clear. My dad would have been very proud of my stepping into this marketing role and my father's approval was something I hungered for. I had temporarily taken my eyes off the Lord's assignment for my life, and turned my focus to the task of people pleasing. My dad would have been delighted if I had chosen the marketing position instead of my God-given appointment of staff missionary, and would have proudly spoken of it over coffee with his friends. But my Heavenly Father had different plans. The world may never speak of the *great and mighty things* my life has produced because, by the world's standards, my *things* probably won't measure up to be *great and mighty*. Yet God may have a Peter or Martin Luther moment planned for the future of this ordinary woman of God. He might choose to do an extraordinary work through me because of my faith and obedience to Christ alone.

Thus far we haven't seen Martin Luther do anything extraordinary, so let's return and see how God used this man mightily. Eventually Martin went to Wittenberg, Germany, as a member of the Augustinian Order. This order was founded in the mid-thirteenth century, named after Saint Augustine, whose writings were very influential in the development of Christian theology. Martin became a staff professor of the prestigious Wittenberg University. With Luther and other well-respected intellectuals on staff, people soon began to speak of *the Wittenberg Theology*.[31] Shortly before Martin's appointment to Wittenberg, he had the unique opportunity to travel to Rome. Historians point to this trip as a turning point in Luther's life. "Luther saw and felt a Rome utterly abandoned to money, luxury, and kindred evils. He was stunned and unable to understand it—but he did not stay in Rome long enough to rebel against it. . . . As the years went by for Luther, and as other things in theology and church organization became clear to him, he remembered the Rome of his visit and could see far more clearly how utterly corrupt was the leadership offered to the great church in 1510."[32]

Luther became increasingly uncomfortable with the church. "He was thoroughly conservative by nature. He loved his tradition, his church and his people. But he was honest. He hated sin in all places, high and low. He would protect his people. He would honor the obligations of his teaching office. He would speak clearly, decisively, directly."[33] This disharmony became so unsettling that by 1517 Luther had written ninety-five theses—propositions he intended to dispute and debate to reform the Catholic Church. Luther had no idea that when he nailed those propositions to the front door of the Wittenberg church he set a new course, not only for his future, but also for the future Protestant movement.

One of the subjects that Luther challenged, was the church's practice of allowing people to purchase a pardon from the church (an indulgence) to go to Heaven by securing their release from purgatory. Luther's reasoning was simple and straightforward. His logic was: if you could pay the priest to free someone from purgatory, and if the Catholic priest was so loving and kind, then why didn't he use all the church's resources to free everyone who was in purgatory (Proposition 82)? Or, why would a holy God allow an enemy of God to purchase the freedom of a devout man in purgatory, but not release that devout man without payment, for love's sake (Proposition 84)?[34]

Luther believed there was **salvation in none other than Jesus Christ** and this belief thrust him into action. He couldn't keep this information to himself. Like Peter and John, Luther could not stop speaking about all he had seen and heard (**Acts 4:20**). Even when faced with excommunication from the Catholic Church, Luther did not back down.

We will talk about Luther again next week. For now, let's keep one fact in the forefront of our minds: God's divine hand is behind the boldness in each of our lives. People have a tendency to give credit to the obedient men and women of God instead of to the One who is truly worthy. Let's remind ourselves of this truth.

6. Read **John 15:5** and fill in the blanks.

   "I am the vine, you are the branches; he who abides in Me and I in him, he bears much fruit; for apart from

   Me _____ can do _____."

God is the One stirring our hearts to bring about His purposes. He takes sold-out servants of the Lord and orchestrates the circumstances in their lives to glorify *His* name and further *His* kingdom. We have had an informative day with Martin Luther. He was quite an inspirational character. We will spend more time with him next week, but for now, let's close with our application questions.

7. How has God spoken to you today? What has God shown you which you can apply to your life? Your church? Your nation?

8. Close today with your prayer to the Lord. Ask Him for an extra serving of wisdom as you walk through these weeks of study. Thank Him for allowing us to have godly examples like Peter, John, and Martin Luther.

*"Trust in the LORD with all your heart and do not lean on your own understanding. In all your ways acknowledge Him, and He will make your paths straight."*
***Proverbs 3:5-6***

# WEEK 2—DAY 5

Last week we began studying about the Puritans (Pilgrims). They were ordinary men and women of God who were compelled to follow God instead of man. They, like Peter and John, understood, "We must obey God rather than men" (**Acts 5:29b**). Today we will begin to focus our attention on one Puritan, William Bradford. Over the next several weeks, we will learn about his journey from England to the Netherlands, then finally to America. Before we begin, let's start with a prayer to the Lord. Ask Him to give you insights into today's lesson only He can give.

William Bradford was born March 19, 1590, in Austerfield, England. Bradford was orphaned by the time he was seven years old. His uncles raised him, but the stress of losing his parents took its toll on young William. As a result, he became ill for an extended period. God used this illness as a great blessing in Bradford's life. Since Bradford could not work on the farm, his uncles thought sending William to a school to learn to read, among other lessons, could help them with drafting of deeds, accounting, and farm business.[35] At this time in history, almost ninety percent of men in Europe were illiterate. The gift of education would set William apart, and with the elite of that time period. The Lord used this gift to shape and mold Bradford for the remainder of his life.

Since there were no schools in Austerfield, William's education was probably administered by Reverend Silvester, a local minister. Bradford would have read books like: *The Praise of Folly* by Desiderius Eramus, *Foxe's Book of Martyrs* by John Foxe, and of course the Holy Scriptures. "[T]he clergy would argue the Bible was "not for any 'Jack & Tom & Will & Dick' to be reading. But by age twelve, Bradford was deeply immersed in the Scriptures. Left frail and weak by his sickness, he found studies more to his liking than farming . . . . [as a result] [H]is reading in the Bible made him wonder if Queen Elizabeth's church was the only right and true way."[36]

During Queen Elizabeth's reign, she established a form of Anglican service for the Church of England. This included mandatory church attendance and rules against unlawful assembly, which was anyone attending a church other than the Church of England. Imprisonment awaited anyone caught in these offenses until they agreed to comply with the Queen's demands. Anyone who chose not to comply after his term of imprisonment would be exiled from England. Finally, if they returned to England after being exiled, they would face execution.[37]

Despite the clearly outlined fate of anyone who defied the queen, by the age of twelve William Bradford was walking sixteen miles each week to attend a reform church in Bayworth, which could have meant imprisonment for the young man. Bradford's uncles did not approve and began to threaten the lad. William was steadfast in his beliefs: "'the wrath of his uncles, nor the scoff of his neighbors . . . diverted him from his pious inclinations.' In fact, Bradford told his uncles, if he was to suffer disaster because of his new beliefs, then he would be suffering 'for a good Cause.' They should neither be angry with him nor feel sorry for him, he insisted, because God had called him to follow in this way, and 'hath given me a heart so to do.'"[38]

William Bradford had the same attitude as Peter and John in **Acts 4,** when the Sanhedrin commanded Peter and John "not to speak or teach at all in the name of Jesus" in **Acts 4:18.**

1.  Write **Acts 4:19-20** below. I know we have already looked at these verses, but repetition will help you memorize this important Scripture.

This would not be the last time Peter and John, or William Bradford, would need to have this strong resolve. This resolve permeated the first church and you will discover it permeated the Pilgrims who arrived on the shores of Cape Cod on the Mayflower.

---

### Questions to Ponder

Do you believe you have the steadfast resolve of Peter, John, and William Bradford? Give your reasoning.

---

King James the First became king in 1603 when Queen Elizabeth died. The Puritans approached the king to ask for reform. The king replied, "'I will [have] none of that!' he thundered; a church in which its members made their own choices about how they were to be governed 'as well agreeth with a Monarchy as God and the Devil. Then Jack & Tom, & Will and Dick shall meete [sic] and at their pleasure censure me, and my Council, and all our proceedings.' James would not be censured. He swore that he would put down anyone who challenged his authority as head of the church. 'I will make them conform, or I will harry them out of the land.'"[39]

Let's remind ourselves who these Puritans were and why King James and Queen Elizabeth felt so threatened by them. Kay Kizer describes them below.

"The Puritans were a group of people who grew discontent in the Church of England [The Anglican Church] and worked towards religious, moral and societal reforms. The writings and ideas of John Calvin, a leader in the Reformation, gave rise to Protestantism and were pivotal to the Christian revolt. They contended that the Church of England had become a product of political struggles and man-made doctrines. The Puritans were one branch of dissenters who decided that the Church of England was beyond reform. Escaping persecution from church leadership and the King, they came to America.

The Puritans believed the Bible was God's true law, and it provided a plan for living. The established church of the day described access to God as monastic and possible only within the confines of 'church authority'. Puritans stripped away the traditional trappings and formalities of Christianity which had been slowly building throughout the previous 1500 years. Theirs was an attempt to "purify" the church and their own lives."[40]

By 1607, five members of the Scrooby church, where Bradford was attending, were called before the Ecclesiastical Commissioners of the province of York. This was a dangerous time. Several of the church members were chained and taken to prison. Many could not leave their homes to even work and buy daily provision, as their homes were watched day and night. After this event, the Scrooby church began to contemplate serious plans for fleeing England. They felt this was their only hope of religious freedom.

2. Young Bradford was seventeen years of age, yet was living out a valuable Scripture Paul taught to the church in Rome. Write **Romans 5:3-5** below.

3. What does this Scripture teach? Fill in the blanks below.

Exult in our _____

Tribulations bring _____

Perseverance brings _____ _____

Proven character brings _____

Why can we hope? _____

When Peter and John spoke the words, "For we cannot stop speaking what we have seen and heard" their hope was not in a governmental system to save them. Their hope was in a God who poured His Spirit out on them. William Bradford's hope was in the same God who poured out the same Spirit on Bradford and the Puritans.

The members of William Bradford's home church in Scrooby were known as Separatists, or extreme Puritans. These Separatists realized their only option for religious freedom was to leave England; therefore, they began selling their belongings and preparing to move to Holland (the Netherlands). The time came for them to leave; they had contracted with a ship. On a late night in 1607 with only what they could carry, they climbed aboard the ship. Instead of heading for freedom, they found themselves headed for imprisonment. The ship's captain had betrayed them; everything was lost, their money, their meager possessions, even their books.

William Bradford's uncles' greatest fears had become a reality. The group was made "'a spectacle & wonder to the multitude, which came flocking on all sides to behold them.' They were dragged before the magistrates of the town and imprisoned; messengers hurried to London to inform King James's [sic] court of the attempted escape."[41] Most were released after a month of incarceration, yet six leaders were kept for trial. Eventually all were sent back to Austerfield, but their lives were altered forever. Most had sold everything to gain passage to Holland and some even returned without having a home to sleep in at night. Most would live in poverty for years, if not the rest of their lives. The Scrooby church was learning the cost of following Jesus.

4. Read **Luke 9:57-62**.

   a. What do these Scriptures teach us about following Christ?

      v. 57-58

      v. 59-60

      v. 61-62

   b. As you have seen, these Scriptures can be broken down into three categories. What words would you use to define these categories?

      v. 57-58

      v. 59-60

      v. 61-62

You may not have used the same three words, but they are a picture of comfort, responsibility, and steadfast dedication. In my own life, when ministry did not appear to go in the direction of my choice, it was at times tempting for me to *look back* to the security of my corporate career. But just as one teaches a horse to plow in straight rows, Jesus taught me to put "blinders" on and move forward in His calling for my life.

   c. Looking at the modern-day church in America how would you rate our alignment with the assertions of Jesus? Explain your answer.

A few of the Scrooby congregation abandoned the idea of fleeing England, but most stood firm and began to make plans for future escape. This time they contracted with a Dutch captain, praying for better results. When the time came to leave they divided into two groups: the women and children, and the men. The women and children arrived before the men and waited in a smaller boat in a creek. The men approached at sunrise, but the tide had turned and the women could not reach the boat. With only half the men aboard, crowds rushed the beach with guns and other weapons. The Dutch captain, fearing the worst, panicked. He abandoned the remaining men and all the women and children. The women watched while the men on the beach were arrested and once again incarcerated. Bradford, among those arrested, had to endure more persecution and difficulties than we in America can fathom. Bradford wrote this, "'was no marvell [sic]'—yet newcomers 'came on with fresh courage, & greatly animated others.'"[42]

The men who escaped began to arrange for people to leave in small groups so as to go unnoticed. By August of 1608 all the Separatists finally made their way to Amsterdam. They began life "'in a comfortable condition, enjoying much sweete [sic] & delightful societie [sic] & spirituall [sic] comforte [sic] together in ways of God, under the able ministrie [sic] and prudent governmente [sic] of Mr. John Robinson & Mr. William Brewster…. So…they grew in knowledge & other gifts and graces of the Spirit of God & lived together in peace & love and holiness.' It must have seemed to Bradford the Separatists had finally found what they had been looking for."[43]

5.  The unity and strength of purpose of the Separatists' new life are similar to the first church in **Acts 2:42-44**. Write this passage below.

It would take another threat of suppression of religious freedoms, twelve years later, to send the Separatists (Puritans) on a journey to America, the New World. We will continue our journey with these Puritans in the coming weeks. For today, we've covered a lot of ground. Think about what you have learned from William Bradford and his friends.

6.  What has God shown you through today's study you desire to apply to your life? Your church? Your nation? How does this correlate with what you learned earlier this week? Write your answers below:

7. Write your closing prayer to the Lord. Thank Him for what you are learning and ask Him for strength to apply it to your life.

*"Consider it all joy, my brethren, when you encounter various trials, knowing that the
testing of your faith produces endurance."*
**James 1:2-3**

# Week 3 Overview

*Pray that you would begin to speak the Word of God with boldness*
**Acts 4:31**

This week we will discover the importance of becoming bold in our faith. You will understand how two distinct types of people react to a bold faith. God's Word teaches, "The wicked flee when no one is pursuing, but the righteous are bold as a lion" **(Proverbs 28:1a)**.

This week we will:

❖ Look at the necessity for boldness in our faith.

❖ Investigate prayer in connection with speaking God's Word with boldness.

❖ Look at possible motivations behind unbelievers' actions and attitudes.

This week's applications include:

❖ Beginning to pray like our first-century brothers and sisters in asking our Father for boldness.

❖ Beginning to look with spiritual eyes for opportunities to be bold in our faith.

❖ Learning from our sixteenth-century believer what was true in biblical times is true today.

This week's verse to memorize:

*"And when they had prayed, the place where they had gathered together was shaken,
and they were all filled with the Holy Spirit and began to speak the word of God with boldness."*
***Acts 4:31***

Fill in the blanks where appropriate.

**Foundational Step:** _____ there is _____ in none other than _____

_____ **(Acts 4:12)**.

**Step 2:** Pray you will begin to speak the Word of God with boldness **(Acts 4:31)**.

# WEEK 3

Pray you would begin to speak the Word of God with boldness.
—Acts 4:31

## WEEK 3—DAY 1

Last week we saw that Peter and John got themselves into quite a sticky situation by proclaiming Jesus as the only source of salvation. Yet, despite their circumstance, they could not stop speaking about what they had *seen* Christ do and what they had *heard* Christ say.

Today we will travel back to Acts 4 and continue to investigate Peter and John to see what else we can learn from them. Before we begin, let's ask the Lord to continue to embed in our hearts the truth that tells us, **There is salvation in none other than Jesus Christ**. Ask Him to show you why this truth is so important in today's society. Ask Him to give you the ability to speak without ceasing and then have the boldness to proclaim His word and everything you have seen Jesus do in your life. Write your prayer below:

You may have noticed this week our application step is to **Pray you would begin to speak the Word of God with boldness.** For most people this is a much-needed prayer. Was boldness something natural for first-century believers? Or did they need God's supernatural ability just as we need it today? Let's see what we can discover.

*Remember:* Last week, the priests, the captain of the temple and the Sadducees arrested Peter and John because they credited Jesus for healing the lame man at the temple. As a result, the Sanhedrin ordered them to stop speaking in the name of Jesus. Let's review what Peter and John said, and then continue from there.

1. Read **Acts 4:17-23**.

   **Acts 4:17** says, "in order that *it* (emphasis added) may not spread any further among the people…." The *it* refers to the healing of the lame man by Jesus through Peter and John.

   a. What was the Sanhedrin trying to prevent from spreading to the people?

   ---

   ### Questions to Ponder

   Do you believe silencing is being used today as a tactic? If yes, how?

   ---

   b. Write Peter and John's response from **Acts 4:19-20**. (Since this is our theme verse we will write it several times throughout the study to help us memorize it.)

   c. What do we learn about the response of the Sanhedrin in **Acts 4:21**?

   d. What do we learn from **Acts 4:21** about the truth of Peter and John's arrest?

   e. Where did Peter and John go when they were released? What did they do?

There was no basis on which the Sanhedrin might punish them! Peter and John had been dragged to jail, brought before the Sanhedrin court and admonished for speaking in the name of Jesus for no just cause. Where is the justice in this!?!

   f. What might have been the Sanhedrin's motivation behind their actions?

g. What can you learn from Peter and John's words to the Sanhedrin in **Acts 4:19-20**?

h. How are the Sanhedrin's actions similar to the actions of people who try to silence the gospel of Christ today?

The suppression of Christ may be more subtle today than in the days of Peter and John, but incrementally, day by day, Christian values are being suppressed. Read below an excerpt from an article from the National Religious Broadcasters Association.

"In recent years, new media companies have been accused of censoring faith-based viewpoints and expressions. In 2010, Apple removed from its iTunes App Store the Manhattan Declaration, a statement of Christian conscience drafted in part by the late Chuck Colson, as well as the app of Exodus International, a leading outreach to individuals, families, and churches impacted by LGBT [Lesbian, Gay, Bi-Sexual, and Transgender] issues.

More recently, Facebook removed from its site a page created by Gov. Mike Huckabee that called for a "Chick-fil-A Appreciation Day" after the chain's president, Dan Cathy, expressed his unabashed support for traditional marriage. The page was taken down for about 12 hours before appearing again. A Facebook representative reportedly said if the company had deleted the page it was because the "content violated our policies not because of public sentiment."

"Clearly, these new media web-based tech companies have, at least in part, contributed to the suppression of free speech," says Craig Parshall, Senior Vice President & General Counsel at the National Religious Broadcasters and Director of the John Milton Project for Religious Free Speech."[44]

These incidents are trivial in comparison to being thrown in jail because you voice the name of Jesus, but they are still very real. Twenty years ago would a company's founder have been ridiculed for supporting traditional marriage in America? What will believers be ridiculed for in five or ten years from now? How long before Christians will be thrown in jail for our biblical beliefs?

Were Peter and John always so bold in their speech? In our first week of study we looked at snippets of Peter's actions when he betrayed Christ. Let's look at this event in more detail.

2. Read **Matthew 26:30-35**.

a. What did Jesus say would happen to the disciples?

b. How many would "fall away"?

c.  What did Jesus say Peter would do?

d.  What did Peter say in his defense (v. 35)?

e.  What did the other disciples say about Peter's comment (v. 35)?

Jesus knew Judas would betray him that very evening and He would soon pay for the sins of the world in a painful death on the cross of Calvary. These twelve men who had spent almost every day of the previous three and a half years with Jesus were all going to betray Jesus in His agonizing hour of death. Peter proclaims, "Even if I have to die with You, I will not deny You." Peter sounded bold, yet we know the true story. Let's go ahead and read what Jesus had already prophesied.

3.  Read **John 18:12-27**.

We all want to be bold for Jesus but when the rubber meets the road, how will you respond? Will you be like Peter in **Acts 4:20** who boldly said, "[F]or we cannot stop speaking about what we have seen and heard?" Or will you be like Peter, who in the midst of great conflict, denied even being a disciple (**John 18:17-27**)? These are great questions to contemplate.

Review today's lesson in your mind. Where do you think you would be on the scale below? Would you deny Christ or would you speak of all you have seen Christ do? Circle a number below.

| 1 | 2 | 3 | 4 | 5 | 6 | 7 | 8 | 9 | 10 |
|---|---|---|---|---|---|---|---|---|---|
| Deny Christ | | | | | Cannot stop speaking | | | | |

Instead of being discouraged by Peter's failure, let him encourage you. God used Peter mightily in His kingdom to bring others to the Lord. We have seen his boldness, yet at one point in Peter's life, he denied His Savior. If you found yourself circling a low number, be encouraged. God did not give up on Peter. He loved him and met Peter where he was and showed him the path to victory. Peter was not unique. If our Lord did this for Peter, He will also do the same for you. Rejoice! God is a loving God who desires victory for His children. Therefore, **Pray you would begin to speak the Word of God with boldness!**

4.  Let's close with our application questions. What has our Lord showed you today to apply to your life? Your church? Your nation?

5.  Write your closing prayer to Him.

*"Therefore everyone who confesses Me before men, I will also confess him before My Father who is in heaven. But whoever denies Me before men, I will also deny him before My Father who is in heaven."*
**Matthew 10:32-33**

# WEEK 3—DAY 2

Yesterday we began to look at our second application step: **Pray you will begin to speak the Word of God with boldness.** Peter and John displayed this step as they stood before the Sanhedrin for preaching Christ to the multitude in the synagogue. As we continue our study of Peter and John, let's begin with our prayer to the Lord. Ask Him for wisdom—not the wisdom of the world but wisdom from our Father from whom all wisdom comes.

Yesterday we left Peter and John in a sticky predicament. They spent the night in jail, then were dragged before the Sanhedrin to answer the charges brought against them. Peter and John, uneducated and untrained, amazed the Sanhedrin with their understanding. The Sanhedrin commanded Peter and John not to speak any further of Jesus and the great miracle performed in His name. Peter and John boldly proclaimed, "Whether it is right in the sight of God to give heed to you rather than to God, you be the judge; for we cannot stop speaking about what we have seen and heard" (**Acts 4:19-20**). What happened next? Let's find out.

1.  Read **Acts 4:24-31.**

    a.  What was the first response of the friends and companions of Peter and John?


    b.  What was the result of the believers' prayers (v.31)?

---

### Questions to Ponder

❖ Did you notice the response of the believers to their persecution? Write your thoughts below.


❖ How do you respond to persecution?


❖ What persecution do you see happening in the United States today?

---

We can learn a lot from the prayers of these first century believers. Let's take a look.

    c.  **Acts 4:24** tells us, "O Lord, it is Thou who didst make the heaven and the earth and the sea, and all that is in them." What does this tell you regarding what the early Christians believed about God?

    d.  Then the people quoted **Psalm 2:1-2**, "Why did the Gentiles rage, and the peoples devise futile things? The kings of the earth took their stand, and the rulers were gathered together against the Lord, and against His Christ." What were the people acknowledging?

From their knowledge of the Old Testament, early believers understood that the visible battles on earth are actually a reflection of the war the enemy wages against God, His Son, and His people. The Ryrie Study Bible tells us, "David (cf. [compare] Acts 4:25) unveils the resolve of world rulers to rebel against the Lord and His anointed King."[45] Therefore, the early church would not have been surprised by the persecution they were receiving from the world leaders.

    e.  The companions turned from Old Testament prophecy to the recent events of Jesus' crucifixion. What did the congregation understand about Jesus' death (vs. 27-28)?

    f.  Those praying made their requests to the Lord (v. 29). List the requests.

      ❖

      ❖

Interestingly, they wanted the Lord to take note of the threats against them, but they didn't dwell for long on the personal attacks. What did they understand about the Lord which could help us when we are rebuked or ridiculed for speaking about Jesus? Let's begin by looking at the words of Jesus and see what principles He taught them to live by.

2.  Write **John 15:20**.

3.  a.  Read **Matthew 5:10-12**.

    b.  What does Jesus tell us in these Scriptures about persecution?

      ❖

      ❖

❖

❖

❖

The miracle of healing the lame man took place shortly after Pentecost. To review the time frame of Acts, remember Pentecost was fifty days after Christ arose from the dead, and ten days after Christ ascended to be with the Father. The first-century Christians were just beginning to understand they too would be persecuted. Peter and John's imprisonment happened just weeks after Christ's ascension. The Sanhedrin jailed Peter and John without just cause. Peter and John heard Jesus say, "Blessed are you when others revile you and persecute you and utter all kinds of evil against you falsely on my account. Rejoice and be glad, for your reward is great in heaven, for so they persecuted the prophets who were before you" (**Matthew 5:11-12 ESV**). Were Peter and John and the believers in Jerusalem the only ones who knew this truth?

4. Read **2 Timothy 3:10-12**.

What did Paul tell those who followed his teaching? Why?

Second Timothy, Paul's last epistle, was written in about AD 64. He was giving Timothy final instructions before Paul was martyred for Jesus Christ. Paul's purpose was to confirm the fact there would be persecution in a believer's life. Paul, once the persecutor, had himself become the persecuted.

Biblical historians place Paul's conversion on the road to Damascus within the first year after Christ's resurrection. Because Paul was himself a persecutor, this coincides with the previous conclusion that persecution of the church began almost immediately after Christ ascended into heaven to be with the Father.

John wrote Revelation on the isle of Patmos. It was the final book written in our divinely inspired Scriptures. Read what *Foxe's Book of Martyrs,* says about the Beloved John:

> John certainly did not live a long life unscathed by pain and suffering. His emotional trials must have been considerable. He lived during times in which those who killed or abused Christians had nothing to fear from the law. In fact, they were sometimes carrying out the law. The painful death of friend after friend must have taken a heavy toll on John. Tradition holds that on one occasion, John was scheduled for boiling in oil. He escaped by divine intervention. His exile on Patmos could have easily been a death sentence. When Emperor Domitian, who had exiled him to Patmos, had died, John was brought back to Ephesus, where he was confined for two years. It is written that he was compelled to drink poison but was unharmed and finally died in peace.[46]

Paul, Peter and John all knew firsthand for a believer in Jesus Christ persecution was a part of life. The church's persecution in the first century spanned from AD 33, beginning at Christ's death, to AD 96 when Domitian, the tyrant Roman emperor, was assassinated by his own court officials. The first-century Christian was well acquainted with the world's mistreatment. What did James tell the church who were scattered abroad because of persecution?

5. Read **James 1:2-4**.

   a. Fill in the blanks below.

   "Consider it all _____ when you encounter various _____ . . ."

   What did James know that trials produce?

   b. What is the result of endurance?

Let's remind ourselves of the response of the early church to trials, tribulation, and persecution. Return to **Acts 4** to begin this investigation.

**Remember:** After Peter and John were released from prison, they found their friends and reported all the events they had endured. Then they began to pray. Notice the order of their prayer:

❖ First, their prayer edified God, proclaiming His power through creation.

❖ Second, the prayer quoted Scripture, verbalizing their knowledge of God's sovereignty and control of the situation. Despite the fact man was devising plans and kings were taking a stand, the first-century church was trusting in the Lord.

❖ Third, they knew God had predestined Christ's death. Herod and Pontius Pilate were just men whom God used to carry out His plan of salvation for humanity.

❖ Fourth, the church brought their petitions to the Lord. They left the threats of the Sanhedrin in the trustworthy hands of the Lord. They prayed for confidence, healing, signs and wonders in order to glorify Jesus' name.

6. Read **Acts 4:31**.

   a. What happened after this congregation prayed?

   ❖

   ❖

The church in Jerusalem was not the only church to speak with boldness. What can we learn from Paul and the church in Thessalonica?

7. Read **1 Thessalonians 2:1-4**.

   Under what conditions did Paul have the boldness to speak the gospel?

The boldness of the first-century church can be convicting. We will continue our discovery from Scripture tomorrow, but for now let's close with our application questions. You've worked hard today.

8. What has our Lord been showing you? Write what you gleaned from this lesson and how you will apply it to your life. Your church. Your nation.

9. Write your closing prayer to the Lord. Pray for boldness and perseverance in your daily Christian walk.

*"On the day I called, You answered me; You made me bold with strength in my soul."*
**Psalm 138:3**

# WEEK 3—DAY 3

Yesterday we began studying our application step. The principle, **Pray you will begin to speak the Word of God with boldness,** may not have taken you by surprise, but the truth of all Christians experiencing persecution and suffering may have left you a little uncomfortable. This is just one reason we will always begin in prayer. We need to ask continually for the Lord to strengthen and encourage us to accomplish the task for which He has called us. Write your prayer below. Ask for the boldness, which only the Lord can provide.

Let's begin by reviewing what we have studied so far:

- ❖ Peter and John could not stop speaking about what they had seen and heard.
- ❖ The Sanhedrin continued to threaten them but could find no basis to punish them.
- ❖ After Peter and John were released from prison, they reported to their companions the events they had endured.
- ❖ The companions began to pray to the Lord about what had occurred.
- ❖ When they finished praying they began to speak the Word of God with boldness.

Peter and John's entire predicament happened because the lame man was healed. Why did this event send the Sanhedrin into such an uproar? This will be our focus today as we move forward. The answer to questions like these will help us understand why we need to **Pray we will speak the Word of God with boldness.**

Today we will travel back to **Acts 3**. This text gives us the details of the events of the lame man's healing. We will not look at the Scriptures regarding the healing but at the events which transpired immediately following the healing. This should prove to be an enlightening day of study.

As you read **Acts 3:9**, understand that Peter and John had just come across the lame man begging alms at the temple. Peter gazed upon him and said, "I do not possess silver and gold, but what I do have I give to you: In the name of Jesus Christ the Nazarene—walk!" (**Acts 3:6**).

1. Read **Acts 3:9-21**.

   a. What was the crowd's reaction?

   b. Who did the people want to credit for healing the lame man?

   c. Who did Peter say was glorified (vs. 13,16)?

**Remember:** Peter was addressing the people clarifying the fact neither he, nor John had any power to make the lame man walk. In this first statement, Peter clearly pointed to Jesus as the one who deserved glory for this miraculous healing.

d. List what Peter said to the crowd in the temple about Jesus (v. 13-15).

❖

❖

❖

❖

❖

❖

e. **Acts 3:16** turns the attention to the healed lame man. On what basis did Peter say the lame man was strengthened?

f. From where did Peter say faith comes (v. 16)?

g. How did Peter say the people acted (v. 17)?

h. What did Peter tell the crowd to do (v. 19)?

Why?

i. What did Peter tell them would happen when their sins were wiped away?

How?

j. For whom did Peter claim Jesus was sent (v. 20)?

Personalize the verse by substituting your name for the pronoun *you*. Think about this exciting information! Jesus Christ was appointed for *you*!

k. What does this passage of Scripture (**Acts 3:13-21**) tell you about the motivation behind Peter's passionate speech?

l.   After studying **Acts 3:9-21**, how would you answer our focus question, "Why did this event send the Sanhedrin into such an uproar?"

### Questions to Ponder

❖  Do you believe the Sanhedrin's response would have been different had Peter and John taken credit for the lame man's healing? Why?

Peter's boldness came from a heart for the lost. His entire motivation was to point people to the Lord's redemptive power. From whom did Peter learn this boldness of calling sin, sin? Let's take a look and see.

2.   Read **John 8:39-46.**

Jesus was once again teaching in the temple and the scribes and Pharisees were there along with the people. The scribes and Pharisees began to test Him in various aspects, trying to catch Him in disobedience to the Law of Moses. The Pharisees claimed they were from Abraham, but Jesus said if they were from Abraham they wouldn't be trying to kill Him.

a.   Who did the Pharisees claim as their Father?

b.   What accusation did Jesus make (v. 40)?

c.   Who did Jesus say was the father of the Pharisees (v. 44)?

d.   Whose desires did the Pharisees want to follow (v. 44)?

e.   What did Jesus say are the desires of the devil (v. 44)?

   ❖

   ❖

   ❖

f.  How is the devil known?

He is the father of _____.

g.  Because they are from the devil, why did the Pharisees not want to believe Jesus (v. 45)?

h.  Jesus had already clearly presented the path to freedom from sin. What had He said to them in **John 8:31-32?** Write it below.

Peter learned his passion for truth from the Savior, Jesus. Through prayer and the Holy Spirit, Jesus gave Peter the boldness to speak His truth to people who were in desperate need of the Savior's redemption. Peter spent three and a half years with the Savior who delighted in revealing His heart to those who would listen. We too need to understand the heart of our Savior. Let's look at a few Scriptures to help us understand why we should boldly proclaim God's Word.

As children, most of us memorized one of the Bible's most well-known verses, "For God so loved the world, that He gave His only begotten Son that whoever believes in Him should not perish, but have eternal life" **(John 3:16).** Yet, many have not looked beyond this verse to find the treasures given to us. The next verses give us great insight into God's actions and man's actions and reactions.

3.  Read **John 3:17-21.**

a.  Fill in the chart below based on the information from the above Scripture.

| God | Those who believe | Those who do not believe |
|---|---|---|
| ❖ | ❖ | ❖ |
| ❖ | | Why? |

b.  What is the judgment?

❖

❖

c.  List what you learn about the contrasting characteristics.

| Those who come to the Light | Men who love darkness |
|---|---|
| ❖<br><br>Why? | ❖<br>❖<br>❖<br><br><br>Why? |

What has God shown you today about His heart for sinners? How does this relate to boldness?

4.  Let's close today by answering our application questions. Why should we speak God's Word with boldness? How should the answer affect your life? Your church? Your nation?

5.  Write your closing prayer to Him. Pray for the Lord to give you His heart for sinners. Pray for the boldness of Peter. Ask the Lord to open the hearts of the people in our nation and around the world to receive His message.

*"God be gracious to us and bless us, and cause His face to shine upon us—Selah.*
*That Your way may be known on the earth, Your salvation among all nations.*
*Let the peoples praise You, O God; let all the peoples praise You."*
***Psalms 67:1-3***

# WEEK 3—DAY 4

Last week we began to look at the life of Martin Luther. We discovered his strong belief in salvation in none other than Jesus Christ propelled him to action. His life was evidence of his belief. Martin was an ordinary man whom God used in extraordinary ways. Today we will continue to examine the life of Luther and discuss how his belief in Christ drove him to speak with boldness the Word of God. Let's begin with our prayer to the Lord. Thank Him for what He is showing you through His Word. His Word is truth.

Last week, we left Martin Luther in 1517 when he nailed his ninety-five propositions to the front door of the Wittenberg church. "The wooden doors of the Cathedral Church were used as the bulletin board, since the church was attached to the school. It was not as though Luther took a hammer, symbolic of revolution, and struck at the portals of this church, symbolic of the whole church. Rather, here was a theology professor and village preacher calling his colleagues to dispute, in correct academic fashion, the fundamental questions of the generation."[47]

Luther's intent was to initiate a conversation to bring about reform in the Catholic Church. His heart and motives were pure. He loved the Lord and he loved his church. His meditation and study of the Word of God had revealed to him the error of the church's ways, and he believed when other leaders saw the truth, which was so evident through God's Word, they too would see the error and want to conform to truth. Luther soon learned his thinking was very naïve.

Let's look again at a Scripture from Week 1 Day 5.

1. Read **Luke 9:57-62**. What three points did Jesus communicate?
   - ❖ v. 57-58
   - ❖ v. 59-60
   - ❖ v. 61-62

Martin Luther had no idea the road ahead would be so difficult, but he was already headed down the narrow path. There were opportunities and temptations to look back, but to do so would mean denying His Lord. Therefore, Luther kept his hand to the plow "fixing His eyes on Jesus the author and perfecter of his faith" (**Hebrews 12:2**).

I too have been naïve when it comes to understanding the cost of speaking God's Word with boldness. Being an *all in* kind of gal, people noticed when I became a Christian. I was not one to keep so great a salvation to myself. God had to reach down really far to pull me out of the pit, so why wouldn't I want to shout about it from the mountaintops? I realized very quickly my hunger for truth and bold style of speaking about all I had seen and heard were a problem for some people; yet "after putting my hand to the plow" there could be no turning back. Often my prayer to the Lord is to help me be faithful to Him. When I write, I often listen to praise and worship music to help keep me focused on the Lord. When I was in the midst of writing my first study, *Bound To Be Free*, my journey was getting very hard, harder than I ever expected. One day I heard a remake of the old song, *I Have Decided to Follow Jesus* by Sadhu Sundar Singh. As I listened, tears flooded my eyes when I heard the words "*Though none go with me, still I will follow. No turning back, no turning back.*" Even if the cost of following Christ was great, I had to keep moving forward, my hand to the plow, without looking back. Martin Luther too, had no idea how great a cost a simple piece of paper with ninety-five propositions would be.

Copies of those propositions spread like wildfire throughout Germany and Europe. People began discussing them, especially the touchy subject of indulgences. You may be asking, "What is an indulgence?" An indulgence was a "full or partial remission of temporal punishment for sins after the sinner confesses and receives absolution [from a Catholic priest]. Under Catholic teaching, every sin must be purified either here on earth or after death in a state called purgatory." In 1095, Pope Urban II was the first known pope to use plenary [complete] indulgences. Pope Urban granted absolution of sins when the petitioner participated in the crusades and confessed their sins. For those who could not afford to go [to] the Crusades, they could offer a cash contribution.[48]

In Luther's time, the pope delegated the privilege of dispensing indulgences. The Castle Church in Luther's Wittenberg, for example, was delegated the rare privilege granting full remission of all sins. Frederick the Wise, elector for the region of the Holy Roman Empire that included Wittenberg, took pride in a large collection of relics (over 19,000 holy bones and 5,000 other items) of saints that supposedly provided the basis for granting indulgences that could reduce stays in purgatory by over 1.9 million years. These treasures were made available to believers on All Saints Day, November 1. By viewing the relics and making the stipulated contribution, the believer could reduce a stay and [in] purgatory while providing much needed financial support for Castle Church and the University of Wittenberg.

Leo X, the pope in 1517, needed funds to complete the building of St. Peter's Basilica in Rome. Leo entered into an arrangement essentially selling indulgence franchises allowing the franchisee to retain about half the funds raised by selling indulgences in return for sending to Rome the other half for Leo's construction project. To encourage indulgence sales, Albert of Brandenburg, one winner of the privilege of selling indulgences, advertised that his indulgences (issued by the pope) came with a complete remission of sins, allowing escape from *all* of the pains of purgatory. Moreover, Albert claimed, purchasers of indulgences could use them to free a loved one already dead from the pains of purgatory he or she might presently be experiencing. The going rate for an indulgence depended on one's station, and ranged from 25 gold florins [one gold florin would be equivalent to $200 today] for Kings and queens and archbishops down to three florins for merchants and just one quarter florin for the poorest of believers.

In proclaiming the special indulgence offered by Albert of Brandenburg, indulgence vendor John Tetzel promoted it with a sermon that included a jingle of his own creation: "*As soon as the coin in the coffer rings, the soul from purgatory springs.*" Tetzel made his way through Germany, entering towns as part of a procession that included local dignitaries, a cross bearing the papal arms, and the papal bull of indulgence carried on a velvet cushion. In the marketplace of each town, Tetzel would offer this sermon:[49]

> Listen now, God and Peter call you. Consider the salvation of your souls and those of your loved ones departed. You priest, you noble, you merchant, you virgin, you matron, you youth, you old man, enter now into your church, which is the Church of St. Peter. Visit the most holy cross erected before you and ever imploring you. Have you considered that you are lashed in a furious tempest amid the temptations and dangers of the world, and that you do not know whether you can reach the haven, not of your mortal body, but of your immortal soul? Consider that those who are contrite and have confessed and made contribution will receive complete remission of all their sins. Listen to the voices of your dear dead relatives and friends beseeching you and saying, 'Pity us, pity us. We are in dire torment from which you can redeem us for a pittance.' Do you not wish to? Open your ears. Hear the father saying to his son, the mother to her daughter, 'We bore you, nourished you, brought you up, left you our fortunes, and you are so cruel and hard that now you are not willing for so little to set us free. Will you let us lie here in the flames? Will you delay the promised glory?' Remember that you are able to release them, for as soon as the coin in the coffer rings, the soul from purgatory springs. Will you not then for a quarter of a florin receive these letters of indulgence through which you are able to lead a divine and mortal soul into the fatherland of paradise?[50]

2. Last week we touched on the propositions that spoke of indulgences. Let's take a closer look at some of these. We will look at Martin Luther's proposition reasoning, and compare them to the Word of God.

| Proposition | God's Word |
| --- | --- |
| 79. To say that the cross-emblazoned with the papal arms, which is set up [by the preachers of indulgences], is of equal worth with the Cross of Christ, is blasphemy. | Ephesians 2:8-9<br><br><br>Titus 3:5 |

| Proposition | God's Word |
|---|---|
| 80. The bishops, curates, and theologians who permit such assertions to be spread among the people will be held accountable for it. | **1 Timothy 1:3-7**<br><br><br><br>**James 3:1** |
| 82. For example: "Why does not the pope empty purgatory, for the sake of holy love and of the dire need of the souls that are there, if he can redeem an infinite number of souls for the sake of miserable money with which to build a Church? The former reasons would be most just; the latter is most trivial." | **1 Peter 1:17-19** |
| 84. Again: "What is this new piety of God and the pope, that for money they allow an impious man who is their enemy to buy out of purgatory the devout soul of a friend of God, when they do not allow that pious and beloved soul to be redeemed without payment for pure love's sake or because of its need of redemption?" | **Luke 16:19-31** |

| Proposition | God's Word |
|---|---|
| 85. Again: "Why are the penitential canon laws long, which in actual fact and practice are long obsolete and dead, now satisfied by the granting of indulgences, as though they were still alive and in effect?" | **Romans 7:5-6** <br><br><br><br> **Galatians 3:10-14** |
| 88. Again: "What greater blessing could come to the Church than if the pope were to do a hundred times a day what he now does only once, and bestow on every believer these remissions and participations?" | **Hebrews 10:10-12** <br><br><br><br> **Hebrews 9:27-28** |
| 89. "Since the pope seeks the salvation of souls rather than money by his pardons, why does he suspend the indulgences and pardons granted before now, since these have equal efficacy?" | **Hebrews 9:22** <br><br><br><br> **2 Peter 3:9** |

Luther was only thirty-four when he wrote his ninety-five propositions. He had certainly learned our second principle—pray you will begin to speak the Word of God with boldness—yet Luther was ill-prepared for the "torrential way these theses (propositions) on indulgences swept through Europe."[51] Luther had another twenty-eight years of ministry ahead of him and many days would be very dark and lonely. He was learning Jesus' words, "No one, after putting his hand to the plow and looking back, is fit for the kingdom of God" (**Luke 9:62**). Some of Luther's greatest contributions to Christianity would occur through those times.

The battle between the Catholic Church and Martin Luther ensued. The battle began with Pope Leo X. (This is the same Leo X written about earlier in this lesson who sold indulgence franchises.) By August 1518, Luther was ordered to appear in person in Rome. One of the core demands of the Catholic Church was for Luther to recant several books he had written. Some of the titles included *On the Babylonish Captivity of the Church* and *The Freedom of the Christian Man.* Luther's defense of his writing was simple: show the error in the books based on God's Word and he would recant, if they could not, then he would not. "I cannot and will not recant anything, for to go against conscience is neither right nor safe. Here I stand, I can do no other, so help me God. Amen."[52]

On May 4, 1521, Luther and his companions were returning from one of his mandatory summons to Rome when a company of armed horsemen forced Luther's carriage to stop. The armed horsemen kidnapped Luther. Word spread quickly of Luther's kidnapping. Many rumored him dead. The kidnappers were actually a group of men who devised this plan for Luther's protection. They had heard rumors of death threats, decided to thwart the plotters, and kidnapped Luther for his welfare. If others, including those who wanted to harm him, thought he was dead, those who sought harm would halt their evil plans.

Luther was well cared for, but restless as summer turned to winter. However, Martin Luther's greatest work can be attributed to this period. Martin began translating the New Testament from the original Greek language into German. Martin labored tirelessly over each word. Although many German translations were available, none had been translated from the original language, and many were in regional dialects. Luther desired a translation that could be understood by everyone from peasants to kings.[53] Between 1534 and 1574, over one hundred thousand copies of Luther's New Testament were printed, and read by millions.[54] It became a bestselling book during this time.

Martin must have understood how Paul felt. Paul spent most of the last eight years of his life in prison for the gospel of Jesus Christ. During that time, he wrote some of his greatest works, which included Ephesians, Philemon, Colossians, Philippians, 1 and 2 Timothy, and Titus. Paul's final book, 2 Timothy, was written just before he was beheaded.

3.  Read **Philippians 1:12-14**.

    a.  What did Paul say was the purpose for his imprisonment?


    b.  How did Paul's imprisonment affect others?

        Non-believers?


        Believers?


Martin Luther's confinement was also used by God to further the gospel, and Martin could proclaim Paul's words, "We know that God causes all things to work together for good to those who love God, to those who are called according to His purpose" (**Romans 8:28**).

The life of Luther is fascinating. If we had time we would linger and glean more from Martin's life, lived out in service to our King, and all it could teach us. Listed below are additional resources you might wish to investigate to learn more about this great hero of the faith.

**Books:**

*Here I Stand: A Life of Martin Luther* (Hendrickson Classic Biographies) by Roland H. Bainton. Published by Hendrickson Publishers Marketing, LLC. Peabody, Massachusetts.

*Martin Luther: The Great Reformer* by Edwin P. Booth. Published by Barbour Publishing Inc., Uhrichsville, Oh.

**Video:**

*Luther*—Released in October 2003. Directed by Eric Till. Luther is played by Joseph Fiennes.

4. What has God shown you today through Martin Luther? And how does his life demonstrate speaking God's Word with boldness? How should studying Martin Luther's life affect the areas of your life? Your church? Your nation?

5. Write your closing prayer to Him. Pray for the Lord to give you His heart of boldness like Martin Luther's. Ask the Lord for the people of His church in our nation and around the world to be willing to speak boldly for Him.

*"But the Jews who disbelieved stirred up the minds of the Gentiles and embittered them against the brethren. Therefore they spent a long time there speaking boldly with reliance upon the Lord, who was testifying to the word of His grace, granting that signs and wonders be done by their hands."*
*Acts 14:2-3*

# WEEK 3—DAY 5

We have journeyed with the Puritans (Pilgrims) from Scrooby, England, to Amsterdam in the Netherlands. Today, we will continue our investigation into how the Pilgrims' Christian beliefs empowered their faith journey. William Bradford will once again take center stage in this adventure. Let's pray and ask the Lord to open our minds and help us see with spiritual eyes His instructions for our lives in this lesson.

Last week we studied the Separatists (Puritans) and their arrival in Amsterdam. Although William Bradford was not among the first to travel there, he, as well as the remainder of the Scrooby congregation, were safely in their new homeland by August of 1608. They fled England for Amsterdam specifically to claim their right to this religious freedom. "Thirty years before the Separatists came to Amsterdam the Dutch had declared no 'inquires should be made into any man's belief or conscience, or any injury or hindrance should be offered to any man on account of his religion.' With this spirit guiding this country—an extraordinary one for its time—the Separatists realized that here they would be free to worship precisely as they pleased, free from the entanglements of the Anglican Church."[55]

Dr. Marshall Foster, president of the World History Institute, in the documentary *Monumental: In Search for America's National Treasure* said it this way, "[The Netherlands] was the only place they could have gone in the entire world that was not under a tyrant [king] who would kill them. [If] They went to France tens of thousands were dying. If they would have gone over to Germany, millions were dying in the streets. If they went up to Scotland, forty thousand or more were dying, even ministers by the thousands were being persecuted and butchered. And so of all the places in the world that they could have gone that year that [Amsterdam] was the one place they could be free, and they could worship God, and they could prepare for the future."[56]

One practice, which was mocked in England, was called "prophecying [sic]." During this time "a few learned men of the congregation discussed a text from the Scriptures," afterward the minister would sum up the discussion to avoid confusion or disagreement. "Bishops for the Church of England suggested that the Separatists had been 'Amsterdamnified by brainlesse [sic] opinions' and that 'a Pope and a Bishop were all one with them.' To the first, the Separatists may not have given an answer. To the second, they would have agreed. A pope and a bishop were all one to them. This sense of democracy they practiced in the Amsterdam church, this sense all Christians could have ideas should be discussed, bishops and archbishops were not the only authorities — these ideas were to carry over into the Plymouth Colony and influence the course of a nation."[57] The Separatists (Puritans) understood Christ was the head of the Church and those who loved Him had His Spirit dwelling in them to guide them into all truth.

**Bible study tip of the week:** When studying a subject in the Bible, try to look up every verse in the Bible related to the subject. This will give you God's perspective on this subject.

1.  Read the following Scriptures and make relevant notes as they relate to Christ's relationship to the church, and the church's relationship to one another.

    a.  1 Timothy 2:5

    b.  Ephesians 5:23-24

    c.  Colossians 1:18

    d.  John 14:16-18

    e.  John 16:13

    f.  Galatians 3:28

During these "prophecying" [sic] discussions, a few of the congregation would argue over the finest points of doctrine. Some quarrels were very public. These disagreements became so loud they shocked even tolerant citizens. Because of the dissension, the decision was made for the majority of the congregation to move to Leyden. **Note:** Leyden is about 22 miles southwest of Amsterdam and known for being one of the most beautiful cities in the world. The burgomeisters (town officials) of Leyden said they would be "pleased to welcome all 'honest' persons who would behave themselves."[58]

King James protested to the burgomeister claiming that the Separatists were fugitives. "The burgomeister brushed aside the protest, saying they would admit any person of any religious faith." The Separatists settled into a quiet life in Leyden amidst the many struggles. Most had to learn new professions when they left England, and housing was not easy to find. The group found themselves in a poor area of the city, many on a street called Stinck Alley. While there, many Separatists lost children due to the poor conditions, fumes, and streets filled with infections.[59] (This would have been about the summer/fall of 1609.)

In 1611, William Bradford turned twenty-one and was now the legal heir to his father's property. Not looking back to the comforts of England, William sold everything there and helped the Separatists move forward in Leyden. He purchased a large, older home, which would be the meeting place for the congregation and home to their minister, John Robinson. Twenty-one other homes were built for the poorest of the congregation. In 1612, Bradford married, Dorothy May, "Dority," daughter of another Separatist family.

Life was still very difficult for many of the Separatists in Leyden. Despite this they were happy with their freedom. However, many were concerned about losing their English heritage. Forty-six of the Separatists had married and many children were born. These children were growing up without knowledge of their parent's homeland, England. As a result, a few families decided to return to England. It was said, they "preferred & chose the prisons in England rather than this libertie [sic] in Holland, with these afflictions."[60]

As a tool to propagate the gospel, the Separatist acquired a printing press. Their plan was to print pamphlets and books to spread the truth of God's Word, even if it was not acceptable to King James. Once their items were printed they put them in barrels and sent them out to sea, praying they would arrive on the shores of England. "In 1619, [William] Brewster anonymously published his *Perth Assembly*, which attacked King James for forcing Scottish Presbyterians to accept the rule of English bishops, [King] James demanded that the author be arrested . . . [Brewster] began hiding in one Separatist home after another, but as the manhunt continued month after month, Bradford and the others soon recognized their elder would forever be a homeless fugitive as long as they remained in Leyden.

". . . a ten-year truce the Dutch had drawn up with Spain was nearing its end. All the citizens of the Netherlands feared the revival of what was a very bloody struggle, but none feared it more than the Separatists. If Spain should be the victor, it would mean the Catholic Church would become the state church. The Inquisition was established in the Netherlands, and rooted out Separatists with intimidation and torture. The persecutions that Elizabeth and James had established in England were fleabites in comparison.

"The Separatist came to believe their time in the Netherlands was nearing an end …. But move on to where?"[61]

The Separatist's journey reminds us of the first church and their great sacrifices to follow Christ.

2.  Read the following Scriptures. Compare what the writer of the early church is teaching with how the Separatist were living, and how it applies to your own life. There are several verses that will emphasize the same application.

| Early Church Teaching | Separatist | How this applies to me |
|---|---|---|
| John 10:14-18 | | |
| John 15:13-14 | | |

| Early Church Teaching | Separatist | How this applies to me |
|---|---|---|
| 1 John 3:16 | | |
| Acts 4:34-37 | | |
| Romans 1:15-17 | | |
| Philippians 2:14-18 | | |
| 1 Peter 2:4-7 | | |

You may be thinking, "The Puritans (Pilgrims) left England, and now they are going to leave Amsterdam. Shouldn't they stay? Wouldn't the Lord want them to persevere under their trials?" Before we close let's look at one more section of verses.

3. Read **Matthew 10:17-26**.

    a.  What did Jesus tell His disciples would happen (vv. 17-18)?

    b.  How did Jesus tell them to act in these situations?

    c.  What did Jesus promise them would happen when they spoke?

They would face difficult times. Families would turn in their own families to the authorities; even fathers would turn in their own children. Many people today believe these Scriptures are speaking of the end times. I don't disagree, yet the principles and precepts still apply to us.

    d.  When persecution comes, what does Jesus tell them to do (v.23)?

    e.  Why did Jesus say this will happen (vv. 24-25)?

    f.  What was Jesus' last exhortation (v. 26)?

Isn't it interesting, Jesus Himself told His disciples to flee from persecution! Throughout history God has used fleeing from persecution as a tool to spread the gospel. His final great commandment was "go and make disciples." Yet, even as faithful as the early church was to our Lord, they grew *comfortable* and chose to stay in their familiar settings instead of fulfilling the command of Christ.

Around AD 60 the Emperor Nero began persecuting the church to further his cause; Nero blamed the Christians for the fire. "This was the fire during which Nero is said to have played his fiddle—because it suited him to clear the slums of Rome for his rebuilding programme [sic]." [62] "To divert the suspicion that he had started it for his own entertainment, Nero accused another party about whom the public were also prepared to believe the worst. Having forced a conviction for arson against certain Christians he conducted mass arrests, and among other tortures burnt his victims alive in public (Tacitus, *Ann.* 15. 44)." [63] Both Peter and Paul died a martyr's death under this persecution. Legend even has them being martyred on the same day, but what was the result of persecution to the early church? As the early church fled to other cities to obtain relief from their suffering, the gospel of Jesus Christ spread to the nations.

Sometimes God instructs His people to stay and deal with persecution, but often the Lord uses difficult events to spread His gospel to a world desperately in need of Him. Just as the Lord used persecution to spread the gospel in biblical times, He also used it in the days of the Puritans. Since Jesus is the same yesterday, today, and forever (**Hebrews 13:8**), then He can do the same today.

The Puritans feared persecution in Amsterdam, so they made the decision to go to a new land. For twelve years, the Puritans lived in the Netherlands, but it was time to find a new land of freedom, a land where the Puritans would be free to worship as they believed. Their desire was a land where they would not live in fear under a tyrant. This would be difficult, since the Netherlands was the only European country allowing such freedom. Therefore, the land they chose was America!

The Separatist' love of God and commitment to sharing His gospel were of prime importance to them. Dr. Marshall Foster said, "They came to propagate the gospel of Christ or the kingdom of Christ to the remotest part of the world. Yea they could be but stepping-stones for the promotion of so great of work… [They have] a generational vision that they can lay their lives down in this wilderness and literally put their faces down in the mud and have their children walk on their back[s] to a better day. That's a generational perspective. In fact, it [their generational vision] was so true of them at the end of Bradford's life he says, 'That this one small light that we have kindled here in Plymouth has shined to this entire nation.' So it happened four hundred years later the liberty the world now enjoys is because these people had the faith to lay down their lives in the wilderness four hundred years ago."[64]

Let's close with our application questions and prayer.

4. What has God shown you today through William Bradford and the Puritans? How are their lives an example of speaking God's Word with boldness? How has studying them affected areas of your life? Your church? Your nation?

5. Write your closing prayer to the Lord. Pray for Him to give you His heart of boldness. Ask the Lord to help you be willing to speak boldly for Him.

*"For whatever was written in earlier times was written for our instruction, so that through perseverance and the encouragement of the Scriptures we might have hope. Now may the God who gives perseverance and encouragement grant you to be of the same mind with one another according to Christ Jesus, so that with one accord you may with one voice glorify the God and Father of our Lord Jesus Christ."*
***Romans 15:4-6***

# Week 4 Overview

*Pray the gospel is "unveiled" to a lost and dying world.*
**(2 Corinthians 4:3-4)**

God's heart is for the lost. Peter teaches, "The Lord is not slow about His promise, as some count slowness, but is patient toward you, not wishing for any to perish but for all to come to repentance" (**2 Peter 3:9**). This week we will study the importance of praying for the Lord to reveal Himself to those who don't know Him. Our responsibility is not results oriented but is all about being obedient to pray and present the gospel.

This week we will:
- ❖ Investigate God's heart for the lost.
- ❖ Discover how the first-century church was obedient to Jesus' Great Commission.
- ❖ Study the two types of responses to the gospel.

This week's applications include:
- ❖ Beginning to pray the gospel is revealed.
- ❖ Looking with spiritual eyes for opportunities to share God's good news.
- ❖ Understanding our role is to be an obedient servant; and we are not held responsible for conversions.

This week's verse to memorize:

*"And even if our gospel is veiled, it is veiled to those who are perishing,*
*in whose case the god of this world has blinded the minds of the unbelieving so that they*
*might not see the light of the gospel of the glory of Christ, who is the image of God."*
**2 Corinthians 4:3-4**

Fill in the blanks where appropriate.

**Foundational Step:** _____ there is _____ in none other than

_____ _____ (**Acts 4:12**).

**Step 2:** _____ you will begin to _____ the word of God with _____ (**Acts 4:31**).

**Step 3:** Pray the gospel is "unveiled" to a lost and dying world (**2 Corinthians 4:3-4**).

# WEEK 4

Pray the gospel is "unveiled" to a lost and dying world.
—2 Corinthians 4:3-4

## WEEK 4—DAY 1

When the principles we are studying are rooted in our hearts and lives, just like Peter and John, we will speak about all we have seen and heard. Let's pray, and then start our next step. Ask the Lord to reveal to you those people around you who need the truth of the gospel, and for Him to open doors for you to share His love with them.

We will build upon our foundation with the next step in this study, **pray the gospel is "unveiled" to a lost and dying world (2 Corinthians 4:3-4).** For the past two weeks, we have studied Acts 4 with Peter and John in custody before the Sanhedrin. For context, we will review the first few verses.

1. Read **Acts 4:1-4.**

   a. Why were Peter and John seized (v. 2)?

   b. What was the effect on those who heard Peter and John's message (v.4)?

We've already seen in **Acts 4:21** the Sanhedrin had no basis to punish them. An event like this would seem unfathomable in the United States today, but read what happened in Dearborn, Michigan. Mark Ellis of *The Persecution Times,* reported on June 19, 2010:

> "Three Christians were arrested Friday evening at the Arab International Festival as they shared their faith with Muslims. The three were arrested by police as they engaged in intense, but respectful dialog in which they proclaimed their faith in Christ.
>
> "'I never thought I would see this in America,' says Steven Atkins, a resident of Toronto, Canada, who was visiting the festival and observed the incident.
>
> The three arrested include Dr. Nabeel Qureshi, David Woods, and Paul Rezkalla. Dr. Quereshi is co-director of Acts 17 Apologetics Ministries. He holds an MD from Eastern Virginia Medical School and an MA in Christian apologetics from Biola University.
>
> "'When Dr. Quereshi was arrested I heard people clapping and applauding, and some said 'Allahu Akbar,' Atkins said. There was a crowd of 15-20 people watching the exchange and subsequent arrest.
>
> "The festival attracts several hundred thousand Arab Americans each year, and some Christian groups find it an ideal venue for Christian outreach.
>
> "This year, the city of **Dearborn banned the distribution of Christian literature** near the festival. Some accused the city of catering to its large Muslim population when the law was passed. On June 17, a three-judge panel from the 6th Circuit Court of Appeals granted an emergency motion on behalf of Pastor George Saieg, allowing him to distribute literature and talk about his faith to Muslims at the festival.
>
> "'It was an intense discussion, but it was not unruly,' Atkins noted. 'There was no threat of violence,' he said. 'It's becoming more restrictive here than in Canada.'"[65]

Read a follow-up article written by Bob Unruh of *World Net Daily.*

> "'This case is a stunning example of the pernicious influence of stealth jihad and Shariah law in America. The city of Dearborn is now a serial violator of Christians' constitutional rights and has wasted hundreds of thousands of dollars in legal fees and costs defending its insidious conduct. Apparently, in Dearborn, where Shariah and jihad is advocated openly, it is a crime to preach the Christian gospel. AFLC is committed to stopping this attack on our Constitution. And the ruling today allows us to do just that,' said Yerushalmi."[66]

The fact the *federal judge agreed* these charges were *based upon fabricated allegations, and the Christians did not have a full and fair opportunity to challenge the claims in the police reports prior to the ruling* shows the correlation with Peter and John being arrested for no just cause. I praise the Lord that these incidents seem to be isolated, but how long until our religious freedoms are stripped from this nation. What can we learn from our first-century Christians that will help us in our journey?

After the Sanhedrin released Peter and John from prison, they took every opportunity to spread the gospel of Jesus Christ. Let's look at an occurrence shortly after they were told, "to speak no more to any man in this [Jesus'] name" (**Acts 4:17**).

2. Read **Acts 5:12-32**. There is so much we could focus on in these Scriptures, but for now we will concentrate on information pertaining to the gospel being unveiled.

    a. Of what did the council (Sanhedrin) remind Peter and the apostles (v. 28a)?

    b. With what did Peter and the apostles fill Jerusalem (v. 28b)?

This scripture is the first evidence of Jesus' disciples beginning to fulfill His final prophecy before He ascended to be with the Father: *"[B]ut you will receive power when the Holy Spirit has come upon you; and you shall be My witnesses both in Jerusalem, and in all Judea and Samaria, and even to the remotest part of the earth"* (**Acts 1:8**). Peter and John were already filling Jerusalem with Jesus' teaching through the power of the Holy Spirit.

    c. Did Peter and John heed the strict command of the council (Sanhedrin)?

    d. What was Peter and John's explanation for disregarding the council (Sanhedrin) (v. 29)?

    e. Does Peter and John's statement, "We must obey God rather than men" sound familiar? Where have we seen this?

Yes, these words had the same meaning when Peter spoke to the Sanhedrin in **Acts 4:19-20**, *"Whether it is right in the sight of God to give heed to you rather than to God, you be the judge; for we cannot stop speaking about we have seen and heard."* Peter's and John's priority was to please the King of Kings and Lord of Lords, not man.

---

### Questions to Ponder

❖ Do you foresee a time coming in the United States when believers will be faced with the difficult choice of obeying the law of the land or the law of God?

❖ Do you see an indication of this happening now? Explain.

---

Read the following excerpts from various articles.

From breitbart.com on May 1, 2013:

"The Pentagon has released a statement confirming that soldiers could be prosecuted for promoting their faith: 'Religious proselytization is not permitted within the Department of Defense . . . Court martials and non-judicial punishments are decided on a case-by-case basis . . .'"[67]

From Christianpost.com on October 26, 2013:

"Cadets reciting the U.S. Air Force Academy (AFA) oath will now have the choice to add "so help me God" to the end of their affirmation, the school confirmed on Friday."[68]

From the Christianpost.com on October 28, 2013:

"The American Center for Law and Justice has challenged the removal of the phrase "so help me God" from the Air Force Academy's Honor Code, which it says is evidence of an "anti-Christians Crusade" against the U.S. military."[69]

Our Christian military men and women will have hard choices to make. Will they stand with the great heroes of the faith or will they heed the demands of men?

f. Let's continue to study Peter and John and learn from their lives. In **Acts 5:30-32**, Peter outlines the gospel. Write the basic gospel information below.

| What do we learn about God? | What happened to Jesus? | What is the result of these events? | To whom is the Holy Spirit available? |
|---|---|---|---|
| ❖ | ❖ | ❖ | |
| ❖ | ❖ | ❖ | |
| ❖ | ❖ | | |

g. If you are unfamiliar with presenting the gospel, Peter's presentation is a wonderful example to follow. Based on this information, on a separate piece of paper, write out a simple presentation of the gospel.

**Acts 5** takes place less than two years after Christ's death, burial and resurrection. Jerusalem was already *filled with the teaching of the gospel*. This was a simple gospel presentation, and Peter spoke to people who had witnessed the death of Jesus. **Matthew 28:11-15** clearly outlines reports to the chief priest of the resurrection of Jesus. Instead of going to see if the reports were true and finding out for themselves whether Jesus was resurrected and walking the earth, they paid *"large sums of money to the soldiers* [to say]… *'His disciples came by night and stole Him away while we were asleep.'"* The men who bribed the guards to lie were the same men Peter accused of placing Jesus on the cross. Peter, John and these men had all witnessed many of the same events, but the influence of these events on their lives was very different!

3.  What key factor(s) influenced the Sanhedrin in their attack upon Peter and John?


In week one we looked at the Greek word *pisteúō,* meaning, *to believe, also to be persuaded of, and hence, to place confidence in, to trust, signifies, in this sense of the word, reliance upon, not mere credence.*[70] The critical difference between Peter and John and the Sanhedrin is *pisteúō.* Peter and John had placed their confidence in Christ and relied on Him. Although the Sanhedrin had witnessed the same events, their eyes were blinded; the truth had yet to be unveiled. They allowed pride and their desire to control to become more important than the truth.

Time will not allow us to unpack the word *unveiled* today. But discovering the meaning of unveil is the main topic of discussion tomorrow. Before we close, let's take a quick look at a key Scripture so you can meditate on it until we meet again.

4.  **2 Corinthians 4:3-4** says:

    *"And even if our gospel is veiled, it is veiled to those who are perishing, in whose case the god of this world has blinded the minds of the unbelieving so that they might not see the light of the gospel of the glory of Christ, who is the image of God."*

    According to this Scripture, why did the Sanhedrin not *pisteúō* even though they had the same opportunities as Peter and John to know Jesus?


The Sanhedrin had the same problem most people have today: the god of this world, Satan, is blinding their minds to the light of the gospel. Is it God's heart for some to know Him and others to be blinded? Let's look up two verses which clearly outline where God stands on the matter. You may be familiar with both verses, but they will serve as an excellent reminder for us.

5.  Write what you learn about God's heart for those who don't know Him.

    a.  **2 Peter 3:9**


    b.  **John 3:16**

**Note:** The word, *believe* in **John 3:16** is the same Greek word *pisteúō* which we have been studying today. Believing (*pisteúō*) is key in any relationship with the Lord.

God's heart is for those who don't know Him; therefore, our hearts need to be seeking those for whom the gospel is still veiled. The American church is filled with programs inside a church building, but the majority of those who don't know Him are not inside the walls of a church building. We must begin to think strategically about where God wants us to go individually to reach people who need Jesus. We need to define our own *Jerusalem, Judea, Samaria, and the outermost parts of the earth.* This may be as simple as opening your eyes to the people who live across the street or your co-workers, but it starts with prayer. When you begin to **pray the gospel is "unveiled" to a lost and dying world,** God will begin to open your eyes to His lost. Ask Him to direct you to them so you can share Jesus with them. There will be no shortage of people to pray for, speak to and show Christ's love to—they will be in every doorway.

Let's close with our application questions and prayer. You have much to ponder.

6. What has our Lord been showing you today? Write what you gleaned from today's lesson to apply to your life? Your church? Your nation?

7. Write your closing prayer to Him. Ask Him to give you a heart for the lost and to open your eyes to those He wants to draw into His kingdom. Begin to pray the gospel is unveiled to your neighbors, your city, and your state.

*"The effective, fervent prayer of a righteous man avails much."*
**James 5:16b** (NKJV)

# WEEK 4—DAY 2

Yesterday we discovered God unveiling the gospel to Jerusalem through Peter and John and the early church. **Acts 5:28** tells us Jerusalem had been filled with the teaching of the church. When Christ ascended to heaven, Scripture tells us 120 persons prayed and waited in the upper room until the day of Pentecost (**Acts 1:12-15**). Listed below is evidence of the evangelism of the early church. **Remember:** Man does the labor; God is the only One who can *unveil* the truth. Pentecost is the day the LORD gave the Holy Spirit to believers as Jesus promised in **John 14:16, 26** and **John 16:7-15**. If you have not previously studied the day of Pentecost, read Peter's explanation in **Acts 2:14-40**.

- ❖ Day of Pentecost—3,000 souls added that day (**Acts 2:41**).
- ❖ Day by day—the Lord was adding to their number those who were being saved (**Acts 2:47**).
- ❖ Healing of the lame man at the Beautiful Gate—the number of men who believed came to be about 5,000 (we do not have the number of women and children) (**Acts 3:1-16, Acts 4:4**).
- ❖ Multitudes of men and women were constantly added to their number (**Acts 5:14**).
- ❖ "You [Peter] have filled Jerusalem with your teaching" (**Acts 5:28**).

There were extraordinary numbers of people coming to know the Lord in Jerusalem. Think of your church, whether small or large, has there been a day when 3,000 men came to the Lord? One might ask, "Why don't we see events like these in our churches today?" The answer could be as simple as, "If we prayed with the faith of the first church, then we would experience events like those!" This, my friend, is why we are studying this week's step (**Pray the gospel is "unveiled" to a lost and dying world**). Let's open by writing our prayer to the Lord. Ask for a passion for His people who are lost and who need someone to lead them to their Savior.

Yesterday we began examine at **2 Corinthians 4:3-4**.

*"And even if our gospel is veiled, it is veiled to those who are perishing, in whose case the god of this world has blinded the minds of the unbelieving so that they might not see the light of the gospel of the glory of Christ, who is the image of God."*

Today we want to take a closer look at this Scripture and corresponding Scriptures which will enlighten us to unveiling the gospel. The Greek word for veil is *kalúptō* meaning *to wrap around, as bark, skin, shell or plaster; to cover up.*[71] How descriptive. Think how impossible it would be to see if tree bark or plaster were covering your eyes. This is how blinded people are when they do not know Christ.

1. Take your answers from **2 Corinthians 4:3-4** above.

    a. To remind ourselves, who is blinding people from the gospel?

    b. Who is the god of this world?

Yes, Satan is the god of this world. When God placed Lucifer in the Garden of Eden, his job was to care for it and protect the garden. Lucifer was the anointed cherub until pride entered his heart and he sinned against our Lord. Lucifer failed at his God-given task, and he continues to fail at the job God gave him *in the beginning* (**Ezekiel 28:12-19**). Thankfully, there is a day coming, one day soon, when Satan will be bound for 1,000 years, then cast into the lake of fire, which has been prepared for Satan and his angels (**Matthew 25:41, Revelation 20:2-3,10**).

    c. According to **2 Corinthians 4:3-4,** what does Satan do to the unbelieving?

    d. What does Satan not want people to see?

    e. If you were to walk into a dark room, what would you do?

Yes, it is logical to turn on the light. Why? Light always overcomes darkness.

2. Let's look at a few Scriptures and see if this principle holds true in God's Word. Make your notes below.

    a. **John 1:5**

    b. **John 1:9**

    c. **John 8:12**

    d. **John 12:46**

e. **Romans 2:19**


f. **1 Peter 2:9**


Satan's fear is believers will bring the light of the gospel into the darkness of this world, the Light (Jesus Christ) will overcome the darkness. We just read our job description, *"A PEOPLE FOR GOD'S OWN POSSESSION, that you may proclaim the excellencies of Him who has called you out of darkness into His marvelous light"* (**1 Peter 2:9b, emphasis added**). Do you know you are God's own possession? Do you see God rescued you out of darkness into light for the purpose of proclaiming His light to those in darkness? Many people want to believe these tasks lie with the pastor or those who have the gift of evangelism, but this is not what the Bible teaches.

Let's look at some additional passages, which will crystalize this truth in our hearts and help us with our task.

3. Read the following verses and write your answers to the questions below.

| Matthew 5:14-16 | Ephesians 5:8-9 | Philippians 2:14-15 |
|---|---|---|
| How are we described? | How is your past described? | What are we told NOT to do? |
| | How are you described today? | ❖ |
| What is the exhortation to us? | | ❖ |
| | | What will our action prove? |
| Why? | How are we to walk? | ❖ |
| | | ❖ |
| | | ❖ |
| What is the result? | What is the fruit of the light? | In what kind of generation do we live? |
| | ❖ | |
| | ❖ | |
| | ❖ | God's goal is that we appear as |
| | | _____ ___ ___ _____. |

Light always overtakes darkness. It doesn't take much light to make a difference . . . . but it is always our job to speak.

4. Read **Romans 1:14-17**.

   a. To whom was Paul under obligation to preach?

     ❖ _____ and _____ .

     ❖ _____ and _____ .

     ❖ Paul was not ashamed of what?

     ❖ What does the gospel have the power to do?

     ❖ To whom is salvation offered?

     ❖ What does the gospel reveal?

     ❖ How is the righteousness of God revealed?

     ❖ How does the righteous man live?

We, like Paul, need to be eager to preach the gospel. We need not be ashamed of the gospel. We need to understand there is power in the gospel. There is an invisible battle for people's eternal souls and we are God's chosen plan to bring the saving power of the gospel to these souls. One of my favorite verses in the Bible is **Isaiah 65:1 (comment added):**

> "I [the Lord] permitted Myself to be sought by those who did not ask for Me;
> I permitted Myself to be found by those who did not seek Me.
> I said, 'Here am I, here am I,'
> to a nation which did not call on My name."

I am so thankful to know we have a God who is seeking us even when we are not seeking Him. I praise Him for His mercy and grace upon my life and the lives of those who receive Him.

Before I went into full-time ministry, I spent most of my business career in sales. It was my job to convince people they needed what I offered. If you are in sales, you know the old saying, "You're only as good as your next sale." Your worth is measured by your performance. You can go from hero to zero in one day. It can be a brutal business. But, I remember the day I realized my Father in heaven does not grade my gospel presentation on the outcome. I am not responsible for the *sale*; I am only responsible for the presentation! There is nothing I can do to make someone accept Christ. This is not my job. How this understanding freed me of such a great responsibility. I believe people often shy away from talking to others about Christ and His saving grace because they are afraid they won't *do it right*. We need to remember we often are the instruments the Lord uses to lead people to God, but only God can change someone's soul and move them from darkness into light.

5.  Let's close by reminding ourselves of two important Scriptures.

    a.  Read **Acts 1:8**.

        "…but you will receive power when the Holy Spirit has come upon you; and you shall be My witnesses

        both in Jerusalem, and in all Judea and Samaria, and even to the remotest part of the earth."

    b.  Change each *you* above to your name.

    c.  Who has the power if they are in Christ Jesus?

    d.  **Read Matthew 28:18-20**.

        "And Jesus came up and spoke to them, saying, 'All authority has been given to Me in heaven and on earth. Go therefore and make disciples of all the nations, baptizing them in the name of the Father and the Son and the Holy Spirit, teaching them to observe all that I commanded you; and lo, I am with you always, even to the end of the age.'"

    e.  Who has the authority?

    f.  Who will be with you?

    g.  How long will Jesus be with you?

How can we have confidence and boldly be light in the midst of a crooked and perverse generation? We have been given the power, as we are under the One who has the authority, the One with the authority has promised us He will be with us! We don't bear responsibility for the results; we are merely responsible for our actions. He has given us all we need, but we must remember the catalyst that sets everything in motion is fervent prayer. Therefore, let's close with our application questions and then **Pray the gospel is "unveiled" to a lost and dying world.**

6. What has our Lord been showing you today? Write what you will apply to your life? Your church? Your nation?

7. Write your closing prayer to Him. Ask Him to unveil your eyes to the ones for whom He wants the gospel to be unveiled. Pray for your neighbors, your city, your state, and your nation.

*"After these things I looked, and behold, a great multitude, which no one could count, from every nation and all tribes and peoples and tongues, standing before the throne and before the Lamb, clothed in white robes, and palm branches were in their hands…. Then one of the elders answered, saying to me, 'These who are clothed in the white robes, who are they, and where have they come from?' I said to him, 'My lord, you know.' And he said to me, 'These are the ones who come out of the great tribulation, and they have washed their robes and made them white in the blood of the Lamb.'"*
***Revelation 7:9, 13-14***

# WEEK 4—DAY 3

The early church was exploding! They had prayed for boldness to speak about all they had seen and heard, and Peter and John were taking every opportunity to present the gospel. We have studied how Satan, the god of this world, has veiled the minds of the unbelieving from the light of the gospel. Today we are going to take a closer look at how to unveil the gospel to a lost and dying world. Let's begin by writing out our prayer. Has God begun to show you people within your sphere of influence who need to have their eyes opened to God's light? Pray specifically for them by name.

We've studied the Greek word veiled, *kalúptō,* meaning *to wrap around, as bark, skin, shell or plaster; to cover up.*[72] This meaning gives us great insight into why people without Christ are incapable of seeing the truth. We have put on our spiritual eyes and can see the invisible battle that we must fight for our friends, neighbors, and even countrymen and women. The battle begins on our knees with prayer. Today we will begin taking a closer look at the word *gospel,* then see how Paul spoke of the gospel to the church at Corinth, and finally study several verses which talk about the gospel. This information will give us better insight into and define our role in sharing the gospel.

The Greek word for gospel is *euaggélion* meaning *"gospel. Originally a reward for good news, later becoming the good news itself. The good news of the kingdom of God and salvation through Christ…in Paul's epistles used of the basic facts of the death, burial and resurrection of Christ and of the interpretation of these facts."*[73] What can we learn from God's Word about the gospel?

1. Read **1 Corinthians 15:1-8**.

    a. Paul was speaking to the church in Corinth. Of what does he remind the church regarding the gospel? Fill in the blanks below.

    ❖ Paul _____ the gospel to the church in Corinth.

    ❖ The church _____ the gospel.

    ❖ The church _____ in the gospel.

    ❖ The church is _____ by the gospel.

    ❖ The church _____ _____ to the Word, unless you believe in _____.

b. How did Paul deliver the gospel to the church?


c. How did Paul describe the gospel?
- ❖
- ❖
- ❖
- ❖


2. What are some other facts we can learn about the gospel? Read the verses below and make notes.

a. **Matthew 24:14**


b. **Mark 8:35**


c. **Mark 13:10**


d. **Mark 16:15**


e. **Acts 15:7**


f. **Ephesians 1:13**


g. **Ephesians 3:6**


h. **Philippians 1:27**


i. **Revelation 14:6**

In 1997, God called me out of corporate America into full-time service to Him. I was on my first overseas, short-term mission trip in southeastern Romania. I was sitting in a village that had no running water, one telephone for 500 families, and one car, which drove over dirt roads with deep crevices where tires had left tracks from driving on the road in the rain. But, they had a post office. When I asked my translator if we could stop by the post office and pick up some stamps, she told me they didn't sell stamps at the post office. I asked what you did at the post office and she looked at me as if I were crazy and replied, "Once a month we go and pick up our mail." Boy, did I ever need an education about life in third-world countries! Yet, somehow God was drawing me to His mission and purpose. There, in that small village, I was reading the book of Acts. Below you will find the verse God used to speak clearly to me about His purpose and plan for my life.

*"But the Lord said to him, 'Go, for he is a chosen instrument of Mine, to bear My name before the Gentiles and kings and the sons of Israel; for I will show him how much he must suffer for My name's sake.'"* (**Acts 9:15-16**)

Not only was Paul a chosen instrument to bear our Lord's name, but so are you and I. You don't have to be in *full-time* ministry to bear our Lord's name. The church body (you and I) are to be the catalyst in which non-believers hear the gospel. Therefore, most of the people hearing the gospel should be people outside the walls of a church building as they are going about their everyday lives, and it's our job to take the gospel, the good news, to unbelievers. As we have studied, we are to be salt and light to the world (**Matthew 5:16**). The purpose of the leaders in the church is to equip the saints for the work of service (**Ephesians 4:11-13**).

## Questions to Ponder

Do you see yourself as God's chosen instrument to share the gospel?

Has today's lesson enlightened you to His purpose for your life?

As you are going about your day, are you actively seeking out people to speak to who need to hear the gospel? If not, why not?

Before we close, review what we studied this week about the words *veiled*, *light*, and *gospel*.

| Veiled | Gospel | Light |
|---|---|---|
| ❖ *kalúptō - to wrap around, as bark, skin, shell or plaster; to cover up*<br>❖ eyes of those who are perishing<br>❖ Satan, god of this world, veils the minds of the unbelieving | ❖ Is described as Christ:<br>  • Died for our sins<br>  • Was buried<br>  • Was raised on the third day<br>  • Appeared to Cephas, the twelve, over 500, and to Paul<br>❖ Is preached<br>❖ Is received by the church<br>❖ Church stands in the gospel<br>❖ Church saved by the gospel<br>❖ Church holds fast to the Word<br>❖ Is to be preached to the whole world<br>❖ If you lose your life for Christ and the sake of the gospel, you shall save your life<br>❖ Must be preached to all the nations<br>❖ Church is commanded to go into all the world and preach the gospel<br>❖ Believers:<br>  • Listened to the message of truth<br>  • Believed in the message of truth<br>  • Are sealed in Him with the Holy Spirit of promise<br>  • Must conduct themselves in a manner worthy of the gospel<br>  • Angel will preach the gospel to all those who live on the earth | ❖ Shines in darkness<br>❖ Jesus is the true light<br>❖ Jesus is the light of world<br>❖ Those who believe in The Light, Jesus, will not remain in darkness<br>❖ We are to be light to those who are in darkness<br>❖ God called you out of darkness into His marvelous light to proclaim Him<br>❖ Believers are the light of the world |

3.  Looking at the above list, what is God emphasizing to you? Write your thoughts below:

4.  Let's close with our application questions. What has our Lord been showing you today? Write what you are going to apply to your life? Your church? Your nation?

5.  Write your closing prayer to Him. Continue to pray for your neighbors, your city, your state, and your nation.

*"You shall do what is right and good in the sight of the LORD, that it may be well with you and that you may go in and possess the good land which the LORD swore to give your fathers, by driving out all your enemies from before you, as the LORD has spoken."*
***Deuteronomy 6:18-19***

# WEEK 4—DAY 4

I am so excited to begin our study today. The fourth day of the remaining five weeks will be spent studying a sixteenth-century hero of the faith, William Tyndale. Many may be familiar with Tyndale Publishing, the company named for this man, but may otherwise have little knowledge of his life. You will be fascinated as you read about the contributions he made that help us even today. If you have ever read an English translation of the Bible, then Tyndale's godly contributions have impacted your spiritual life as well as enriching other aspects of your life. Of course, before we dive in, prepare your heart for the Lord's message, pray and ask Him to reveal His message of grace and truth for you.

Look at the chart below. The timeline indicates Martin Luther's life events, which we have studied, and William Tyndale's birth date. We will continue to use the timeline as we proceed. As we add events to the chart, think of how God uses His people for His plan, to save others whom He has marked out for eternity.

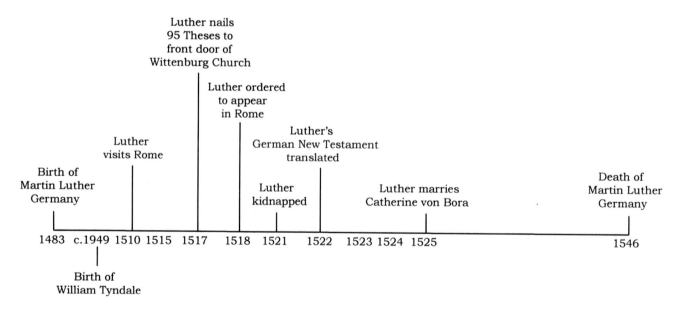

William Tyndale was a remarkable man. The mystery of his early life will never be known. "There is no documentary evidence of him at all until he took his Oxford BA in his late teens. No record exists of when or where he was born ... [but] the most likely year of his birth, 1494."[74] Most believe he was born of the Gloucestershire Tyndales.

Tyndale was born following a turbulent time in England's history. A civil war raged for many years between the Lancaster and York families for the throne of Britain. This war was known as the *War of the Roses* (1455-85). The name came from roses used as a symbol expressing loyalty to one family or the other. Red roses were used for the Lancaster family and white roses represented the York family. For up to thirty years after this war, people used alias names to protect their family in case the wrong royal family came into power. This was the case for the Tyndales who took the name Hutchins or Hytchyns. Henry Tudor, a member of the House of Lancaster, was crowned King Henry VII and within a year married Elizabeth of York, the daughter of the late King Edward IV. This marriage, uniting the two families, temporarily ended major conflicts.

Tyndale's education indicated his family was at least moderately prosperous. Most believe Tyndale began his academic education in 1506, at the tender age of twelve, where he left home under the name of William Hytchyns. The first written record of Tyndale's life was in 1512 when he graduated from Magdalen College with a bachelor of arts degree. Young William would have been about eighteen years old. In 1514 Tyndale was ordained as a Catholic priest. Tyndale received his master's degree from Oxford, in 1515, at the age of about twenty-one, and he most likely continued theology studies there. He stopped using the alias Hytchyns and resumed using the Tyndale family name.

We will never fully know the contributions Tyndale made to the English language. But words like: network, seashore, waves, inexcusable, refused, rose-colored, lost, stiff-necked, and busybody all came from William Tyndale and these are not even his biblical contributions.[75] In addition, "he [Tyndale] made phrases which have gone deep into English-speaking consciousness. For example, for the Hebrew grammatical form of the possessive known as the construct, he greatly extended the English 'the + noun + of + the + noun' ('the birds of the air, the fish of the sea')."[76] As you can see, the basic structure of the English language we use today came from William Tyndale. "There is perhaps some truth to the maxim 'without Tyndale, no Shakespeare.'"[77] By the end of Tyndale's life he would know, speak, and understand eight languages. These included English, Greek, Hebrew, Latin, German, Spanish, French, and Italian. It was said, "[W]hichever he [Tyndale] speaks, you might think it his native tongue!"[78]

When I began researching William Tyndale, I realized Tyndale, at his core, was a man of conviction. Yet his convictions brought upon him tribulation. This rings true through the Scripture, "Indeed, all who desire to live godly in Christ Jesus will be persecuted" (**2 Timothy 3:12**). Tyndale reminded me of Nehemiah, a man in the Bible with similar troubles. Both were humble men who wanted only to serve their God, and in doing so the people around them would be served. Neither would ever understand what a great a contribution for their Lord they would make to their generation and subsequent generations.

**Bible study tip of the week**—When studying a book or chapter of the Bible, it is important to determine what kind of book it is. For instance, the book of Nehemiah is one of many history books in the Old Testament. Books can be more than one "type." For example, Daniel is both a book of history and prophecy. Many of the New Testament books are epistles or "letters." You would not study a history book in the same manner as an epistle. Many times epistles have exhortations, warnings, and instructions. You might want to make a list of what each teaches you. On the other hand, history books give an account of what took place. Watch for the flow of the events, focusing on the people, and plots.

Let's study Nehemiah so we can better understand Tyndale.

1. Read **Nehemiah 1:1-11**.

    a. What did Nehemiah ask his brother Hanani (v. 2)?

b. What did Hanani report to Nehemiah (v. 3)?

  ❖

  ❖

  ❖

c. When Jeremiah heard the news what did he do?

  ❖

  ❖

d. On the chart list what you learn about God, Israel, and Nehemiah's prayer (v. 5-11).

| What Nehemiah knew about God | What Nehemiah said about Israel and himself | How did Nehemiah pray to God and make supplication for Israel? |
|---|---|---|
| | | |

e. What did the chart teach you about Nehemiah?

f.  What did the chart teach you about Israel?

g.  What was Nehemiah's job (v.11)?

A cupbearer was a "high ranking royal official primarily in charge of serving wine to the king. Since he was close to the person of the king, who feared intrigue [conspiracy] and the possibility of poisoned food, the cupbearer was required to be a man of irreproachable loyalty capable of winning the king's complete confidence."[79] God had placed Nehemiah in a strategic position to accomplish the Lord's design. As with Nehemiah, Tyndale was in a strategic position, he was given the gift of an advanced education, which was rare in the sixteenth century. This allowed Tyndale to accomplish the task the Lord had planned for him.

When Nehemiah heard of the conditions of Jerusalem and that the people were in great distress, Nehemiah immediately understood he needed to be part of the solution, rather than do nothing. Like Nehemiah, Tyndale felt doing nothing was not an option. Tyndale was an avid Bible student and studied it in the original languages of Greek and Hebrew. The more Tyndale engrossed himself in his studies three things became evident:

❖  Tyndale's biblical views were in opposition to the sixteenth century church in England.
❖  Tyndale's conviction grew for English-speaking people to have a Bible in their language.
❖  If English-speaking people had a Bible in English, this would allow the people to read the Bible for themselves and not rely on the teaching of the church, some of which was false.

Many of the issues Tyndale had with the church were the same Martin Luther had with the church. The Catholic Church served both England and Germany which embraced the false teaching and use of indulgences. **Remember:** the church defined an indulgence as money paid to the church in exchange for granting full or partial remission of the punishment of sin. Faith in Christ alone was at the core of Tyndale's convictions; this was in stark contradiction to the teaching of indulgences. "If he [Tyndale] were to continue preaching and writing that salvation was by faith alone, in opposition to the teachings of the church, he would likely be burned at the stake. Yet if he remained silent, the uneducated Englishmen with whom he had grown up and tens of thousands like them would never hear the truth."[80]

William Tyndale, like Nehemiah, was moved by the conditions of his people. Tyndale became a man who gave up his life to serve those who could not serve themselves. Tyndale not only studied the Bible, but he believed what it said and took action upon God's words.

2.  Note what you learn from the following verses:

    a.  **John 15:13**

    b.  **1 John 3:16**

As we continue to study William Tyndale's life, these verses will become a powerful testimony of how God's Word impacted his life. Our action step this week is **pray the gospel is "unveiled" to a lost and dying world (2 Corinthians 4:3-4).** Tyndale knew the best way for people to be transformed by the power of the gospel was for the people to be able to read God's Word themselves. William's desire was for mankind to be healed by God's Word and he lived out this truth daily.

Tyndale studied at Cambridge from 1517 to 1521. During this time Martin Luther's Ninety-Five Theses made its way from Germany to England. Some claim Luther had great influence on William. However, the fact that Tyndale agreed with many of Luther's biblical conclusions and aligned himself with Luther's biblical philosophies is a more accurate statement. In 1520, Cambridge officials who disagreed with Luther burned copies of his books. William either witnessed these events or heard about them from other students.

The man who had the most influence on William Tyndale's life was the Dutch scholar Desiderius Erasmus. Erasmus had once been at Cambridge while teaching and working on his Greek New Testament. And young William chose to walk the same halls as Erasmus a few years later.

The political climate of the times in which Tyndale lived also had influence on his future. "In the spring of 1509, when Tyndale was finishing his first year of studies at Magdalen College, King Henry VII died and his eighteen year-old son became King Henry VIII …. While Henry VII had left England more secure and stable than it had been in centuries … more experienced rulers in France and Spain could easily exploit England's young monarch."[81] King Henry VII first-born son, Arthur, died shortly after he had married Catherine of Aragon, the daughter of the powerful Spanish king and queen, Ferdinand II and Queen Isabella I. The marriage was a strategic alliance between countries. When Arthur died, Henry VII pledged that his second son, Henry VIII, in marriage to Catherine when Henry VIII turned eighteen, therefore maintaining the alliance. Henry married Catherine shortly after he was crowned king. Henry appeared to be a good-natured young man (as long as he got his way). "Two days after his coronation, he arrested two of his father's ministers and promptly executed them. He began his rule seeking advisers on most matters, and would end it with absolute control. After Henry declared his supremacy, the Christian church separated, forming the Church of England. Henry instituted several statutes outlining the relationship between the king and the pope and the structure of the Church of England: the Act of Appeals, the Acts of Succession and the first Act of Supremacy, declaring the king was 'the only Supreme Head in Earth of the Church of England.' These macro reforms trickled down to minute details of worship."[82] Although the term Divine Right of Kings was not in use until the time of King James, about 100 years later, the spirit of the Divine Right of Kings was in full force.

This was the political environment in which William Tyndale lived until his death in 1536. As we continue in our study of Tyndale, you will understand better why this information is important. William Tyndale was a man who never wanted to become political, yet the politics of the time kept pursuing him. The closer Tyndale came to fulfilling his God-given purpose of translating the Bible into English, the more his world collided with a world he never sought.

We will continue our study of William Tyndale each week. But for now I hope you are recognizing how Tyndale's passion for sharing the Word of God in the language of the ordinary people in England continues to change the world today.

3.  Before we close, write the following events of Tyndale's life on our chart on page 126.

    a.  1515 - Tyndale received his master's degree from Oxford

    b.  1517 - Tyndale began his studies at Cambridge

    c.  1521 - Tyndale complete his studies at Cambridge

Let's answer our application questions and prayer.

4.  What have you learned today that God wants you to apply to your life? Your church? Your nation?

Close today with your prayer. Ask the Lord to continue to teach you what you need to know about unveiling the gospel to the world.

*"For whatever was written in earlier times was written for our instruction,*
*so that through perseverance and the encouragement of the*
*Scriptures we might have hope."*
**Romans 15:4**

# WEEK 4—DAY 5

Has God opened your spiritual eyes to the lost around you? Even though today is our final day of study for this important subject, I pray your life will continue to be impacted for God's beloved who have not yet come to know Him. Jesus said, "I have other sheep, which are not of this fold; I must bring them also, and they will hear My voice; and they will become one flock with one shepherd. For this reason, the Father loves Me, because I lay down My life so that I may take it again. No one has taken it away from Me, but I lay it down on My own initiative. I have authority to lay it down, and I have authority to take it up again. This commandment I received from My Father" (**John 10:16-18**). Even though this reference is speaking about a people group (the Gentiles), the concept still applies today. Before we continue our journey with the Pilgrims, write your prayer to the Lord. Ask Him to continually stir your heart for His sheep who are still lost. Ask Him for a willing heart to lay down your life so that others may come to Him.

On August 5, 1620, the Puritans set sail for the New World, three years from when they first realized they needed to leave the Netherlands. In 1617, they contacted Captain John Smith, who had previously made a voyage to the New World in 1614. The Puritans' decision to move to America meant someone had to travel to England.

Two key elements from England needed to be acquired for their journey. First was the financial backing of the London Company, which had financed the Jamestown Colony in 1607, but more importantly they needed a "patent [land grant or permit] from the King [James] of England to settle his land. They hoped if James was willing to send convicts and the condemned to the New World, he would be willing to allow them to go as well."[83] Considering the difficulties they had with the King, the patent would not be easily obtained.

William Brewster was still in hiding from King James and his life was in danger if he traveled to England; William Bradford was still considered too young to handle such an important affair. Therefore, the Puritans selected John Carver and Robert Cushman to plead their cause before the London Company and the king.

Carver and Cushman sought out Sir Edwin Sandys of the London Company, also known as the First Virginia Company. The meeting with Sir Edwin went exceedingly well. He was excited "a group of people were willing to travel to Virginia; if they added health to a dying colony, it meant profits for both the London Company and the king himself. But there was a sticking point: the Separatists insisted upon a statement to insure their religious freedom in the New World. Edwin Sandys assured Cushman and Carver such a promise would not be difficult to obtain."[84]

Robert Naunton, the secretary of state, met with King James on behalf of the Puritans to acquire the land patent. He promised their request for religious freedom would not be an issue. "When the proposal was finally brought to the king, he seemed to agree enthusiastically. 'What profits may arise in the parts to which they intend to go?' he asked, perhaps demonstrating why he was so enthusiastic. When he was told that they would be fishermen, the king declared, 'So God have my soul, 'tis an honest trade. It was the Apostle's own calling.'

"But as so often happened with the Separatists, happy beginnings did not always lead to equally happy endings. The next day [King] James suggested the Separatists meet with the bishops from the Church of England to discuss their differences. The folk in Leyden, many of whom had visited British prisons, would have none of that. The result was, James would not issue the patent for reasons of state, though privately he promised if the Separatists would go to Virginia even without the charter, he would … not molest them, provided they carried themselves peaceably …. With such a 'sandy foundation,' many argued, they could not proceed. But others like Bradford were not yet ready to yield [give up], recognizing it was God, and not the king, who would lead them in this new adventure. Besides a charter with a 'seale as broad as the house floor' was no guarantee; a king could revoke a charter at his whim. They must depend on God's providence, and not on the blessings of kings or bishops."[85]

The Puritans knew they needed to be dependent on God's providence. *Webster's Dictionary* defines providence as, "divine guidance or care."[86] I've also heard it defined as, "God's divine care, control and guidance over a life, situations and circumstances; making one ready for future events" (source unknown).

The Puritans' story reminds me of the Israelites just after they left Egypt. I am sure William Bradford knew this story well. Let's take a look.

1. Read **Exodus 13:21-14:8**.

   a. Who led Israel with a cloud by day and fire by night?

   b. Where did the Lord lead the people in **Exodus 14:2**?

   c. What would Pharaoh say of the Israelites (v. 3)?

   d. Whose plan was it for Israel to be camped in front of the Red Sea when the Egyptians came chasing after them?

   e. Whose plan was it for Pharaoh's heart to be hardened?

The Israelites were in quite a sticky situation! Yet, it was the Lord who led them into their circumstances. If you know the story, then you know the Israelites grumbled and complained. They questioned Moses to see if he had brought them there purposely to die in the wilderness. Of course, Moses, servant of the Lord, told Israel not to fear and that the Lord would be their salvation. Then Moses spoke very profound words.

f. Fill in the blanks from **Exodus 14:14**.

The _____ will _____ for you while _____ keep _____.

We know God did indeed rescue Israel in a powerful way by parting the Red Sea and having them walk to the other side on dry land. Finally, God drowned their enemy, the Egyptians, in the Red Sea. What might have been God's *providence* and plan in this situation? What was His purpose?

2. Read **Exodus 14:18**. What did the Lord want Egypt to know?

3. Read **Exodus 14:30-31**.

   a. What did the Lord allow Israel to see concerning their enemy?

   b. What was the response of the people concerning the Lord?

   c. What two things were said about Israel's relationship with the Lord.

   d. How did their opinion of Moses change?

Just as the Lord led the Israelites to their critical juncture, the Lord led the Puritans to theirs. William Bradford believed they would move forward. Figuratively speaking, they would follow the pillar of cloud by day and fire by night just like the Israelites had.

---

### Questions to Ponder

When you encounter a "Red Sea" circumstance, what is your normal response?

What have you learned from Moses and the Puritans to help you in your next "Red Sea" moment?

---

Two years passed while Separatists continued to pursue their vision of gaining religious freedom in America. They finally obtained the patent from King James by hiding their identities. It was a patent which, ultimately, would not be used. The group was approached to form a seven-year, joint stock agreement with London Merchant Adventures. The expectation was for exports (like furs) from the New World to go back to England to be sold to pay off the investors. Even after the Pilgrims set sail for America, there continued to be setbacks and difficulties. The *Speedwell*, a ship purchased by the Pilgrims for their new fishing business, had to be abandoned in England because of leaks and lack of seaworthiness. This would not only affect their journey to America, but also the proposed business of becoming fishermen.

With only the *Mayflower*, chartered by the Merchant Adventures, to make the journey, twenty people had to abandon the dream of traveling to the New World. Some were grateful for the opportunity to stay because they were miserable because of seasickness or they feared they might die at sea.

William Bradford first used the term "pilgrims" to describe himself and his band of Separatists as they set sail from Holland. "So they left that goodly and pleasant city, which had been their resting place for nearly twelve years; but they knew they were pilgrims, and lifted up their eyes to the heavens, their dearest country, and quieted their sprits."[87] Over the years, the name stuck.

By the time the *Mayflower* landed in America, on November 10, 1620, the Pilgrims had spent sixty-six days at sea and four months living on the ship—arriving months behind schedule. This meant they were too late to plant crops, and the only food they would have until spring was what they could catch or kill. The Pilgrims knew they were headed into a difficult winter. They just didn't understand how difficult a winter it would be.

Only one passenger died on the journey, but by the spring of 1621, forty-five of the 102 passengers had succumbed to the harsh winter. Dority, William Bradford's wife, was the first to die after their arrival in America; she was found floating close to the Mayflower about a month after they landed, her cause of death unknown.

Despite their great difficulties, the Pilgrims were grateful. Bradford "hoped that his children—and the children of all the fathers on that voyage—could say,

> 'Yea, let them which have been redeemed of the Lord, shew how he hath delivered them from the hand of the oppressour. When they wandered in the deserte wilderness out of the way, and found no citie to dwell in, both hungrie, and thirstie, their sowle was over- whelmed in them. Let them confess before the Lord his loving kindness, and his wonderfull works before the sons of men.'

Like the Hebrew children who wandered so long in the desert wilderness, the Pilgrims were coming to set up a new country, a new way of living. And they trusted in God to see it established."[88]

Just before the Pilgrims walked on the shores of their new home, they gathered together with the "strangers" (those aboard the ship who did not come with the Puritans from Leyden) and discussed a "body politik" at the suggestion of their Leyden pastor, John Robinson. The result was the Mayflower Compact.

4.  Read the body of the Compact (in modern spelling).

"Having undertaken, for the glory of God, and advancement of the Christian faith and honor of our King and Country, a voyage to plant the first colony in the northern parts of Virginia, do by these presents, solemnly and mutually in the presence of God, and of one another, covenant and combine ourselves together into a civil body politic, for our better ordering and preservation and furtherance of the ends aforesaid; and by virtue hereof to enact, constitute and frame such just and equal laws, ordinances, acts, constitutions and offices, from time to time, as shall be thought most meet and convenient for the general good of the Colony: unto which we promise all due submission and obedience.

IN WITNESS WHEREOF we have hereunder subscribed our names at Cape Cod, the 11 of November, . . . Ano Dom. 1620."[89]

a. What reasons did they give for coming to America?

   ❖

   ❖

   ❖

b. What was their intent in forming the civil body politic (politik)?

   For better _____ and _____.

c. What was the purpose of the Compact?

d. Whose interest were they to have when they met?

After Plymouth's first governor, John Carver, died in April of the first spring, the dwindling group chose William Bradford as their leader. William was taught under the watchful eyes of William Brewster and their Leyden pastor, John Robinson. Bradford's leadership skills had surfaced on the ship when conflicts arose. Until then he had not been looked upon as a leader.

One can only imagine how Brewster felt about Bradford's appointment. From the time of Bradford's boyhood, Brewster had been an instrumental figure. Bradford looked upon Brewster as a surrogate father. Now Brewster took on the leadership role in the church and Bradford took the leadership role in government; both served in these roles faithfully for near the rest of their lives. Bradford served as governor all but five of the next thirty-seven years until his death in 1657.

Bradford's leadership style was decisive and immediate, partly because of the vast needs of the colony, but foremost because of Bradford's "confidence that the Lord had led him to this point and would use him to establish a Christian commonwealth. It would be a commonwealth where all things would be guided by principles from the Scriptures . . ."[90] Bradford combined the Lord's wisdom with his God-given talents and temperament to establish the colony. He had confidence in the Scriptures, just as had many other men and women who have been used mightily by the Lord. Let's take a look at a few.

5.  Note below how these Scriptures apply to the biblical person, Bradford, and yourself. You may not have answers for every section.

| Scripture | Biblical Figure, Bradford, and Yourself |
|---|---|
| | *Paul* |
| Acts:13:2 | |
| Romans 1:1 | |
| Galatians 1:14-17 | |
| | *David* |
| Psalm 4:3 | |
| | *David/Solomon* |
| 2 Chronicles 6:5-10 | |

| Scripture | Biblical Figure, Bradford, and Yourself |
|---|---|
| | *Jeremiah* |
| Jeremiah 1:4-9 | |
| Jeremiah 1:17-19 | |
| | *Ezekiel* |
| Ezekiel 2:1-7 | |
| | *Esther* |
| Esther 4:14 | |

6. After looking at these Scriptures, do you believe God is providentially involved in the direction of your life? Explain.

Bradford invested his life in the Plymouth Colony. He remarried and had four children in addition to John, his son from his first wife. He also raised several orphans in the colony. In the ensuing years, other colonies were established nearby which outgrew the small Plymouth. Plymouth never reached over 3,000 people, while the close by Massachusetts Bay Colony (modern-day Boston) had swelled to 15,000. By 1647, Bradford, who had kept a diary of colony life, was so discouraged he stopped writing. "Two centuries passed before his words were published. He did not know he had written a great account not only of the planting of a colony, but of God's loving providential care of a people who tried to carry out a vision they had found in the Scriptures. Bradford thought he had failed in this vision; he did not understand how much he had succeeded."[91]

Bradford reminds us of Abraham, another servant of the Lord who did not get to see the fulfillment of the Lord's promise. God's promise to Abraham is still being fulfilled over 4,000 years later. Although Bradford "felt that he had failed in Plymouth, he had not. His was the first of the colonies to succeed in New England, and it provided the model for all the rest. The Pilgrim vision of church life would last to the present time and give rise to thousands and thousands of congregations, who would choose their own ministers and their own way of worship. The principles by which he governed may be found demonstrated today during any New England spring, where the people of a township gather together to vote on how they shall be governed. The mutual roles of church and government played out in America today come not from the strong colony of Massachusetts Bay, but from Plymouth.

"The vision of Plymouth survives because of William Bradford, a man of God who grabbed onto a continent and never let go."[92]

7. Let's close with our application question. What has our Lord been showing you today? Write what you are going to apply from this lesson to your life. Your church. Your nation.

8. Write your closing prayer to the Lord. Continue to pray for your neighbors, your city, your state, and your nation.

*"And what more shall I say? For time will fail me if I tell of Gideon, Barak, Samson, Jephthah, of David and Samuel and the prophets, who by faith conquered kingdoms, performed acts of righteousness, obtained promises, shut the mouths of lions … And all these, having gained approval through their faith, did not receive what was promised, because God had provided something better for us, so that apart from us they would not be made perfect."*
**Hebrews 11:32-33, 39-40**

# Week 5 Overview

*Humble yourself, pray, seek, and repent to God for healing in our land.*
**(2 Chronicles 7:14)**

Most people in the United States would agree our country is in a crisis. However, the real disagreement is in how to solve the crisis. If we, as Christians, want our country to change, we must understand change begins with ourselves. We cannot expect unbelievers to act in a godly fashion; it's an impossibility. It's like asking a dog to act like a fish! Christians are the catalyst for transformation of a nation.

This week we will:

❖ Study the Hebrew words for *humility, pray, seek,* and *repentance.*
❖ Study God's response to believers who humbled themselves.
❖ Look at how God interacted with people and nations in the Old and New Testaments.

This week's applications include:

❖ Praying the church will humble themselves before the Lord.
❖ Understanding the role of humility in the life of a believer.
❖ Understanding the believer's role in changing a nation.

This week's verse to memorize:

*"If My people who are called by My name humble themselves and pray and seek My face and turn from their wicked ways, then I will hear from heaven, will forgive their sin and will heal their land."*
***2 Chronicles 7:14***

Fill in the blanks where appropriate.

**Foundational Step:** _____ there is _____ in none other than _____

_____ **(Acts \_\_\_\_\_)**.

**Step 2:** _____ that you will begin to _____ the Word of God with _____ **(Acts \_\_\_\_\_)**.

**Step 3:** _____ the _____ is "_____" to a lost and dying _____
**(2 Corinthians 4:3-4)**.

**Step 4:** Humble yourself, pray, seek, and repent to God for healing in our land **(2 Chronicles 7:14)**.

# WEEK 5

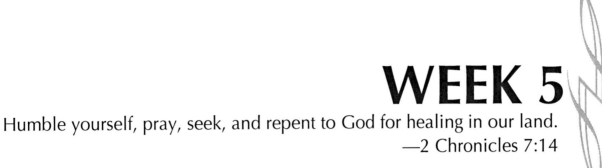

Humble yourself, pray, seek, and repent to God for healing in our land.
—2 Chronicles 7:14

## WEEK 5—DAY 1

We are halfway through our journey my friend. Have you found yourself talking about this study with your friends and family? Are you encouraged and convicted at the same time? We at *Words of Grace & Truth* would love to hear your comments; you can e-mail us at biblestudy@wogt.org. Before we begin, write your prayer to the Lord. Ask Him for a heart that is solely His.

This week our action step is to **Humble yourself, pray, seek, and repent to God for healing in our land.** In our key verse, **2 Chronicles 7:14**, the Hebrew word for *humble* is *kâna'. This verb occurs thirty-six times [in the Old Testament]. It denotes bringing a proud and recalcitrant [obstinate or disobedient] people or spirit into subjection … Two key references are Lev. 26:41 and 2 Chr. 7:14 which indicate that so long as a person, or nation, is arrogant and self-sufficient, God can do nothing for them.*[93]

1. Write **2 Chronicles 7:14** below. You might already know this verse, but it is always good to refresh our memories.

Read **Leviticus 26:41-42**.

What happens if their [Israel's] hearts become humble?

---

### Questions to Ponder

❖ What does the world teach about being proud versus being humble? Do these Scriptures contradict what the world is teaching on this subject? Write your thoughts below.

---

As we study God's Word, we must always consider how it applies to us. *Bible study is not about information; Bible study is about transformation.* If we just gain information without applying God's Word to our lives, then we are being prideful and exalting ourselves. This is not pleasing to Christ, nor is it a good representation of Him to a world desperately in need of finding Him.

We will look at the context of **2 Chronicles 7:14** later this week but keep the definition of *humility* at the forefront of your mind. Today, we will read about Stephen, then study a man named Saul and the first church to see how they humbled themselves and brought themselves under submission to God.

As the early church grew, their needs outgrew the management ability of the twelve apostles. Therefore, the church chose seven men to assist the twelve with the needs of the church. This would allow the twelve to devote themselves to prayer and to the ministry of the Word. In my opinion, one of the most poignant stories in the Bible is in **Acts 6 and 7**. These Scriptures describe Stephen as a "man full of faith and of the Holy Spirit" (**Acts 6:5**). Stephen and six others were chosen to oversee *the service* of the church. Today, we would call these men deacons or elders.

**Acts 6:8** tells us Stephen was "full of grace and power, [and] was performing great wonders and signs among the people." Because of this, some men in the synagogue rose up and began to argue with Stephen. **Acts 6:10** tells us, "They [Sanhedrin] were unable to cope with the wisdom and the Spirit with which he [Stephen] was speaking." Once again, the tactic of using false statements was their strategy; "they secretly induced men to say, 'We have heard him speak blasphemous words against Moses and against God'" (**Acts 6:11**). The men in the synagogue stirred up the people, dragged Stephen before the council, and brought false witnesses against him. As he stood before the council it is said about Stephen, "the Council saw his face like the face of an angel" (**Acts 6:15**).

As the high priest began to question him, Stephen said, "Hear me, brethren and fathers" (**Acts 7:2**). Stephen then gave an eloquent dissertation on the children of Israel from Abraham, to Joseph, to Moses, to Joshua, and finally to David.

Stephen spoke clearly of Israel's unwillingness to be obedient, and in **Acts 7:51** Stephen proclaimed, "You men who are stiff-necked and uncircumcised in heart and ears are always resisting the Holy Spirit; you are doing just as your fathers did." As you can imagine, this statement, although truthful, was not well received. The Bible tells us the crowd began to gnash their teeth at Stephen and drove him out of the city to be stoned. Then **Acts 7:58b-60** tells us,

". . . the witnesses laid aside their robes at the feet of a young man named Saul. They went on stoning Stephen as he called on the Lord and said, 'Lord Jesus, receive my spirit!' Then falling on his knees, he cried out with a loud voice, 'Lord, do not hold this sin against them!' Having said this, he fell asleep."

We will study Acts 6 & 7 in greater detail in our final week of this study. Today our focus will be on Saul. Who was this man, Saul, who stood idly by and watched as Stephen, this servant of the Lord, was martyred for Jesus Christ? The next mention of Saul begins in **Acts 9**.

2.  Read **Acts 9:1-20**.

    a.  What was Saul's plan when he went to the high priest (vv. 1-2)?

    b.  Who interrupted Saul's plan?

    c.  Whom did Jesus say Saul was persecuting? What can you learn from His statement?

    d.  Whom did Jesus send to Saul? And what was his first response?

    e.  What did the Lord say to Ananias to comfort his fears?

    f.  Before whom did the Lord say Saul would bear Jesus' name?
        ❖
        ❖
        ❖

g. What did Saul do when Ananias restored his sight and the Lord filled Saul with the Holy Spirit?

- ❖ (v. 18)
- ❖ (v. 19)
- ❖ (v. 20)

h. The word humbled is not used, but the actions of Saul and Ananias show humility/obedience before the Lord. Write them below in the appropriate column.

| Saul | Ananias |
| --- | --- |
|  |  |

Imagine if Ananias had not humbled himself and obeyed God. Think of the blessing he would have missed! I assure you, if Ananias had said, *no*, God had someone who would have said *yes* to His call. Humility brings obedience and obedience brings blessings, not only to you, but also to others.

3. What was the result of their obedience? Read **Acts 9:21-28**.

a. What was the reaction of those who met Saul after his encounter with Jesus?

b. What do we learn about Saul (v. 22)?
   - ❖
   - ❖
   - ❖

c. What was the Jews' reaction to Saul proving Jesus was the Christ?

d. How did Saul escape?

e.  What was the reaction of the believers in Jerusalem?

   ❖

   ❖

f.  Who came to Saul's rescue?

g.  What is the last thing we are told about Saul (v. 28)?

The persecutor became the persecuted! Saul became Paul (**Acts 13:9**). He wrote more books in the New Testament than anyone else. His act of humbling himself before the living God turned the world upside down for Jesus Christ. A murderer and accuser of the brethren turned into a great man of God. He preached to Jews, Gentiles and kings. **Remember** the definition of *humility*: *kâna'—It denotes bringing a proud and recalcitrant* [obstinate or disobedient] *people or spirit into subjection . . . so long as a person, or nation, is arrogant and self-sufficient, God can do nothing for them.*[94] Before Paul's Damascus Road experience, he was proud, arrogant, and self-sufficient. Once Paul encountered Jesus, he became a man who was dependent upon the One who would mold, shape, and use him. Later, we will see in more depth how God used this humble man.

4.  Who do you know who is like Saul and needs a Damascus Road experience? Are you praying daily for God to reveal Himself to them and for them to be transformed by the greatness of our Lord's mercy? Note below at least one person who comes to mind.

5.  There is certainly a lot of information to contemplate, my friend. Let's close with our application questions. What has the Lord shown you from today's lesson to apply to your life? Your church? Your nation?

6. Write your closing prayer to Him; include the name(s) you wrote in question five. Pray that God will give you a heart for the Saul's in your area, and that He will send someone, if not you, to meet them where they are and show/tell them, the love of Christ.

*"When the Gentiles heard this, they began rejoicing and glorifying the word of the Lord; and as many as had been appointed to eternal life believed. And the word of the Lord was being spread through the whole region."*
**Acts 13:48-49**

# WEEK 5—DAY 2

Yesterday we learned the Hebrew word for *humility, kâna'*. We studied two men in the early church, Saul and Ananias, who humbled themselves before the Lord and, as a result, the Lord chose to use them mightily for His kingdom. We observed how their humility led to obedience and their obedience led to blessing others as well as themselves. Open with your prayer to the Lord. Ask Him for a heart of humility. Let Him know you want to be His servant.

1. Before we jump into **2 Chronicles,** let's do a quick comparison of what God teaches on pride and humility. Look up the following verses and note what God shows you. (There may only be a reference to either pride or humility.)

| Verse(s) | Pride | Humility |
|---|---|---|
| **2 Chronicles 32:24-26** | | |
| **Proverbs 11:2** | | |
| **Proverbs 29:23** | | |
| **Daniel 4:23-37** | | |
| **Matthew 23:12**<br><br>**Note:** Jesus is speaking to His disciples. | | |
| **James 4:6** | | |

| Verse(s) | Pride | Humility |
|---|---|---|
| 1 Peter 5:5-6 | | |

The basic definition of *pride* in Hebrew is *to lift up or to be proud.*[95] **Remember** what we saw yesterday in the definition of *humility: so long as a person, or nation, is arrogant and self-sufficient, God can do nothing for them.*[96]

---

### Questions to Ponder

❖ Do you believe America is a nation (as a whole) of people humbling themselves to the Lord or being prideful?

❖ What do you believe will be the consequences of our actions?

---

Let's turn our attention to **2 Chronicles**. If you have already studied *Leaders, Nations, and God* you have a good overview of Solomon's prayer to the Lord.

2. Read **2 Chronicles 6:14-42**. Look over the following chart and see the *highlights* of what Solomon said to and about the Lord. Then write what this tells you about Solomon's belief in or about God and how this relates to this week's step **Humble yourself, pray, seek, and repent to God for healing in our land.**

| Solomon said to or asked of the Lord | Solomon said about the Lord | What does this teach us that Solomon believed about the Lord? | How does this show humility, prayer, seeking the Lord or repenting? |
|---|---|---|---|
| | **(v. 14)**<br>• God of Israel<br>• No god like Thee<br>• Keeps covenant<br>• Shows lovingkindness to servants who walk before Him | | |

| Solomon said to or asked of the Lord | Solomon said about the Lord | What does this teach us that Solomon believed about the Lord? | How does this show humility, prayer, seeking the Lord or repenting? |
|---|---|---|---|
|  | **(v. 15)**<br>• Kept what was promised to father David |  |  |
| **(v. 17)**<br>• Let Your Word be confirmed which You spoke |  |  |  |
|  | **(v. 18)**<br>• Will God dwell with mankind on earth?<br>• Heaven cannot contain Thee |  |  |
| **(v. 19)**<br>• Have regard to the prayer of Thy servant<br>• Listen to the cry and to prayer Thy servant prays |  |  |  |
| **(v. 21)**<br>Listen to supplications of<br>• Thy servant<br>• Thy people Israel<br>Hear Thou and forgive |  |  |  |
|  | **If/Then Clauses** |  |  |
| **If:** | **Then:** | What does this teach us that Solomon believed about the Lord? | How does this show humility, prayer, seeking the Lord or repenting? |
| **(v. 22-23)** A man sins against his neighbor and takes an oath before Your altar in the Lord's house | Hear from heaven, act, and judge.<br>• Punish the wicked and bring his way on his own head<br>• Justify the righteous |  |  |

| Solomon said to or asked of the Lord | Solomon said about the Lord | What does this teach us that Solomon believed about the Lord? | How does this show humility, prayer, seeking the Lord or repenting? |
|---|---|---|---|
| **(v. 24-25)** Israel is defeated before an enemy because they have sinned and:<br>• Return to Thee<br>• Confess Thy name<br>• Pray<br>• Make supplication before Thee | • Hear from heaven<br>• Forgive the sin of Thy people<br>• Bring them back to the land which Thou hast given to them | | |
| **(v. 26-27)** Heavens are shut up and there is no rain because they have sinned and:<br>• Pray<br>• Confess Thy name<br>• Turn from sin | • Hear from heaven<br>• Forgive the sin<br>• Teach them the good way to walk<br>• Send rain on Thy land | | |
| **(v. 28-31)** There is/are:<br>• Famine<br>• Pestilence<br>• Blight or mildew<br>• Locust<br>• Grasshopper<br>• A siege by their enemies<br>• Plague or sickness<br>• Prayer or supplication made | • Hear from heaven<br>• Forgive according to a man's way<br>• That they may fear You and walk in Your ways | | |
| **(v. 32-33)** Foreigner comes to the temple to pray to You | Hear and do what the foreigner calls to Thee: Why?<br>• All the peoples of the earth will know Thy name<br>• Nations will fear Thee<br>• Nations may know the Lord's house | | |
| **(v. 34-35)** Israel goes out to battle against their enemies and they pray | Hear from heaven and maintain their cause | | |

| Solomon said to or asked of the Lord | Solomon said about the Lord | What does this teach us that Solomon believed about the Lord? | How does this show humility, prayer, seeking the Lord or repenting? |
|---|---|---|---|
| **(v. 36-39)** Israel sins against Thee, Thou art angry, and Israel is taken captive to a land near or far and they:<br>• Repent—say they have sinned<br>• Return to Lord with all their heart, their soul<br>• Pray | Hear from heaven their prayer and maintain their cause, forgive Thy people who have sinned against Thee | | |

What a prayer! I love studying the prayers of those in God's Word; there is so much to learn from them. It was clear Solomon knew who the Lord was, what the Lord had said to his father David, and what Solomon believed the Lord could and would do. Tomorrow we will study the Lord's response to Solomon's prayer. Remember Solomon's if/then requests because we will look at the Lord's response to see how it aligns with Solomon's belief system.

**Bible study tip of the week**: If/then statements are conditional clauses or statements. It is always important to look at what God says when He uses if/then clauses. These clauses can express implications, provide an explanation of a consequence, a result or conclusion.

3. Before we close with our application questions and prayer, think about how Solomon's prayer relates to our application step **humble yourself, pray, seek, and repent to God for healing in our land.** Write your thoughts below.

4. What has the Lord shown you from today's lesson to apply to your life? Your church? Your nation?

5. Write your closing prayer to Him.

*"When he was in distress, he entreated the LORD his God and humbled himself greatly before the God of his fathers. When he prayed to Him, He was moved by his entreaty and heard his supplication, and brought him again to Jerusalem to his kingdom. Then Manasseh knew that the LORD was God."*
**2 Chronicles 33:12-13**

# WEEK 5—DAY 3

Yesterday we studied Solomon's prayer to the Lord and, as promised, today we will look at the Lord's response to Solomon's prayer. There is much to learn, so let's make sure our hearts are prepared to hear what our Savior wants to teach us. Ask the Lord for a heart of humility and wisdom for the days ahead.

After Solomon finished the prayer to the Lord in **2 Chronicles 6:14-41,** fire came down from heaven and the glory of the Lord filled His house. Israel worshiped the Lord and gave praise to Him saying, "Truly He is good, truly His lovingkindness is everlasting" (**2 Chronicles 7:1-2**). After they had dedicated the temple, the Lord appeared to Solomon. Let's read what happened.

1. Read **2 Chronicles 7:12-22.**

   a. Complete the chart with the Lord's if/then statements.

| I [The Lord] have chosen this place for Myself as a house of sacrifice. | |
|---|---|
| If: | Then I [The Lord] will: |
| (v. 13)<br>•<br>•<br>•<br><br>(v. 14) If My people who are called by My name will:<br>•<br>•<br>•<br>• | (v. 14)<br>•<br>•<br>• |
| (v. 17)<br>•<br>•<br>• | (v. 18)<br>• |
| (v. 19)<br>• | (v. 20)<br><br>• |

b. What does the Lord's response to Solomon's prayer tell you about Himself?

c. If Israel is uprooted from their land and cast away from the Lord, what question will they ask about Israel and the temple ("this land" and "this house," v. 21)?

d. How will they answer their own question (v. 22)?

e. What warning did this give to the other nations as they saw what God was willing to do to those He loved?

Solomon's prayer to the Lord gives us an indication he knew and understood the Lord's precepts (God's laws and commandments). The Lord gave a clear outline of how Israel could stay in right relationship with Himself and the consequences if they decided to go their own way. You may know Solomon developed a divided heart and led Israel away from the Lord. The result was a divided kingdom. Moreover, as the Lord had promised, He sent Assyria to conquer the Northern Kingdom and Babylon to conquer the Southern Kingdom. Indeed, it was said about Israel, "Because they forsook the LORD, the God of their fathers who brought them from the land of Egypt, and they adopted other gods and worshiped them and served them; therefore He has brought all this adversity on them" (**2 Chronicles 7:22**).

---

### Questions to Ponder

❖ Do Solomon's prayer and the Lord's response have any lessons for America today? If so, what do you believe the implications are?

---

We've spent a lot of time this week studying the word *humble*, but our action step this week is **humble yourself, pray, seek, and repent to God for healing in our land.** Let's take a closer look at the additional concepts of praying, seeking, and repenting.

❖ Pray—Hebrew word *pālal—to pray (to God), entreat, make supplication; to intervene, interpose, intercede … Of the total number of occurrences, eighty instances are reflexive thus expressing the idea of interceding for or praying on behalf of someone (Num. 21:7; Deut. 9:20; 1 Sam. 12:23). In other words pālal has a reciprocal meaning between its subj. and its obj.*[97]

❖ Seek—Hebrew word *bāquah*—*to search out … spec.*[specifically] *in worship or prayer; by impl.*[implication] *to strive after; ask; beg; beseech, desire, enquire.*[98]

❖ Repent—Hebrew word *shūv*—*to turn around (figuratively); to turn to Jehovah (i.e., a spiritual return to the Lord, Num.14:43; Deut. 30:2; 1 Kgs. 8:34; 2 Chr. 30:9; Ps: 22:27; Is.19:22; Hos. 12:6; Joel 2:12, Amos 2:12.)*[99]

What a list! First, we are to humble ourselves by bringing ourselves under subjection to the Lord. Second, we are to intervene for our nation. Third, we are to strive after the Lord. Then, we are to spiritually return to the Lord. What might this look like in practice? The best way to answer this question is by considering at someone who embodies what the Lord instructed when He said, "[If] My people who are called by My name humble themselves and pray and seek My face and turn from their wicked ways, then I will hear from heaven, will forgive their sin and will heal their land" (**2 Chronicles 7:14**).

As I was praying about whom to use as an example, one man jumped into my mind—Daniel. Yes, the same Daniel who would not defile himself by eating the king's food and who found himself in a den of lions because he was praying to the Lord. King Nebuchadnezzar from Babylon captured Daniel, at the approximate age of fifteen, along with others from Jerusalem. Their captivity was a direct result of the Southern Kingdom, Judah, being unfaithful to the Lord. Judah did evil in the sight of the Lord and sought after foreign gods; therefore, the Lord allowed King Nebuchadnezzar to plunder them. They had also failed to give the land rest as the Lord commanded. **Leviticus 25:4** tells us, "During the seventh year the land shall have a Sabbath rest, a Sabbath to the Lord; you shall not sow your field nor prune your vineyard." Judah had cultivated the land for 490 years but had failed to listen to the Lord's instruction to allow the land to rest every seventh year. Because they had ignored the Sabbath rest seventy times, the Lord declared seventy years of captivity (70 x each 7th year = 490).

By the time Daniel prayed in **Daniel 9**, *sixty-nine years had passed*. Daniel was in his mid-eighties and he would soon enter into his eternal rest. What can we learn about how to pray from Daniel, a man of great faith?

2. Read **Daniel 9:1-3**.

   a. What time reference are we given—what year and what king?


   b. What did Daniel understand?


   c. What prophet of the Lord was mentioned?


   d. Read **Jeremiah 25:12**.

      *"Then it will be when seventy years are completed I will punish the king of Babylon and that nation,' declares the* Lord, *'for their iniquity, and the land of the Chaldeans; and I will make it an everlasting desolation.'"*

e. What conclusions can you make?

Daniel studied the Word of the Lord, through the prophet Jeremiah, and discovered the Lord had decreed seventy years of desolation/ruin for Judah. Darius the Mede had already overtaken the Babylonian throne as the Lord decreed. Daniel had been in captivity for sixty-nine years, so he knew freedom was near.

f. In light of what Daniel had learned, how did he respond (**Daniel 9:3**)?

When Daniel learned relevant information pertaining to his people, he took action. God will always have a remnant who will serve Him. In King David's time it was the sons of Issachar. It was said they were, ". . . men who understood the times, with knowledge of what Israel should do . . . [men] with an undivided heart" (**1 Chronicles 12:32-33**). **Daniel 11:32b** tells us, "but the people who know their God will display strength and take action." Daniel was a man who understood the times; he had knowledge of what needed to be done, he had an undivided heart for the Lord, and he was taking action. Let's dissect Daniel's prayer and discover how a hero of the faith prays.

3. As you read **Daniel 9:4-19**, complete the chart.

| The Lord | Israel |
|---|---|
| *His character* | *Actions & results* |
| *His discipline towards Israel* | *Daniel's requests to the Lord* |

What is the Lord showing you about how to humbly pray for yourself, others, and our country?

Daniel was a man who humbled himself before the Lord. He prayed, interceded, and beseeched the Lord on behalf of Judah. He confessed their sin and agreed with the Lord's consequences for sin. Daniel fervently prayed for Judah to spiritually return to the Lord. He was a man who knew the character of the Lord and pled on behalf of Judah. He didn't ask for action for the sake of Judah but for the sake of the Lord's own name. We can learn much from a prayer like Daniel's.

4.  Let's answer our application questions. What have you learned today to apply to your life? Your church? Your nation?

5.  Close with your prayer. Ask the Lord to give you a heart for repentance for yourself, your church, and your nation. Let Him know you want to seek Him earnestly.

*"So the princes of Israel and the king humbled themselves and said, "The Lord is righteous." When the Lord saw that they humbled themselves, the word of the Lord came to Shemaiah, saying, "They have humbled themselves so I will not destroy them, but I will grant them some measure of deliverance, and My wrath shall not be poured out on Jerusalem by means of Shishak."*
**2 Chronicles 12:6-7**

# WEEK 5—DAY 4

Last week we began our study of William Tyndale. Haven't you found him to be a remarkable man? Today we will look at the Bible and continue observing Tyndale's life for the purpose of discovering all we can for application to our lives. Begin your time with prayer. Ask the Lord to show you through the lives of William Tyndale and others how to humble yourself before the Lord.

Observe the timeline of Martin Luther and William Tyndale. Notice how God worked in their lives simultaneously to bring about His purpose. At the end of today's lesson we will add additional events from Tyndale's life.

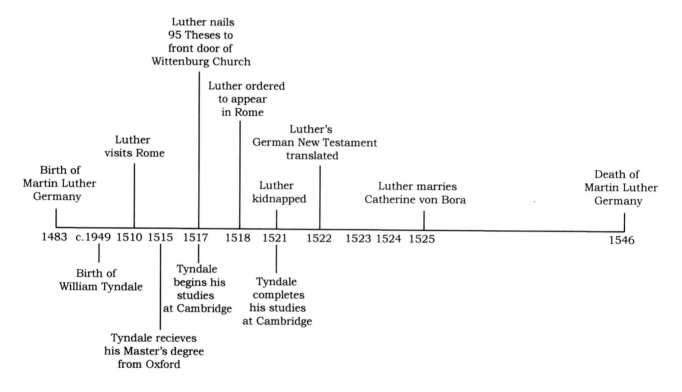

Last week we studied the period of William Tyndale's early life. We laid the groundwork for the environment in which Tyndale labored for the Lord. We paralleled Tyndale with Nehemiah and saw how God showed them both a circumstance that needed to be rectified (Nehemiah securing the Jerusalem wall and Tyndale translating the Bible into English). Finally we saw how God burdened their hearts with a passion to complete the task given them. Today, we will discover how the important work of translating the Bible into English consumed Tyndale's life.

By the summer of 1521 Tyndale was about twenty-seven years old. After graduation he accepted a position in Gloucestershire, his presumed hometown. While most thought Tyndale was wasting his education tutoring the children of Sir John Walsh, Tyndale considered it an excellent opportunity to continue studying Greek.

The work at the Walsh home was very easy, they provided Tyndale with room and board, and he had plenty of time for his own pursuits.

While in Gloucestershire, records show Tyndale also preached. "Like most preachers of his day, Tyndale recited the text of his sermon in Latin and then preached in English. What made his words stand out was his teaching of salvation as a free gift from God and people are saved through faith rather than works. The friars were not pleased with Tyndale's words. If the people actually began believing salvation was a free gift, what would happen to the whole system of selling relics and indulgences? Would people tolerate paying the taxes imposed on them by the church for use of church lands? Tyndale's teachings threatened many of their sources of income. . . . The friars worried if the church lost its hold on the people of England because of Tyndale's teachings, society would disintegrate."[100] As much as Tyndale tried to live a quiet life, his biblical views and convictions continued to lead him into the spotlight.

As tutor to the Walsh children, Tyndale was invited to take dinner with the family. Conversation usually centered on the gossip heard of the royal court and family, politics and, of course, religion. Religion was a dangerous subject in 1521. Heresy against the church was a capital offense and "the number of people accused of heresy was rising. In 1521, the bishop of London tried forty-five cases, and burned to death five people who were convicted."[101]

Sir John and his wife often hosted dinner parties. "The older churchmen who joined in these discussions did not have the advantage of Tyndale's education. They did not appreciate a man not yet thirty years old pointing out to them verses of Scripture contradictive to what they were advocating nor did they like him doing it in front of two of the most influential people in the region—Sir John and Lady Anne. These churchmen, along with the Franciscan friars in Bristol, came up with a way to deal with the young upstart who was causing them so many problems. Tyndale's enemies complained to [John] Bell [the bishop's chancellor] saying the young tutor was guilty of heresy. Not only did they report the parts of Tyndale's teachings which they felt threatened the church, but they also made up things he never said. Tyndale knew precisely what kind of danger he faced. It might result in his death. Tyndale prayed as he made his way to the site of the hearing, asking God to give him the strength to be faithful. He was charged with being 'a heretic in sophistry [the use of reasoning or arguments that sound correct but are actually false], and heretic in logic, [and] a heretic in his divinity.'"[102]

The Scriptures alone became Tyndale's defense, and Chancellor Bell found himself in quite a dilemma. If Bell agreed with Tyndale, the verdict would highlight the error in the theology of the mass of clergy who had accused Tyndale and undermine the authority of the church. Yet if Bell condemned Tyndale of heresy some of the most powerful families in the area would be offended, first and foremost his employer, Sir John Walsh. Bell compromised by releasing Tyndale, after Bell had properly threatened him. "Tyndale himself wrote, 'when I came before the chancellor, he threatened me grievously, and reviled me, and rated me as though I had been a dog.'"[103] This was truly a David and Goliath moment. Tyndale stood alone against the powerful system.

Tyndale was at a crossroads, "if he was to continue preaching and writing salvation was by faith alone, in opposition to the teachings of the church he would likely be burned at the stake. Yet if he remained silent, the uneducated Englishmen with whom he had grown up and tens of thousands like them would never hear the truth. Tyndale's life-mission was declared. He would translate the New Testament into English. Such a work would allow everyone to hear the 'process, order, and meaning' of the Bible in a language they understood'. With the blessing of the Walshes, William Tyndale set off for London in the summer of 1523. He was filled with optimism and hope—and he was totally unprepared for the devious politics of the Tudor court."[104] **Remember:** the Tudor court was the court of Henry VIII and those who served him.

Tyndale was a man who had prepared to the best of his ability for the task of translating the Bible into English. William was an intelligent young man who had spent the majority of his life studying. This made him exceptionally equipped for the task upon which he was embarking; yet, he was not prepared! William Tyndale was not prepared for the trials to come. He was not prepared for the political environment in which he found himself, both inside and outside of the church. He was not prepared for the isolation forced upon him.

The pattern of God calling the unprepared to do great things was also evident in biblical times. God used men and women who were often unequipped for the task to which He called them. Read the list of those through whom God did mighty works.

Those who KNEW they were unprepared:

- ❖ When God called Moses, he said, "Please, Lord, I have never been eloquent, neither recently nor in time past, nor since Thou has spoken to Thy servant; for I am slow of speech and slow of tongue. . . . Please, Lord, now send the message by whomever Thou wilt" (**Exodus 4:10, 13**). In other words, send anyone except me!

- ❖ When God called Gideon to be the deliverer of Israel, he said, "O, Lord, how shall I deliver Israel? Behold, my family is the least in Manasseh, and I am the youngest in my father's house" (**Judges 6:15**).

- ❖ When God called Jeremiah, he said, "Behold, I do not know how to speak, because I am a youth" (**Jeremiah 1:6**).

Those who THOUGHT they were prepared but were not:

- ❖ When the Lord came to Jonah and said, "Arise, go to Nineveh the great city, and cry against it." Jonah chose instead to go to Tarshish *from* the presence of the Lord (**Jonah 1:2-3**). The fact that Jonah chose to disobey the Lord, indicates that Jonah thought he knew more about what was good for Nineveh and himself than God did, thus making Jonah a man who thought he was prepared, but was not.

- ❖ Jesus said to Peter, "Truly I say to you, that you yourself this very night, before a cock crows twice, shall three times deny Me. . . . Peter said to Him, 'Even if I have to die with You, I will not deny You!'" (**Mark 14:30-31**). We know that Peter fulfilled Jesus' prophecy in **Mark 14:72**.

- ❖ The remaining ten disciples agreed with Peter when he said he would not deny Jesus (**Mark 14:31**). *All* eleven disciples fled when Jesus was arrested. Only John returned to be present at the crucifixion of Jesus Christ.

One can see a pattern in God's use of ill-equipped believers—in biblical times, in the days of William Tyndale, and still today. When my husband and I arrived in Romania in 2002 with the mission to live full-time and spread God's Word to the people of southeastern Romania, I thought I knew what to expect. I had traveled the previous five years to the countries of Romania, Ukraine, Moldova, Colombia, Venezuela, Peru, Mexico, and Zimbabwe helping to plant churches, disciple people, and lead women's conferences. I helped lead teams of people from churches in America to serve with churches around the world. What better preparation could there have been than this for a full-time assignment in Romania? Yet the truth was, no matter how much preparation I had, nothing equipped me for my time in Romania. I am sure many of God's servants say the same today. William Tyndale, many others, and I learned the lesson Paul taught: *total dependence upon God is essential to accomplish His work.*

1.  Read **2 Corinthians 12:1-11**.

    a.  What was given to Paul to keep him from exalting himself (v. 7)?

    b.  How many times did Paul pray to the Lord to rid himself of this thorn?

    c.  What did the Lord tell Paul (v. 9)?

    d.  What was Paul's new mind-set (vv.9-10)?

    Paul would rather _____ in his _____

    that the _____ of Christ may _____ in me.

    ❖  Paul was content in

    •

    •

    •

    •

    •

    ❖  Paul knew when he was _____, then he was _____.

    e.  Who did Paul say he had become (v. 11)?

    f.  What did Paul call himself (v. 11)?

Of all the men in the New Testament, Paul could have boasted in how equipped he was for God's work. Yet, God wanted Paul to be dependent upon Him and not think highly of himself. Whether you think you are equipped or know you are ill equipped, the Lord will bring you to a place where you, like Paul, believe, "Your power, O Lord, is perfected in my weakness" (**2 Corinthians 12:9**). This was true in the days of Tyndale, and it is also true for us. The result is by the time we accomplish what the Lord places in our heart there can be no mistake His power accomplished the task. When God accomplishes His work through ill-equipped people it shines light on the One who is worthy of receiving the credit. Our Lord deserves ALL the glory.

Paul said he was content with his weakness, insults, distress, persecutions, and difficulties for Christ's sake. By the end of Tyndale's life he, too, endured insults, distress, persecution, and difficulties. Tyndale's passion is heard through a statement he made in defense of his teachings. In a debate with an educated man, the man claimed, "We were better be [sic] without God's law than the pope's." Tyndale passionately replied, "I defy the Pope and all his laws; if God spare my life ere many years, I will cause a boy that driveth the plough, shall know more of the Scripture than thou dost."[105]

Nehemiah was a man who also knew opposition and he continues to be a great biblical example to parallel Tyndale. Let's see what we can learn.

2. Read **Nehemiah 4:1-15**.

   a. How did Sanballat respond when he heard Nehemiah and the Jews were rebuilding the wall around Jerusalem?

   b. What did Sanballat and Tobiah say about Nehemiah's efforts?

      The questions—

       ❖

       ❖

       ❖

       ❖

       ❖

The statement—

   c. If you were to use one word to describe what Sanballat and Tobiah were trying to do through their words, what word would you use?

You probably chose an adjective such as intimidate, undermine, ridicule, demoralize.

d. How did Nehemiah pray for his oppressors?

e. Did Nehemiah allow the enemies' ridicule to stop the work the Lord called him to do?

f. When Sanballat and Tobiah found their tactics ineffective, what did they do (vv. 7-8)?

g. Again, how did Nehemiah respond?
   - ❖
   - ❖

h. What did the enemies want to do (v. 11)?
   - ❖
   - ❖

i. What happened to the Jews who were rebuilding the wall (v. 14)?

j. What did Nehemiah do to calm their fears (vv. 13-14)?
   - ❖
   - ❖

k. Who intervened for Nehemiah? What happened (v. 15)?

l. What did the Jews do (v. 15)?

We can learn much from Nehemiah's leadership and how he handled adversity. I'm sure you noticed prayer (dependence upon God) was key to his success. You should also have noticed after prayer there was always action. Godly men and women know the faith aspect of prayer is action! Nehemiah took action and placed guards on the wall day and night. He also did not allow fear to stop progress on the wall.

Both Nehemiah and Tyndale were men who humbled themselves before the Lord. They were men who moved forward in faith expecting God to heal their land. Next week you will discover just how much opposition William Tyndale had when he took on the daunting task of translating God's Word into English. Like Nehemiah, Tyndale was a man who took action when adversity struck.

3.  Return to the chart on page 158. Add the following events to the timeline.

    a.  1521—Tyndale began employment with Sir John Walsh in Gloucestershire.
    b.  1523—Tyndale left Gloucestershire for London to begin his English New Testament translation.

You've had a productive day. Let's close with our application questions and prayer.

4.  What has the Lord shown you through William Tyndale and Nehemiah that you can apply to your life? Your church? Your nation?

5.  Close with your prayer to the Lord. Ask Him to give you a heart of repentance and the willingness to move forward in faith with the Lord's plans for your life. Lastly ask Him to give you an expectant heart while fervently praying that He will heal your land.

*"O my God, in You I trust, do not let me be ashamed; do not let my enemies exult over me."*
**Psalm 25:2**

# WEEK 5—DAY 5

What a week we have had! For our final weeks on Day 5s we will continue our study of the colonies but will fast forward to the eighteenth century, just a few decades before the American Revolution. We will learn what was taking place at this time and its impact on the future of the United States. Let us begin in prayer and ask the giver of wisdom, Jesus Christ, to open our eyes, hearts, and minds to the truth He wants to impart into our lives.

When the Pilgrims (Puritans) landed in America in 1620, the population of the colonies was just over 2,300. In about 100 years, the colonies had swelled to over 900,000 people.[106] What had become of the dream of William Bradford and the pilgrims of a land where religious freedom could flourish and the common man was free from government control, and people were free to worship without fear of persecution? Most importantly the Puritans wanted freedom from a governmental church, which commanded what they believed and how they worshiped. What impact did the church have on the people who were flooding to this new land? Was William Bradford's dream of living in a land commanded by Scripture becoming a reality? Or did that dream die with Bradford? We will spend the next four weeks answering these important questions. Time is short, so let's get started!

Thomas S. Kidd in his book *The Great Awakening* said, "by the late seventeenth century many Puritans had become convinced that New England had entered a period of protracted [delayed] spiritual decline, as apparent passivity and immorality replaced religious fervor and holiness. Worried pastors wondered whether New Englanders had exchanged true, heartfelt Christian commitment for mere formality and obligatory church attendance."[107]

This apathy caused many pastors in the 1720s to call for special meetings to fervently pray for the Holy Spirit to energize the churches and for revival to break out within the colonies. In *Revival*, Richard Owen Roberts wrote, "revival is like a prairie fire ignited by a bolt of lightning from the heavens. Without organization, advertising, or even sometimes human leadership, revivals have altered the hearts of men, the social attitudes of millions and the destinies of nations. On these precious occasions God Himself has stepped into the stream of history and done a work so mighty and wonderful that thereafter the mere retelling of God's acts is sufficient to excite expectation and longing in the hearts of the faithful."[108]

---

### Questions to Ponder

Do you think that revival is needed in the hearts of humanity and your nation?

What do you believe has contributed to the spiritual decline of your country?

Do you believe a heartfelt Christian commitment has been replaced with mere formality and obligatory church attendance for the average church attender? Why or why not?

---

The word revival refers to the rebirth of a person. Jesus spoke of this rebirth in his teaching to Nicodemus in John 3. Let's take a quick look.

1.  Read **John 3:1-8**.

    a.  What did Nicodemus understand about Jesus?

**Note:** Although Nicodemus did not have the ability at this moment to comprehend Jesus was God, the Son of God; he did understand Jesus was an anointed teacher from God; therefore, Nicodemus would value the teaching of Jesus. **Remember**: Nicodemus sought out Jesus.

    b.  What did Jesus tell Nicodemus?

When Jesus said, "Truly, truly, . . ." He was testifying to Nicodemus telling him, "Yes, you are correct, I am a teacher from God and I am telling you one must be born again."

    c.  What two questions did Nicodemus ask?
        ❖

        ❖

d. What two ways did Jesus say one must be born?

❖

❖

e. Jesus elaborated on the two births. Fill in the blanks.

That which is born of the _____ is _____.

That which is born of the _____ is _____.

f. What illustration did He use?

g. The illustration refers to which birth?

Based on Jesus' illustration, the second, or spiritual birth, is one in which physical eyes cannot see. Yet, one clearly knows it exists and can observe the effects or results of a spiritual birth, just as one *cannot see* the wind but *can observe* the results of the wind.

h. From our brief examination of **John 3:1-8** how would you describe the two births?

Water—

Spiritual—

Yes, the first birth, or water birth, describes the birth every human has experienced. We celebrate this birth every year with family and friends. It is the day our age clock started, the day our mothers gave birth to us.

The second, or spiritual birth, Nicodemus could not comprehend, is one reserved for people who accept Jesus as Savior and live out a life of obedience to Him. Like the wind it is a birth unseen by the eye, yet can clearly be identified.

The church, in 1720, began to pray for this type of revival or rebirth. Pastors began praying a true passion for the Savior would replace the passivity of the eighteenth-century church. They prayed for true regeneration, true spiritual conversions within and outside the church.

The revival of the 1700s became known as *The Great Awakening*. Most Christian historians attribute the genesis of the movement to Jonathan Edwards' Northhampton Church. Fourteen years of prayer preceded this great spiritual revival.

*The Great Awakening* began in a crisis situation. The young people in Edwards' area were distraught over the untimely deaths of some of their friends. Edwards began to minister to those young people and encouraged them to consider what their eternal destiny would be if they, as their friends had, died. Edwards asked whether they were truly born again. A passion began growing in the youth, which could not be contained. Soon the adults were also pursuing God with great abandon. Many who had been passive before were now intense.

In Jonathan Edwards' book, *A Faithful Narrative of the Surprising Work of God*, he describes the Great Awakening:

> "There was scarcely a single person in the town, old or young, left unconcerned about the great things of the eternal world. Those who were wont to be the vainest and loosest, and those who had been disposed to think and speak lightly of vital and experimental religion, were now generally subject to great awakenings. And the work of conversion was carried on in a most astonishing manner, and increased more and more; souls did as it were come by flocks to Jesus Christ. From day to day for many months together, might be seen evident instances of sinners brought out of darkness into marvellous light, and delivered out of an horrible pit, and from the miry clay, and set upon a rock, with a new song of praise to God in their mouths."[109]

This great manifestation of God was preceded by fourteen years of fervent prayer. This week's action step, **humble yourself, pray, seek, and repent to God for healing in our land (2 Chronicles 7:14)** embodies this strategy. The principle is clear, if we believe our nation has deteriorated spiritually, the cure for our sickness begins with prayer. This principle was true in biblical times, it was true in the 1700s and it is true today. Let's see what we can learn from Scripture.

2. Read **Acts 1:1-14**.

   a. What event was taking place?

   b. What instruction did Jesus give them (v. 4)?

   c. After Christ ascended into heaven, where did His disciples (male and female) go and to what did they devote themselves?

Ten days later during the Feast of Weeks, (a Jewish Holiday celebrated fifty days after The Feast of Firstfruits), the disciples (about 120) were praying in the upper room. A noise came from heaven along with a great wind, and all were filled with the Holy Spirit. This was the Helper who was promised to them by Jesus in **John 14:16-17**.

3. Read **John 14:16-17**.

"I will ask the Father, and He will give you another Helper, that He may be with you forever; that is the Spirit of truth, whom the world cannot receive, because it does not see Him or know Him, but you know Him because He abides with you and will be in you."

a. According to **John 14:16-17**, how long will the Helper/Holy Spirit, be with a believer?

b. Who cannot receive the Helper?

c. Why would a believer know the Helper?

The 120 disciples were praying and waiting just as Jesus instructed them after His ascension. The Helper was given on The Feast of Weeks; today we know this holiday as Pentecost. The prayers of the faithful disciples on Pentecost ushered in the promise of the Spirit of God. You have already learned 3,000 were saved on Pentecost when Peter spoke to the crowds. Revival revived the first church as those early Christians struggled through the difficult days following Christ's death and resurrection. The movement of the first church was bathed in prayer. We have seen this over and over in the past few weeks.

4. Listed below are a few examples of the prayer life of the early church, and God's movement in each situation. As you read the Scriptures underline the word pray or prayer.

"They were continually devoting themselves to the apostles' teaching and to fellowship, to the breaking of bread and to prayer" (**Acts 2:42**).

"Now Peter and John were going up to the temple at the ninth hour, the hour of prayer" (**Acts 3:1**).

"And when they had prayed, the place where they had gathered together was shaken, and they were all filled with the Holy Spirit and began to speak the word of God with boldness" (**Acts 4:31**).

"But we will devote ourselves to prayer and to the ministry of the word" (**Acts 6:4**).

"And these they brought before the apostles; and after praying, they laid their hands on them" (**Acts 6:6**).

"But Peter sent them all out and knelt down and prayed, and turning to the body, he said, 'Tabitha, arise.' And she opened her eyes, and when she saw Peter, she sat up" (**Acts 9:40**).

"On the next day, as they were on their way and approaching the city, Peter went up on the housetop about the sixth hour to pray" (**Acts 10:9**).

"Cornelius said, 'Four days ago to this hour, I was praying in my house during the ninth hour; and behold, a man stood before me in shining garments'" (**Acts 10:30**).

"He [Peter] said, 'Cornelius, your prayer has been heard and your alms have been remembered before God (**Acts 10:31**).

"So Peter was kept in the prison, but prayer for him was being made fervently by the church to God" (**Acts 12:5**).

"And when he realized this [people fervently praying for Peter], he went to the house of Mary, the mother of John who was also called Mark, where many were gathered together and were praying" (**Acts 12:12**).

"Then, when they had fasted and prayed and laid their hands on them, they sent them away" (**Acts 13:3**).

These are just a few examples of our first church and how they prayed. How important was prayer to the first church? Yes, it was vital to their existence. God used prayer to breathe life into the first church. This is why the eighteenth-century church began to pray fervently for fourteen years. They patiently waited and asked God to breathe life into the eighteenth-century church as He did into the first-century church.

Several years ago I attended a meeting where a well-known Christian speaker asked a question after her presentation. She wanted everyone to raise a hand if they had heard in recent months the same message revealed to them in their quiet time with the Lord as she had just communicated. God might not have used the same words but the core of the message held true. Eighty percent of the people held up their hands. She explained this was the work of the Lord for that season. God gives the same message to many different people at the same time when He is communicating a truth relevant for that time in history.

I have been encouraged because everywhere I turn, prayer is being emphasized. I receive e-mails weekly about new prayer groups beginning. My church has intensified our prayer life. Everywhere I turn in the Christian community prayer is a strong focus. This tells us a need for prayer is God's message to believers today. Step up your prayer life. Focus on the greater work, prayer. The solution to a passive church is simple to understand and yet can be very difficult to apply. It begins with you and me. For a revival to sweep our nation—**Humble yourself, pray, seek, and repent to God and HE will heal our land.**

5. What has the Lord been showing you through the early and eighteenth-century church that you need to apply to your life? Your church? Your nation?

6. Close with your prayer to the Lord. Thank Him for what He is revealing to you through *ACTs420NOW*. Thank Him for godly men and women who have gone before us to lead the way.

*"Heed the sound of my cry for help, my King and my God, for to You I pray. In the morning, O Lord, You will hear my voice; in the morning I will order my prayer to You and eagerly watch."*
**Psalm 5:2-3**

# Week 6 Overview

*Persevere by going and telling America and the world until our land is healed.*
## (Isaiah 6:8-11)

Have you noticed each week's principle gets a little more difficult to apply to your life? Being a believer in Jesus Christ is not for the faint of heart. Salvation and receiving the grace of God are free, but living out your faith can be costly.

This week we will:

- ❖ Study God's plan for people to know about Him.
- ❖ Study God's message to Isaiah.
- ❖ Study how God worked in the New Testament church to fulfill His purpose.

This week's applications include:

- ❖ Understanding you are the solution to making disciples.
- ❖ Understanding your response to Jesus should always be, "Here I am, Lord; send me."
- ❖ Understanding our responsibility to share the gospel does not end until the day we see Christ Jesus.

This week's verse to memorize:

*"Then I heard the voice of the Lord, saying, 'Whom shall I send, and who will go for Us?' Then I said, 'Here am I. Send me!' He said, 'Go, and tell this people: "Keep on listening, but do not perceive; keep on looking, but do not understand." Render the hearts of this people insensitive, their ears dull, and their eyes dim, otherwise they might see with their eyes, hear with their ears, understand with their hearts, and return and be healed.' Then I said, 'Lord, how long?' And He answered, 'Until cities are devastated and without inhabitant, houses are without people and the land is utterly desolate.'"*
### Isaiah 6:8-11

Fill in the blanks where appropriate.

**Foundational Step:** _____ there is _____ in none other than

_____ _____ **(Acts** _____**)**.

**Step 2:** _____ you will begin to _____ the Word of God with _____ (**Acts** _____).

**Step 3:** _____ the _____ is "_____" to a lost and dying _____

(**2 Corinthians** _____).

**Step 4:** _____ yourself, _____, seek, and _____ to God for _____ in our land (**2 Chronicles 7:14**).

**Step 5:** Persevere by going and telling America and the world until our land is healed (**Isaiah 6:8-11**).

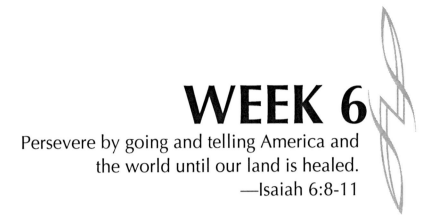

# WEEK 6

Persevere by going and telling America and
the world until our land is healed.
—Isaiah 6:8-11

## WEEK 6—DAY 1

**Psalm 90:12** teaches, "So teach us to number our days, that we may present to You a heart of wisdom." Time is short, we must spend our days seeking His wisdom. Write your prayer to the Lord. As you do, thank Him for the wisdom which He imparts to you day by day.

When Jesus asked Peter in **Matthew 16:16-17** who He was, Peter responded, "[T]he Christ, the Son of the Living God." Then Jesus said to Peter, "Blessed are you, Simon Barjona, because flesh and blood did not reveal this to you, but My Father who is in heaven." As with Peter, our Father who is in heaven reveals to you the truth of what you have been learning through this study.

When you read the statement, **Persevere by going and telling America and the world until our land is healed**, the task may seem overwhelming. We need to take comfort in the fact, God's plan is not our plan. The concept came from the Creator of the universe; therefore, His plan will succeed. Just for a moment let's fast forward to the end of the story and see the outcome of HIS redemptive sacrifice.

1. Read **Revelation 5:8-10**.

    a. Who did Jesus purchase for God with His blood?

    b. What are they called?

Over 2,000 years ago, the spotless Lamb was sent from God to purchase men and women from every tribe, tongue, people, and nation. Why? Because Christ was and is the only One worthy, the only One capable of purchasing you and me.

2. Read **Revelation 7:9-12**.

   a. What constitutes the great multitude?

   b. Where is this great multitude standing?

   c. Did this event take place in heaven or on earth?

These are such rich Scriptures. I would love to linger here and really dig into every word. Maybe one day soon we can sit down together and spend in-depth time in the book of Revelation. However, for now, we have clearly seen one day "a great multitude, which no one could count" (**Revelation 7:9**) will stand before Jesus in heaven and before the throne of God. Rest assured, God's plan and your effort will see fruit. Isn't it nice to know you are on the winning team! Sometimes, with all the trials and daily distractions, it is easy to lose sight of this truth.

Let's look at how God worked in the New Testament church to fulfill His purpose. Now that we have reminded ourselves of God's truth, we can boldly walk forward in the Lord's plan. As you walk through today's lesson think about:

❖ How the methods and people God uses today are similar.
❖ How the methods and people God uses today are different.

Before Jesus went to the cross, He promised to send His followers the Helper (Holy Spirit). The Helper's job was to teach the followers of Christ and bring to their remembrance what Jesus had already taught them. Jesus promised the disciples that the Helper would be with them forever (**John 14:16, 26**).

After Jesus arose from the dead and just before He ascended to the right hand of the Father, He instructed His disciples to *wait* "for what the Father had promised [the Holy Spirit]" (**Acts 1:4**). There were approximately 120 people who waited together in the upper room (**Acts 1:15**). Then the day came. Let's look at this first "telling."

3. Read **Acts 2:1-11, 41**.

   a. What was the day?

About 1,400 years before the events in Acts Chapter 2, God established seven Jewish holidays under Levitical law. God created the feasts/festivals for His chosen people, the Jews of the Old Testament, to celebrate aspects of His relationship with His people and as prophetic illustrations of future events.

*Passover* (Passover, Unleavened Bread, and Firstfruits) celebrated in Israel's first month (March-April) was the Lord's protection and provision for Jewish households marked by a spotless lamb's blood on the doorframe in Egypt. This first Passover killed all the firstborn in the land without the mark on the door (**Leviticus 23:5-14**). The fulfillment of Passover and Unleavened Bread was Christ's sacrifice on the cross! His blood delivers believers from sin (**1 Corinthians 5:7**). The only way for sin to be purged is for Christ to cover our sin. He fulfilled this on the cross and our acceptance of Christ's forgiveness through salvation in Christ alone. The fulfillment of Firstfruits was Christ being raised from the dead after His crucifixion, never to die again. One day, we too, will be raised from the dead, never to die again (**1 Thessalonians 4:13-17**).

*Pentecost*, the Feast of Weeks or Harvest was celebrated in Israel's third month (May-June), welcomed the summer harvest, and required a new grain offering (**Leviticus 23:15-21**). This promise was fulfilled when the Holy Spirit came at Pentecost, and Peter preached to the crowds gathered for the feast. That day 3,000 were saved (**Acts 2:1-47**). Pentecost happened fifty days after Passover.

The *Feast of Tabernacles* (Feast of Trumpets, Day of Atonement, and Feast of Booths/Tabernacles) was celebrated in Israel's seventh month (September-October). This festival began with the trumpet's blowing to signify a holy convocation for the people. Nine days later Israel would cleanse themselves of their sins. Finally on the fifteenth day of the month there would be a seven-day celebration in the wilderness where the Israelites would live in tents/booths (**Leviticus 23:23-44**). The Feast of Trumpets was fulfilled on May 14, 1948 when Israel became a nation. God is regathering His people in preparation for the final Day of Atonement, which is yet to be fulfilled. This will happen when Israel will repent and look to Jesus as Messiah. The Feast of Booths/Tabernacles will be fulfilled when Christ descends from heaven to rule and reign on earth for 1,000 years (**Ezekiel 36:28, Romans 11:25-29, Zechariah 14:16-19**).

Let's return to Acts 2. Notice what the result is through His plan.

b. What happened on this day of Pentecost (v. 4)?

c. What happened when they spoke? Who was responsible (v. 6)?

d. What was the reaction of the multitude?

e. In what language did the multitude hear the disciples speak (vv. 8, 11)?

f. What did the crowd hear the disciples describe (v. 11)?

Once this occurred Peter took over and addressed the crowd. He reminded them of many familiar Scriptures in the Old Testament. He reassured the crowd this event had been spoken about by the prophets of old, and now they were witnessing God's promise being fulfilled. He gave a summation of Jesus' life and a clear explanation of His atonement for the forgiveness of sins and the promise of the gift of the Holy Spirit to all who were saved. Peter then called for the people to repent and receive forgiveness in Jesus' name.

g.  What was the result of these events (**Acts 2:41**)?


Let's look at other events in which a gospel presentation was given. We need to take the 10,000′ flyover approach instead of the "dig deeply in the Scriptures" approach, as there is much to absorb. We will examine a few of the Scriptures in more detail in the final weeks of our study.

4.  Read **Acts 2:42-47**.

    a.  To what were the disciples devoting themselves?

    ❖

    ❖

    ❖

    ❖

    b.  How did they spend their days (v. 46)?


    c.  What was the result of this effort? Who was responsible?


Approximately eight years after Pentecost, Peter had the same dream/vision three times. In this dream, the Lord told Peter to eat meat considered unclean by Levitical standards. Peter refused and said he had never eaten anything unclean. After the third time, the Lord said, "What God has cleansed, is no longer consider unholy." Then the Lord told Peter three men would come looking for him and he should go with them. When the Gentile men found Peter, they were surprised he would go with them willingly because the Lord had set apart the Jews from the Gentiles. Then, through God's word, Peter revealed he expected them to come because God had instructed him. When they arrived in Caesarea at the home of Cornelius, a Gentile centurion, Peter gave a presentation.

5.  Read **Acts 10:34-11:1**.

    a.  What did Peter learn about God?

b. Who does the Lord welcome?

c. To whom was the word of God sent (v. 36)?

d. Who did the prophets say would receive forgiveness of sins (v. 43)?

e. On whom did the Holy Spirit fall (v. 44)?

f. Why were the circumcised believers amazed?

g. What did the brethren in Judea hear (v. 11:1)?

**Note:** In the *Believer's Study Bible,* W. A. Criswell says, "The radical change in Peter's attitude toward other ethnic groups is a case of almost instant release from prejudice. He lapsed but one time as far as the Scriptures show [**Galatians 2:12**]. This experience for Peter [and others] was necessary in spite of Jesus' ministry to Gentiles, which Peter surely witnessed (**Matthew 8:5-13**)."[110] (Emphasis mine.)

---

### Questions to Ponder

Have you ever allowed a prejudice of a people group, socio-economic status or other factors stop you from sharing God's redemptive message of salvation?

What action do you need to take?

---

Acts 13 relates how Paul and Barnabas began their first missionary journey. While they were preaching in Pisidian, Antioch (modern-day Turkey), they started down a path that would change the world.

6. Read **Acts 13:42-52**.

    a.  Where did Paul and Barnabas go to meet the people?

    b.  Why did the Jews get jealous?

    c.  What did Paul and Barnabas believe (v. 46)?

    d.  What was the result of the Jews rejecting Paul and Barnabas' teaching?

    e.  What was the reaction of the Gentiles?

    f.  What did those who rejected the gospel do to Paul and Barnabas?

    g.  How did Paul and Barnabas react to the persecution?

On Paul's second missionary journey, he preached his way through Greece and reached Athens. Notice how Paul addressed his audience. The "them" in **Acts 17:16** refers to Silas and Timothy.

7. Read **Acts 17:16-34**.

    a.  What were the two locations where Paul reasoned with the locals (v. 17)?

    b.  What was the response of the philosophers (the educated)?

    c.  What did the "others" say (v. 18)?

    d.  Where did they take Paul?

    e.  What did Paul observe about the Athenians (vv. 22-23)?

        ❖

        ❖

f. What reactions did Paul receive to his declaration (v. 32)?

❖

❖

g. What was the response of those who chose to hear Paul again?

Are you noticing a pattern? Wherever Paul proclaimed the gospel, some rejected it while others listened. We too, should expect rejection when we proclaim salvation in Christ alone. We should also expect others to listen. Once Paul left Athens, he traveled to Corinth, about 45 miles from Athens. There he met a Jewish couple, Aquila and Priscilla.

8. Read **Acts 18:1-11**.

a. With whom did Paul begin to associate when he arrived in Corinth? Why?

b. What did Paul do when Silas and Timothy arrived?

c. What was Paul's response when the Jews rejected him?

d. How long did Paul stay in Corinth after the Lord encouraged him to continue to speak and assured him that he would not be harmed? And what was Paul's primary purpose?

9. Let's take a quick look at what these Scriptures have in common. Think about how they relate to your life.

a. How did Peter and Paul speak when they made their presentations? (You may want to look back at **Acts 13:46, Acts 17:22-23, Acts 18:6.**)

b. How did Peter and Paul respond to the reaction of the crowd to whom they were speaking? (You may want to look back at **Acts 10:44-45, Acts 13:45-48, Acts 17:32-33, Acts 18:6.**)

c. How does/should this apply to you?

Today we have looked at the early church leaders. We have seen how they were respectful yet spoke the truth with boldness. Although they were not always received positively, they continued to spread the Lord's message, even if it meant moving to a different location or people group. They were not experiencing anything Christ did not experience; therefore, we too should expect rejection by some when we boldly speak God's redemptive message.

Let's close with our application questions and prayer.

10. What has God shown you in today's lesson you will apply to your life? Your church? Your nation?

11. Write your prayer to the Lord. Ask Him to bring to mind people who need to hear His redemptive message, to send people into your path, and to give you the boldness to speak HIS message.

*"How then will they call on Him in whom they have not believed? How will they believe in Him whom they have not heard? And how will they hear without a preacher? How will they preach unless they are sent? Just as it is written, 'How beautiful are the feet of those who bring good news of good things!'"*
***Romans 10:14-15***

# WEEK 6—DAY 2

Yesterday was a powerful day of study. Simply reading God's Word can lead to great wisdom. Today will be another rich, exciting day. We will delve into to the Old Testament to discover what the Lord told His people through the prophet Isaiah. Write your prayer to the Lord asking Him to open your mind to His wisdom, His ways, and His plans.

Have you ever wanted to be used by the Lord but didn't think you were qualified? Now that you are six weeks into *ACTs420NOW*, I pray you realize if you are a believer in Jesus Christ you are as qualified as Peter and Paul! I hope this is a comforting and challenging thought. Today, we will look at another of the Lord's servants who was eager to serve yet didn't feel qualified, yet, he too, was eager to serve. If you are not familiar with the Old Testament book Isaiah, you are going to love it. We will take small bites of this ancient book so as not to get overwhelmed while discovering how relevant it is for our daily lives.

Start today by examining the text. It amazes me how much can be learned by simply slowing down and looking at what the Lord says. Don't just read the words, but meditate and ask the who, what, when, where, why, and how questions.

**Bible study tip of the week**: Do not focus on what you don't understand right now. Instead, focus on the truths that *are* revealed to you today through His Word. Pray for the Lord to reveal more to you in His time.

1.  Read **Isaiah 6:1-11**.

    What a message! Let's begin to break it down piece by piece.

    a.  Who did Isaiah see? Where was He?

    b.  What were the Seraphim saying?

    c.  What was Isaiah's first response? What does this tell you about Isaiah's character and his thoughts on his position with the Lord?

d. What was taken from the altar and how?

e. What is Isaiah in assurance of in verse 7?

"… the coal was a token of forgiveness since fire symbolized cleansing and purification and the altar was the place where purification was made."[111]

f. What was the Lord's question to Isaiah? What does this tell you about the Lord?

g. What was Isaiah's response? What does this tell you about Isaiah?

h. What was the message the Lord told Isaiah to tell Judah (vv. 9-10)?

i. If they began to see with their eyes and hear with their ears, and understand with their heart, what would happen?

j. How long was he to speak to the people?

k. What do these Scriptures tell you about God? About Isaiah?

God–

Isaiah–

What a message! The Lord is calling Isaiah to be His messenger in the year of King Uzziah's death (about 739 BC). If you have studied *Leaders, Nations, and God* you might remember King Uzziah. Although the Bible tells us he was a man who did right in the eyes of the Lord, in his later years he became prideful and reaped the consequences of his actions.

What can we learn about Judah (the Southern Kingdom of Israel) during the time God called Isaiah? What was their relationship to the Lord?

2. Read **Isaiah 1:2-6**.

   a. What is the Lord's attitude toward Judah?

   b. What is the attitude of Judah toward the Lord?

   c. How does the Lord describe Judah (vv. 3b-4)?

   d. How is the head described? How is the heart described?

      Head –

      Heart –

   e. Why are they described as sick and faint and to what degree?

Judah was in bad shape. They revolted against the Lord, they were weighed down with sin, and they were rebellious. Judah's eyes were dim, their ears were dull, and their hearts could not understand. God told Isaiah to minister to these people. They were God's OWN people, No wonder Isaiah didn't feel prepared!

---

**Questions to Ponder**

Do you see any similarities between the people in Isaiah's time and the people in your city, country, or church today?

Is God's heart and message the same today as it was in the time of Isaiah? If so, what should your response be?

---

Isaiah asked the Lord how long he was to prophesy to the people. In **Isaiah 6:11** the Lord answered, "Until cities are devastated and without inhabitant, houses are without people, and the land is utterly desolate." This verse gives us insight into the impending judgment Judah was facing. Did God want to leave them in their devastation? Let's study a few more Scriptures and learn the Lord's continuing message to His people.

3. Read **Isaiah 5:13-24**.

   a. Where were the Lord's people going? Why?

   b. How will the Lord be exalted (v. 16)?

   c. What do the *woes* teach us (vv. 18-23)?

      ❖

      ❖

      ❖

      ❖

   d. What are the roots of Judah's problem (v. 24)?

   They have _____ the _____ of the Lord.

   They have _____ the _____ of the Holy One of Israel.

4. Read **Isaiah 1:17-20**.

   a. What could Judah learn?

   b. What were they to seek?

   c. The Lord said, "Though your sins are as scarlet, they will be white as snow; though they are red like crimson, they will be like wool." What does this tell you about the heart of the Lord (**Isaiah 65:1**)?

   d. What will happen to Judah if they turn to the Lord and obey (v. 19)?

   e. What will happen if Judah refuses the Lord and rebels (v. 20)?

The Lord keeps the perfect balance of judgment and mercy. His heart is always for mercy, but when people choose their own way He has no alternative other than judgment.

5. Read **Isaiah 30: 15-18**.

   "For thus the Lord GOD, the Holy One of Israel, has said, 'In repentance and rest you will be saved, in quietness and trust is your strength.' **But you were not willing, and you said, "No**… Therefore those who pursue you shall be swift … Until you are left as a flag on a mountain top and as a signal on a hill. Therefore the Lord **longs to be gracious** to you, and therefore He **waits on high to have compassion on you.** For the Lord is a God of justice; how blessed are all those who long for Him" (emphasis mine).

   a. List what God wants for people.

   b. Who is responsible for the compassion or judgment one receives?

**Isaiah 6:10** tells us when the people begin to see with their eyes, hear with their ears, and understand with their hearts the result will be healing. The Hebrew word for *healing* is *râphâ*. *The meaning is straightforward in virtually all passages…a human subject is generally the object of the healing… The themes of healing and restoration as connotations of râpâ are combined in the usage of* **Isa. 53:5**, *'With [H]is stripes we are healed.' In many of the occurrences, it is God who causes healing or afflicts with disease or catastrophes which cannot be healed but by divine intervention.*[112] (Emphasis mine).

*Râphâ* is the same Hebrew word studied in **2 Chronicles 7:14**, last week. What does God mean when He says He will heal their land? We want to continue to build upon the principles we are learning. The Hebrew word for *land* is *erets; it is used in many phrases, such as 'people of the land' unlike 'admāh referring to soil, earth, ground, land, and country.*[113]

6. Review the definition of *râphâ* above. Based on the context of **Isaiah 6:10** and **2 Chronicles 7:14** and using the Hebrew definitions, do you believe the word *land* in **2 Chronicles 7:14** is referring to the land itself or the people of the land?

   "[If] My people who are called by My name humble themselves and pray and seek My face and turn from their wicked ways, then I will hear from heaven, will forgive their sin and will heal their land" (**2 Chronicles 7:14**).

   "Render the hearts of this people insensitive, their ears dull, and their eyes dim, otherwise they might see with their eyes, hear with their ears, understand with their hearts, and return and be healed" (**Isaiah 6:10**).

When God speaks of healing land in **2 Chronicles 7:14**, He is speaking of healing the spirit and soul of His people. God's heart is always for people. God's heart is always for compassion, and restoration despite the sinful condition of the people He is pursuing. Throughout the Bible, God used judgment with the intent of turning people to repentance and reconciliation with Him.

ACTs420NOW

7. Write **Isaiah 65:1-2**.




Over the past two days we have seen some common threads when it comes to the principle **Persevere by going and telling America and the world until our land is healed.** Let's look at the chart below.

| Reference | Event | Result(s) |
|---|---|---|
| **Acts 2:1-11, 41** | Peter gave a message to Jews and proselytes (Gentiles who take the Jewish covenant). They were of many nations: Cyrene (northern Libya), Asia (Turkey), Rome (Italy), Cretans (Greece), and Arabs (Saudi Arabia). | Three thousand souls were added that day. |
| **Acts 2:42-47** | Believers were continually devoting themselves to teaching, fellowship, breaking bread, and prayer. | The Lord added believers to their fellowship day by day. |
| **Acts 10:34-11:1** | Peter took the gospel message to the Gentiles. | *All* Gentiles who heard and believed received the Holy Spirit. |
| **Acts 13:42-52** | The whole city of Pisidian, Antioch (central Turkey) assembled to hear Paul's word from the Lord. | ❖ The Jews who were filled with jealousy blasphemed Paul and began to persecute him. ❖ Many others believed. ❖ The Word of the Lord was spread through the whole region. |
| **Acts 17:16-34** | Paul stood before the men of Athens and gave his message of repentance. | ❖ Some sneered. ❖ Some joined him and believed. |
| **Acts 18:1-11** | Paul taught in Corinth. | ❖ Those in the synagogue blasphemed Paul. ❖ Paul turned to the Gentiles who received the word of the Lord; Paul stayed one year and six months teaching the Word of God. |
| **Isaiah 6:1-11** | Isaiah accepted God's call to be His man to the people of Judea and Jerusalem. | |

God's plan is to use God's people to bring God glory. This is the pattern we have seen in Acts and when God asks the pointed question, "Who will go for Us?" in **Isaiah 6:8**.

186

8. Read **Romans 10:14-15**. What is Paul's four-point exhortation in order for the people to be saved? (**Note**: you might find it helpful to begin in verse fifteen and work backwards.)

   ❖

   ❖

   ❖

   ❖

The preacher *must* be sent, the message *must* be preached, the message *must* be heard, and the message *must* be believed. From our study we have learned the job of telling America the good news of the gospel might be fraught with trials and tribulations. The road was difficult for Jesus, Peter, Paul, and Isaiah. Despite the difficulties, it is a road we must travel as believers of Jesus Christ. The method of delivery may change but the message must remain true. Jesus Christ is the Savior of the world. As we learned in Week One, there truly is **salvation in none other than Jesus Christ (Acts 4:12).**

What were the Lord's final words to Isaiah in Isaiah 6, which will encourage us in this task?

9. Read **Isaiah 6:12-13**. Although God will remove men far away from Judah, what will always remain (v. 13)?

   ❖ Write "God kept a tenth (or remnant) for Himself" in the empty results box beside **Isaiah 6:1-11** in question seven.

God had reserved a remnant, a tenth, who would remain in the land; they would become a holy seed. My friend, no matter the rejection you may encounter in presenting God's message, there will always be a remnant, people God is setting apart for Himself. Just think, you get to be a part of His work! Despite the hardships, you get a front row seat in heaven when the saints are ushered into the kingdom of God. What a blessing! I have seen firsthand the miracle of salvation and it never loses its wonder.

10. What has the Lord revealed to you today through Isaiah that you can apply to your life? Your church? Your nation?

11. Write your closing prayer to the Lord. Continue to ask God to bring people into your life with whom you can share His good news of redemption.

*"Then He said to His disciples, 'The harvest is plentiful, but the workers are few. Therefore beseech the Lord of the harvest to send out workers into His harvest.'"*
***Matthew 9:37-38***

# Week 6—Day 3

**Isaiah 5:13** teaches, "My people go into exile for their lack of knowledge." We need to be attentive and seek the Lord's knowledge. We need to be diligent to soak up every morsel of truth the Lord has for us. As always, begin today with your prayer to the Lord. Ask Him to bathe you in His truth for the days ahead.

There is no greater example than Christ Himself when it comes to "going and telling." **Matthew 9:35-38** explains the heart of our Lord. These verses walk through what Jesus was doing, how He felt, and His plan to redeem the situation.

1. Read **Matthew 9.** Note the event(s) and the result(s), then answer the probing questions.

   a. **Matthew 9:1-8.**

| Main Event | Overall Result |
|---|---|
| Example: Forgives paralytic man's sins, then tells him to rise and walk | Example: Multitude glorified God who had given such authority to men |

   i. What was Jesus' first concern (v. 2)?

   ii. What was the reaction of the scribes?

   iii. What was the response of the multitude after Jesus healed the paralytic?

   iv. What can I learn from Jesus about how to respond to people?

   b. **Matthew 9:9-13.**

| Main Event | Overall Result |
|---|---|
|  |  |

i. Jesus <u>chose</u> to spend His time with whom; and who did Jesus take with Him?

ii. Who did Jesus say needed a physician?

iii. What did Jesus want the Pharisees to learn?

iv. What do you believe Jesus wanted to teach His disciples? What do you believe He is trying to teach you?

c. **Matthew 9:14-17.** Note: The disciples of John (the Baptist).

| Main Event |
|---|
|  |

i. To whom was Jesus ministering (v. 14)?

ii. What was Jesus communicating when He spoke about the bridegroom?

iii. What was Jesus communicating when He spoke about garments and wineskin?

d. **Matthew 9:18-26.**

| Main Event(s) | Overall Result(s) |
|---|---|
|  |  |

i. How did Jesus treat those who *interrupted* His day?

ii. When did Jesus' *ministry* take place? Did Jesus work on appointments?

iii. What was Jesus teaching His disciples during these teachable moments? What is He teaching you?

iv. How did the crowd's laughter affect Jesus? What can you learn from His actions/attitude?

Jesus' ministry took place as He went about His day. There were no appointments or "scheduled" healings. People who are desperate need to have the freedom to interrupt! We need to learn from Jesus and begin to see with spiritual eyes those the Lord is placing in front of us each day. We must learn these people are not interruptions but opportunities to be Jesus.

e. **Matthew 9:27-31.**

| Main Event | Overall Result |
| --- | --- |
|  |  |

i. The two blind men (as well as the others in Matthew 9) sought out Jesus. Why do you believe the blind men did this?

ii. Are people seeking you out because they see Jesus in you? Do they believe you have the answers that can bring healing to their spirit and soul?

f. **Matthew 9:32-34.**

| Main Event | Overall Result |
| --- | --- |
|  |  |

What did the Pharisees say regarding Jesus casting out demons?

g. **Matthew 9:35-38.**

| Main Event(s) | Overall Result(s) |
|---|---|
| | |

i.   Where did Jesus go?

ii.  What did He do?
     ❖
     ❖
     ❖

iii. What did He see? How did He feel? Why?

iv.  What problem did Jesus communicate to His disciples?

v.   What was Jesus' solution?

Yes, you and I are the solution to Jesus' proclamation to His disciples when He said, "The harvest is plentiful, but the workers are few, therefore beseech the Lord of the harvest to send out workers into His harvest" (**Matthew 9:37-38**). Jesus' final command was not only, "Go and make disciples", but He also modeled this throughout His ministry (**Matthew 28:19**).

Jesus' entire motivation welled up from a heart of compassion. Everything we have studied has been to prepare our hearts to have compassion on those who need Jesus. He said, "It is not those who are healthy who need a physician, but those who are sick" (**Matthew 9:12**). When we have compassion we are compelled to take action and share God's redemptive plan with those who are sick. If there were a gauge to measure compassion, how high would your meter read? Dealing with the sick is not a task for the fragile of mind and spirit. We must have the mind and heart of Christ for this God-sized task.

The salvation of America and the nations is how the world will be healed, but it begins with telling them about Jesus. Jesus will begin with their spirits, the invisible part of man in need of a relationship with God. Man's spirit was separated from God in the Garden of Eden when man chose to sin. When the spirits of the people are healed, the land will begin to heal. This process is the focus of the first Bible study I wrote, *Bound To Be Free*. The entire eight-week study is dedicated to God's healing transformation.

---

**Questions to Ponder**

Do you believe the American church as a whole is committed to reaching the sick in spirit Jesus spoke of in **Matthew 9:12?**

Do you believe the American church as a whole has a heart of compassion for the sick in spirit Jesus spoke of in **Matthew 9:36?**

What role are you, or do you need to play in Jesus' plan for leading the sick sheep to the Shepherd?

---

The Greek word *ĕkballō, send away (forth, out),*[114] is used in **Matthew 9:38** when Jesus told the disciples to beseech Him to send out workers. Although the meaning is straightforward, *ĕkballō* is used most in the New Testament in reference to Jesus sending out or casting out demons. Three occurrences of the word *ĕkballō* provide interesting insight into the word.

2. Read **Mark 1:9-12**. The English word(s) for *ĕkballō* are italicized and underlined.

"In those days Jesus came from Nazareth in Galilee and was baptized by John in the Jordan. Immediately coming up out of the water, He saw the heavens opening, and the Spirit like a dove descending upon Him; and a voice came out of the heavens: 'You are My beloved Son, in You I am well-pleased.' Immediately the Spirit *impelled* Him to go out into the wilderness (emphasis mine)."

a. Who was responsible for impelling (*ĕkballō*) Jesus into the wilderness?

b. Who will compel (*ĕkballō*) us to go and tell?

3. Read **Acts 13:50** and **Acts 16:37**. The English word(s) for *ĕkballō* will be italicized and underlined.

"But the Jews incited the devout women of prominence and the leading men of the city, and instigated a persecution against Paul and Barnabas, and *drove* them out of their district" (**Acts 13:50**).

"But Paul said to them, "They have beaten us in public without trial, men who are Romans, and have thrown us into prison; and now are they *sending* us away secretly? No indeed! But let them come themselves and bring us out" (**Acts 16:37**).

a.  In each of these verses who wants to send (*ĕkballō*) whom away?

These verses give us a contrast between Christ sending out the disciples and the world wanting to send the disciples away. The same passion used by God's Spirit to send you out is the same passion the spirit of the evil one is going to use to send you away or drive you out.

b.  Understanding some may not want to receive the gospel message, to whom should your allegiance be?

c.  What is your responsibility?

This week we have studied and found Peter and John, Paul, and Isaiah all accepted the call to "go and tell." The road for those faithful men of God was not easy, and the road may not be easy for us, but we are not the One who chooses the difficulty of the path. Our job is to be like Isaiah and say, "Here am I. Send me!" (**Isaiah 6:8**). And like Isaiah we must persevere "until the cities are devastated … and the land is utterly desolate" (**Isaiah 6:11**). We are to be *yes* men and women for Jesus!

4.  What have you learned from today's lesson that God wants you to apply to your life? Your church? Your nation?

Close today with your prayer. Ask Jesus to help you become/or to continue to be a yes man or woman for Him. Let Him know you are willing to go where He will send you. Sometimes the most difficult place is next door!

*"Philip ran up and heard him reading Isaiah the prophet, and said, 'Do you understand what you are reading?' And he said, 'Well, how could I, unless someone guides me?' And he invited Philip to come up and sit with him."*
***Acts 8:30-31***

# WEEK 6—DAY 4

As we begin, let us pray we will continue to hunger for His Word. It is His Word, which transforms us into useful vessels for Him (**Romans 12:2**). Most often He works in us before He works through us. Ask Him to transform you to become the useful vessel for the good works *He* prepared for you before the foundation of the earth (**Ephesians 2:10**).

Timelines can be very helpful in seeing God's plan in history. Once you have studied the details, you can step back and look at the big picture. During these times God can show you new things about Himself. Look at the timeline below with the information we added from the previous weeks. At the end of today's lesson we will fill in additional details.

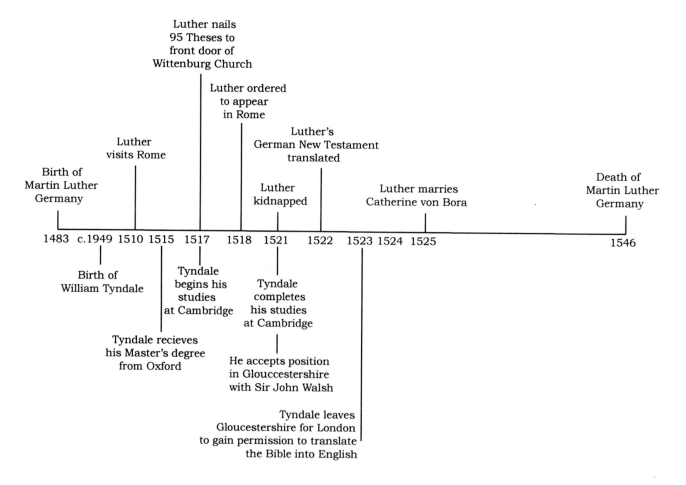

Last week we left William Tyndale as he was leaving Gloucestershire for London. He spent two years as tutor to the children of Sir John and Anne Walsh. Tyndale was brought before the chancellor for heresy, knowing if convicted of the charges he could be burned at the stake. A compromise was reached between the local priest's desires and the desires of Tyndale's wealthy supporters. Tyndale was severely threatened and then released. This trial left Tyndale even more convinced the people in England needed a Bible in their own language. By the time Tyndale began translating the Bible into English, the Bible had already been translated into German, French, Italian, Catalan, Spanish, Portuguese, Czech, and Dutch. Tyndale felt English was far behind and should not be left out.[115]

The persecution of Tyndale reminds us of the persecution of Peter and John. Remember, Peter and John stood before the Sanhedrin and were questioned on whose authority they were preaching Jesus. At the conclusion of their trial, "When they [the Sanhedrin] had threatened them further, they let them [Peter and John] go (finding no basis on which to punish them)…" (**Acts 4:21, comment added**). It is amazing that the very same tactics were used over and over again, and continue even today.

Today the religious threats in America can be more subtle and there is no fear of being physically beaten, yet they are real threats. One such threat comes from the Internal Revenue Service (IRS) against churches and other religious non-profit organizations. The Johnson Amendment was attached to a tax bill passed in 1954. This amendment states that non-profit organizations cannot support or oppose any political candidate. Although LBJ never intended the bill to be used against churches and religious organizations, today the IRS threatens to remove non-profit tax status if these organizations endorse or denounce candidates from the pulpit or publicly.

Erik Stanley, in his September 14, 2011 article, *What is Pulpit Freedom Sunday All About?* explains, "Since 1954, the IRS has been tasked with enforcing the Johnson Amendment. And it has issued pronouncements on how it should be enforced that are so vague even lawyers like to argue over what they mean. The IRS has gone so far as to say that churches cannot 'directly or indirectly' participate in a campaign, yet the IRS refuses to define what 'indirect participation' is. The IRS refuses to say with any certainty where the line is between what a pastor [or religious organization] can and cannot say from the pulpit and instead says that it will 'consider all the facts and circumstances' after the fact to determine whether the law was violated.

"Basically, the IRS has committed itself to *not* advising pastors in advance what speech from the pulpit violates the tax code. It will only tell them after the fact whether what they said crossed the line."[116]

Even though the threat is subtle, it is very real. The message is don't talk politics in the church, but if you do, we, the IRS [the government], will decide if you can remain a non-profit. When the IRS refuses to outline clear guidelines, one is left to guess where the line is actually crossed. Therefore, most shrink back from speaking due to fear of the revocation of their tax status.

1. Whether you lived in biblical times, the 1500s or present day, Paul's words ring true for the committed believer. Write **2 Timothy 3:12** below.


William Tyndale left for London in 1523, knowing he had to address two important issues upon arrival. First was obtaining permission to translate the Bible into English, and second was obtaining a patron (financial supporter) for translating and printing the New Testament. The political environment in London brought to light just how ill prepared Tyndale was. Tyndale believed the letter of introduction from Sir John Walsh and the demonstration of his proficient skills in translating Greek to English would allow him to easily step into a position with the bishop of London, Cuthbert Tunstall. With repeated failures to gain permission to translate the Bible into English, Tyndale realized this God-ordained task was not going to be as easy as he had anticipated. Tyndale was learning politics also ruled within the church.

"The political climate in London was at an all-time worse for taking on the controversial task of creating an authorized translation of the Bible into English. To begin with, all Europe was abuzz with the story of the German priest, Martin Luther. Printed versions of his Ninety-five Theses had been in circulation for six years, but his teachings had gone far beyond simply questioning the practice of indulgences. Luther condemned the pope's claims of authority over spiritual and political events. He preached the priesthood of all believers, not just the ordained."[117] In 1521, during Tyndale's stint as tutor in Gloucestershire, Martin Luther was excommunicated, declared a heretic and was in danger of being executed if apprehended.

"[T]he last thing either Wolsey [Cardinal of the Church] or the king [King Henry VIII] wanted was anything that smacked of Lutheran ideas spreading throughout the land. An English language translation of the Bible might encourage people to draw their own conclusions about the Christian faith rather than follow official church teachings. And independent thinking in the religious arena could easily lead to independent thinking in the area of politics, resulting in a weakening of the king's power."[118]

Time after time Tyndale's attempt to obtain an official patron failed. Therefore, Tyndale went ahead and moved forward with his mission of translating the New Testament into English, knowing execution could be his fate. Tyndale weighed the cost and moved forward. Although Tyndale used Luther's translation as one of his many sources, he often selected wording different from Luther's.

Another issue at the forefront of Tyndale's mind was how to get the English Bible printed. "London had at most five printers . . . [and] no English printer in his right mind would print an English translation of the Bible without official permission from the church. Even asking for such permission would draw unwanted attention to his religious beliefs and political sensibilities."[119]

Because of the political environment in England, Tyndale made the decision to make his way to Germany in the spring of 1524. There he could work in the company of men like Martin Luther who would be sympathetic with his mission. Even traveling to Germany required permission from the king. "Controlling the movement of their people was one method rulers used to censor the ideas coming in and out of their countries. Tyndale neither sought nor received such approval. . . . One of the first things William Tyndale did upon reaching the German states was change his name. . . . On May 27, 1524, a strange name appears in the copy of the registers of the University of Wittenberg: *Guillelmus Daltici ex Anglia* or *William Daltici of England*. In a common practice of the day, William Tyndale disguised his name by simply reversing the syllables of his last name; Tyndale became Daltin."[120]

---

### Questions to Ponder

Do governments control people's movements today? Explain your answer.

Do you see other means of control by governments around the world or in America? Explain your answer.

---

As the months passed, Tyndale's vision of an English New Testament was nearing reality. Unlike Luther who had almost twenty different German translations to consider when he translated his German New Testament, Tyndale had none, not even Wycliff's Bible. Tyndale's main sources were "Erasmus's Greek New Testament, the Latin Vulgate, and probably Luther's German translation."[121]

By the summer of 1525 Tyndale began to think about who would publish for the English New Testament. He had been blessed from his time in Wittenberg but he knew he needed to move forward.

Tyndale wrote a friend in England just before he left, requesting he send the money left for the underwriting and printing of the English New Testament. Without the promised support of many English merchants the English Bible would never become a reality.

Tyndale was at the stage of translation where he needed another pair of eyes to help check the manuscript. Each page needed to be proofread before it went to the printer. Another problem presented itself after it went to print, proofing the printer. In the 1500s, printing presses were manually set. This meant each letter had to be manually set on the press for each page. Therefore not only did the manuscripts have to be proofread before they went to the printer, each page had to be proofread once the type was set, before it was printed!

"Because of the nature of his work, Tyndale was looking for someone who was well-educated—knowing Latin, English, and possibly some Greek. The only available assistant was William Roye, a young man with whom Tyndale obviously had problems. . . . Roye was academically qualified for the job, but his temperament presented problems. . . . He was known for being hotheaded and untrustworthy."[122]

Tyndale chose Peter Quentel of Cologne, Germany, to print the English Bible. Cologne was one of the largest cities in Germany at the time, and a strategic river location. Once printed, the Bibles journeyed to England via the Rhine River. "Every day, Tyndale and Roye visited Quentel's print shop to proofread the work. . . . The inside margins were full of biblical cross-references and the outside margins featured notes commenting on the text. In many ways, the layout of the New Testament resembled Luther's German New Testament, although it was a much smaller book because it did not include the Latin and Greek text as well.

"Things seemed to be going well. Tyndale's dream of a New Testament for the English ploughman was before his eyes becoming a reality. But a suspicious customer soon reminded the two Englishmen of just how vulnerable they were to danger. [A man by the name of John] Cochlaeus was in the habit of peppering Europe with pamphlets attacking Martin Luther. While at Quentel's shop one day, Cochlaeus overheard a conversation about the English Bible. Curious for more information, he struck up a friendship with some of Quentel's employees, taking them out one evening for drinks. When Cochlaeus learned what was going on in the print shop, he told the authorities so they could take action. Somehow, after the senate secretly ordered Tyndale and Roye arrested and their materials seized, the two Englishmen learned of the plan. In the dead of night, they hastily grabbed all the completed signatures they could carry, along with their books and manuscripts, and headed by ship about 125 miles south on the Rhine River to the city of Worms. They might have escaped capture for the moment, but their secret was now widely known."[123] A completed signature was a signature verifying the page had been proofed by the author/translator and a number assigned to it since each sheet was printed separately.

Now Henry VIII and Cardinal Wolsey knew of Tyndale's English New Testament work. "It would not be so easy to smuggle the books in after they were printed. But this was not Tyndale's immediate concern. He needed to find a new printer, and didn't have as much money as he had started out with because of the fees paid to Peter Quentel. He also was still stuck with William Roye for an assistant, and it may well have been that Roye's boastfulness had contributed to their discovery by the Roman Catholic authorities in Cologne. Worms, which had only four years before been the scene of Martin Luther's famous hearing at the Diet, now stood solidly behind the reformers. It welcomed Tyndale and Roye. The two men completed the printing of the New Testament probably early in 1526 with the assistance of printer Peter Schoeffer."[124]

Are you gaining a new appreciation for reading the Bible in your own language? Stories like William Tyndale's need to be told for us to understand the cost great men and women of God made throughout the ages in order for you and me to read God's Word and worship freely today. We cannot appreciate their sacrifice if we do not know their cost.

For the past two weeks we have paralleled Tyndale with our biblical man Nehemiah. We want to learn all we can from both men. We will see the pattern of how evil works, but more importantly how God works through godly people. Identifying how evil operates is just as important as recognizing God's actions. When we recognize evil we can learn to combat and disable it. Evil will not be able to take us by surprise, immobilize us, or keep us, from the work God has for our lives.

Last week we found Sanballat and Tobiah furious when they found out Nehemiah was rebuilding the wall of Jerusalem. We learned from Nehemiah's leadership—when the attacks came, fervent prayer began. Nehemiah was a man who knew God and knew to leave the enemy in God's capable hands. As for Nehemiah and the workmen on the wall, their jobs were to be laser focused on their task. Nehemiah placed reinforcements at the weakest places in the wall and reminded the Israelites of God's greatness; therefore, there was no reason to fear. All these events took place about halfway through the rebuilding of the wall.

Today, we will study **Nehemiah 6:1-15**. Nehemiah and his team are close to completing the work. Let's find out what happens.

1. Read **Nehemiah 6:1-15**.

   a. What did Sanballat and the rest of the enemies want Nehemiah to do when the work was almost complete?

   b. What was their true motivation?

   c. What was Nehemiah's response?

   d. How many times did Sanballat try to get Nehemiah to go and meet him?

   e. When Nehemiah would not listen to Sanballat, what did he do (v. 5)?

   f. What did Sanballat's letter say?

g.  What was Nehemiah's response?


h.  What did Nehemiah understand about Sanballat's plan (v. 9)?

   ❖

   ❖


i.  What was Sanballat's final scheme to get Nehemiah to sin (v. 10)?




j.  How did Nehemiah respond to Sanballat's plan?




Sanballat was relentless! He sent men four times to try to get Nehemiah to come down from the wall. An additional messenger was sent with a letter reporting lies about Nehemiah's intentions. Finally, Sanballat sent a man to try to get Nehemiah to sin by entering the temple where only the priests were allowed.

2.  We learned that Nehemiah was acting righteously by not entering the temple. Read **Proverbs 28:1**. How else did Nehemiah show that he was a righteous man?




Had Sanballat been successful in his evil plot and caused Nehemiah to sin, Sanballat would have destroyed Nehemiah's character and rendered his work ineffective. If you haven't noticed, Sanballat's tactics were intimidation and fear. *Fear* or *frightened* is used seven times in the first six chapters of Nehemiah, four in chapter six alone.

Fear was an effective tool in biblical times, it was an effective tool in Tyndale's time, and it is effective today.

3.  Think about how differently Nehemiah and Tyndale would have impacted their culture had they allowed fear to incapacitate their work. Make notes below.




4.  Think about your life. Have you ever let fear undermine you? What did you learn from Nehemiah or Tyndale to prevent this from happening in the future?

5.  Add the following events to the timeline on page 194.

    a.  1523 Tyndale left Gloucestershire for London

    b.  1524 Tyndale left London for Germany

    c.  1525 Tyndale left Germany to find printer for the English New Testament

    d.  1526 Tyndale's English New Testament completed

6.  What has the Lord been showing you through William Tyndale or Nehemiah to apply to your life? Your church? Your nation?

Close with your prayer to the Lord. Thank Him for what He is revealing to you through *ACTs420NOW*. Thank Him for raising up men and women like Nehemiah and William Tyndale. We can reflect on how they ran the race and learn from their strengths and weaknesses. Thank Him for godly men and women who have gone before us to lead the way.

*"Therefore, since we have so great a cloud of witnesses surrounding us, let us also lay aside every encumbrance and the sin which so easily entangles us, and let us run with endurance the race that is set before us, fixing our eyes on Jesus, the author and perfecter of faith, who for the joy set before Him endured the cross, despising the shame, and has sat down at the right hand of the throne of God."*
**Hebrews 12:1-2**

# WEEK 6—DAY 5

We've arrived at another Day 5, my friend. How time seems to fly and the days seem to get shorter. Yet, there are still 24 hours in a day and 365 days in a year. Could it be we are caught up in the busyness of the world, which distracts us from our true calling—knowing and fellowshipping with HIM? I pray you join me in asking our Father to help us prioritize our life in a way that is pleasing to Him.

Last week we began to study the Great Awakening era. While it is important to understand there was an awakening in Europe during this time period, our focus will be on the movement in the colonies and how this movement impacts us today. To review, the awakening in the colonies began with Jonathan Edwards' Northhampton church in 1734, yet Edwards was not the most well-known pastor associated with this movement of God. That honor goes to George Whitefield.

Whitefield attributes his "new birth" to a sermon he heard at Oxford University in England by John and Charles Wesley in 1735. By 1738 Whitefield had traveled to the colonies, bringing with him an innovative preaching style which he pioneered, called the outdoor meeting, usually held in tents. Whitefield felt church buildings had limited seating and were bound by the traditions of each denomination. Outdoor events could attract large crowds and the message could exclusively focus on salvation, or as Whitefield called it the "*new birth.*"

As a child I had the privilege to attend many old-fashioned tent revivals. Thanks to today's technology, Christian organizations are not limited to one location. Huge crusades are held in multiple cities, and viewed simultaneously through the power of live television or the Internet. Hundreds of thousands of people can come together and hear a modern-day Whitefield preach without traveling from their hometowns. Today the strategy may have changed but the intent still takes precedence—gather large amounts of people and present a message focused on the *new birth.*

Whitefield adapted strategies from the theater, using dramatic techniques to deliver powerful and emotional sermons. "He also adapted strategies of advance publicity and advertising to create excitement in the towns to which he was coming."[125] People flocked to his meetings and there were thousands of reported conversions.

One such conversion was Nathan Cole. In 1740, Cole and his wife attended Whitefield's outdoor revival in Connecticut. A messenger was going house to house announcing Whitefield would preach in one hour. As soon as Cole heard the news he dropped his plow and ran to get his wife. Fearful they might be late, they rode his horse as fast as they could into town. Cole gave this account of the event:

"When we came within about half a mile or a mile of the Road that comes down from Hartford[,] Weathersfield and Stepney to Middletown; on high land I saw before me a Cloud or fogg (sic) rising; I first thought it came from the great River, but as I came nearer the Road, I heard a noise something like a low rumbling thunder and presently found it was the noise of Horses feet coming down the Road and this Cloud was a Cloud of dust made by the Horses feet . . . I could see men and horses Sliping (sic) along in the Cloud like shadows . . . every horse seemed to go with all his might to carry his rider to hear news from heaven for the saving of Souls, it made me tremble to see the Sight, how the world was in a Struggle . . .

When I saw Mr Whit[e]field come upon the Scaffold he looks almost angelical . . . And my hearing him preach, gave me a heart wound; By Gods blessings; my old Foundation was broken up, and I saw that my righteousness would not save me . . .

It pleased God to bring on my Convictions more and more, and I was loaded with the guilt of Sin, I saw I was undone forever; I carried Such a weight of Sin in my breast or mind, that it seemed to me as if I should sink into the ground every step; and I kept all to myself as much as I could; I went month after month mourning and begging for mercy. I tried every way I could think to help myself but all ways failed . . .

God appeared unto me and made me Skringe [Cringe] before whose face the heavens and the earth fled away; and I was Shrinked into nothing: I knew not whether I was in the body or out, I seemed to hang in open Air before God, and he seemed to Speak to me in an angry and Sovereign way why won't you trust your Soul with God; My heart answered O yes, yes, yes; before I could stir my tongue or lips . . .

When God appeared to me everything vanished and was gone in the twinkling of an Eye, as quick as A flash of lightning; But when God disappeared . . . everything was in its place again and I was on my Bed. My heart was broken; my burden was fallen of[f] my mind; I was set free, my distress was gone . . . I got along to the window where my [B]ible was and I opened it and the first place I saw was the 15ᵗʰ Chap: John—on Christs (sic) own words and they spake to my very heart and every doubt and scruple that rose in my heart about the truth of God's word was took right off . . ."[126]

Many other written testimonies of God working in individual's lives during the Great Awakening have been recorded. Yet, the *new birth* was just one aspect of God's mighty work during this time. "Many reported experiencing such visits to heaven, where angels of Jesus himself showed them whether their name was written in the Book of Life. Others encountered the devil and witnessed the torments of the damned in hell."[127]

The Great Awakening emphasized the work of the Holy Spirit living inside of each believer. This was in stark contrast to the traditional church with a college-educated pastor who had absolute authority over the congregation. During this awakening, common people became exhorters and lay preachers, some were even ordained without college credentials. "Traditional . . . social hierarchies built on class, race, education, and gender"[128] began to weaken.

In an era when women found it difficult to have any voice, a woman named Mercy Wheeler became a well-known figure. Wheeler, unable to walk since a childhood illness, came to prominence at a 1743 revival meeting while she was listening to a sermon about Jesus healing people. She thought if such miracles could happen to people in biblical times why couldn't they happen now. At the end of the service she repeated to herself—"*If thou wilt believe, thou shall see the Glory of God.*"[129] Immediately she began to walk and for years to come had a platform to exhort Scripture.

The Great Awakening was not without criticism. Those who criticized the movement were called *antirevivalists*. Their first criticism was the revivals were just about emotional experiences and the meetings had no real substance. Secondly, the clergy were fearful the movement would break down their authority. The antirevivalists called those in the awakening *radical evangelicals or dissenters*. The colonies were birthed under British authority; therefore, the Church of England was still the official state church of the colonies. As the conflict escalated between the two groups, the radical evangelicals began to break away from the established church. As new churches emerged, they faced fines and were harassed by the government. These churches resented paying taxes to support the Church of England.

Many of these radicals went one step further from being separatist to becoming Baptist! Although Baptists were established in the colonies, their numbers were quite small. Baptists disagreed with the Church of England's stand on infant baptism. "The Baptist viewed the ritual as a symbolic representation of conversion, which could be experienced by people old enough to understand their sinfulness and their need for the new birth. . . . No one better demonstrated the journey from radical evangelicalism, to separatism, and finally to becoming a Baptist, than the great Baptist leader Isaac Backus. . . . Backus called for freedom to practice Christianity as each person saw fit, with no government penalties or interference."[130]

The men and women of the Great Awakening remind me of the first church we have been studying. Let's take a look at the commonalties of the men and women of the Great Awakening and the first church.

1. Read the following verses and note similarities between the first church and our Great Awakening Christians. We have already studied many of these verses.

   a. Note how the traditional and social hierarchies that were built on class, race, education, and gender began to weaken.

| Scripture | 1st Century Church |
| --- | --- |
| Acts 4:13 | |
| Acts 8:5 | |
| Acts 10:34-35 | |
| Acts 11:1-3 | |
| Acts 13:46-48 | |
| Acts 15:7-9 | |

| Scripture | 1st Century Church |
|---|---|
| Acts 17:6 | |
| Galatians 3:28-29 | |

Do you see these Scriptures relate to the Great Awakening church? Explain your answer.

b. Note below how evangelicals began to break away from the established religious practices (strict Judaism).

| Scripture | 1st Century Church |
|---|---|
| Acts 4:5-7 | Who interrogated Peter and John? |
| Acts 4:18-20 | What was the answer Peter and John gave? |
| Acts 13:5, 14-15, 44-46 | |

Do you see these Scriptures relate to the Great Awakening church? Explain your answer.

c. Note below how early Christians understood their sinfulness and their need for the new birth.

| Scripture | 1st Century Church |
|---|---|
| Acts 2:38 | |
| Acts 4:12 | |
| Acts 5:31 | |
| Acts 11:18-21 | |

Do you see these Scriptures relate to the Great Awakening church? Explain your answer.

d. Note below who had assumed absolute authority over their congregation.

| Scripture | 1st Century Church |
|---|---|
| Acts 4:15, 18-20 | |
| Acts 5:27-29 | |
| Acts 6:12-7:1 | |

Do you see these Scriptures relate to the Great Awakening church? Explain your answer.

e. Note below how God brought the people to flock to meetings where there were thousands of reported conversions.

| Scripture | 1st Century Church |
|---|---|
| Acts 2:41, 47 | |
| Acts 4:4 | |
| Acts 11:17-18, 21, 24 | |
| Acts 13:49 | |

Do you see these Scriptures relate to the Great Awakening church? Explain your answer.

f. As new churches developed, they faced fines and began to get harassed by the government.

| Scripture | 1st Century Church |
|---|---|
| Acts 5:40-42 | |
| Acts 12:1 | |
| Acts 13:50 | |

Do you see these Scriptures relate to the Great Awakening church? Explain your answer.

g.  God performed healings.

| Scripture | 1st Century Church |
|---|---|
| Acts 3:1-8 | |
| Acts 8:6-8 | |
| Acts 9:36-43 | |

Do you see these Scriptures relate to the Great Awakening church? Explain your answer.

h.  Dependence upon the Holy Spirit.

| Scripture | 1st Century Church |
|---|---|
| Acts 4:13 | |
| Acts 4:31 | |
| Acts 13:9 | |
| Acts 13:52 | |

Do you see these Scriptures relate to the Great Awakening church? Explain your answer.

The *radical evangelicals* or *dissenters*, began to send missionaries south, where they were more free from the trials and persecutions taking place in the northern colonies. Hugh Bryan, a convert under George Whitefield, not only ministered to the plantation owners but believed he was "chosen to lead slaves out of their captivity. . . . By the 1750s, significant numbers of African Americans in the South experienced the new birth and joined evangelical congregations. . . . When the irritable (non-evangelical) Anglican itinerant Charles Woodmason visited the rural Carolinas in the late 1760's he found the area crawling with evangelicals. . . . By the time of the Revolution, evangelicals represented only a minority of the southern population, but their quick growth heralded the future transformation of the South into America's 'Bible Belt.'"[131]

God used persecution to further the gospel during the 1700s just as He did in biblical times. Paul's life was threatened several times after he spent time in certain cities preaching the gospel and discipling the people. Those who did not believe devised plots to kill him. But before the unbelievers could succeed, Paul fled to another location (Iconium—**Acts 14:1-7**; Paul's trip from Jerusalem to Rome—**Acts 21:17-28:31**).

Also in AD 64 the Roman Emperor Nero burned Jerusalem and accused the Christians of this callous act. Nero ordered Christians to be arrested, tortured, and put to death in horrifying ways for the entertainment of the Roman citizens. Christians fled the city because of the persecution they were receiving. Peter wrote to the church in 1 Peter and describes the church as "aliens, scattered throughout Pontus, Galatia, Cappadocia, Asia, and Bithynia, who are chosen" (**1 Peter 1:1**). As aliens scattered abroad they took their faith with them.

Self-preservation forced the first-century church to leave the comfort of Jerusalem and finally obey the command of Jesus in **Acts 1:8** which says, "But you will receive power when the Holy Spirit has come upon you; and **you shall be My witnesses** both in Jerusalem, and in all Judea and Samaria, and even to the remotest part of the earth" (emphasis mine).

God used each of these situations to further His kingdom. We must remember God did not cause these circumstances but He allowed them. **Romans 8:28** (emphasis mine) resonates when it teaches, "And we know that God causes all things to work together for good to those who love God, to those who are called according to *His* purpose.

---

### Questions to Ponder

Can you think of an instance where God has used persecution today to further the gospel? Give an example.

Does this lesson change your perspective on persecution? Why or why not?

---

Often, I'm asked why I am so passionate about sharing the history of people like Martin Luther, William Tyndale, and our American heritage. The answer is simple: it matters; it is important! If we believe God is the same yesterday, today, and tomorrow, is it not important to see how He has worked in days past? Then our spiritual eyes will be open to what our Lord is doing around us. Our lenses will become crystal clear, and the fog will lift and the Son will shine through. We as believers of Jesus Christ need to know how He works. When we compare history side by side with biblical history the answers become obvious.

Our Great Awakening saints certainly were people who **Persevered and went to America proclaiming the gospel and praying for the land to be healed.** Next week we will look at how this Great Awakening influenced the thought process for the American Revolution. You do not want to miss the final weeks!

2. Let's close with our application question. What has our Lord been showing you today? Write what you are going to apply to your life. Your church. Your nation.

3. Write your closing prayer to the Lord. Continue to pray for your neighbors, your city, your state, and your nation.

*"Make your ear attentive to wisdom, incline your heart to understanding;*
*for if you cry for discernment, lift your voice for understanding."*
***Proverbs 2:2-3***

# Week 7 Overview

## Love your enemies and pray for those who persecute you
### (Matthew 5:44)

"You have heard it was said, 'You shall love your neighbor and hate your enemy.' But I say to you, love your enemies and pray for those who persecute you . . . For if you love those who love you, what reward do you have? Do not even the tax collectors do the same?" (**Matthew 5:43-44, 46**). Jesus' words were not easy to live out in biblical times and are not any easier today. This week we can be comforted by Jesus' words, "Blessed is a man who perseveres under trial; for once he has been approved, he will receive the crown of life which the Lord has promised to those who love Him" (**James 1:12**).

This week we will:

- ❖ Study God's purpose in loving our enemies.
- ❖ Study how Old and New Testament figures acted and reacted to persecution.
- ❖ Study the Greek words for *love* and *persecution*.

This week's applications include:

- ❖ Understanding demonstrating love to our enemies will attract some of them to Jesus Christ, which brings glory to God.
- ❖ Determining to glorify God through your life.
- ❖ Equipping ourselves with God's truth on this difficult subject.

This week's verse to memorize:

*"But I say to you, love your enemies and pray for those who persecute you."*
**Matthew 5:44**

Fill in the blanks where appropriate.

**Foundational Step:** _____ there is _____ in none other than

_____ _____ (**Acts** ____).

**Step 2:** _____ you will begin to _____ the Word of God with _____ (**Acts** ____).

**Step 3:** _____ the _____ is "_____" to a lost and dying _____

(**2 Corinthians** ____).

**Step 4:** _____ yourself, _____, seek, and _____ to God for _____

in our land (**2 Chronicles** ____).

**Step 5:** _____ by _____, and _____ America and the world until our

land is _____ (**Isaiah 6:8-11**).

**Step 6:** Love your enemies and pray for those who persecute you (**Matthew 5:44**).

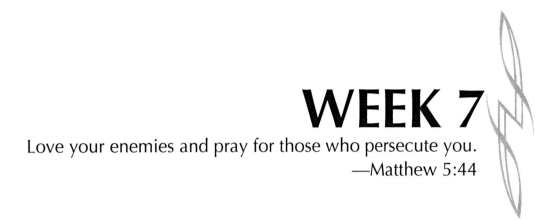

# WEEK 7

Love your enemies and pray for those who persecute you.
—Matthew 5:44

## WEEK 7—DAY 1

If you read the title of our lessons this week, **Love your enemies and pray for those who persecute you,** you may be thinking, "Easier said than done!" Yes, this is true, yet this principle is straight from God's Word; therefore, we must be diligent to understand and apply all His truths, even this one, to our lives. Let's prepare our hearts to hear what the Spirit of the Lord wants to teach us today. Write your prayer below.

Once a believer begins to **Persevere and go and tell America and the world** the gospel, one thing is certain, some form of persecution will begin. This was true in biblical times and it is true today. The apostle Paul *guaranteed* Timothy in his final letter, "Indeed, all who desire to live godly in Christ Jesus will be persecuted" (**2 Timothy 3:12**). We must remember that Paul wrote this not only for Timothy but also for us.

Paul wanted Timothy to come quickly because Paul knew his time was short. Paul penned his final letter to Timothy in AD 64, (some biblical historians say as late as AD 67). Shortly afterward, the Roman government executed Paul for the cause of Christ. Because Paul was a Roman citizen, they could not hang him on a cross like Christ therefore he was beheaded.

Did you know that America has more Christians than any other country in the world today? But Christians in America represent only eleven percent of the *world's* population of Christians.[132] Although most Christians in America are unfamiliar with persecution, such as was suffered by the first-century church, today 100 million Christians are being persecuted each year in over sixty countries around the world.[133] Because 159,960 Christians on average are martyred each year for the cause of Christ,[134] we need to understand the why's, the how's, and the result of persecution. Why? It may be coming soon to a neighborhood near you.

There is no greater example in the first-century church to teach us the principle of **Loving your enemies and praying for those who persecute you** than Saul, whom you now know as Paul. In Week 5, Day 1, we studied Paul's conversion. He held the coats of the men who stoned Stephen, the first recorded Christian martyr. We discovered once Paul encountered Jesus, his life was radically changed and the persecutor became the persecuted. Paul spent the rest of his life boldly proclaiming Jesus Christ in every nook and cranny of the ancient world. Paul said in his letter to the Romans, "from Jerusalem and round about as far as Illyricum I have fully preached the gospel of Christ" (**Romans 15:20**). Illyricum includes parts of modern-day Kosovo, Montenegro, Macedonia, and most of Albania, a country very close to my heart. Paul traveled over 1,000 miles one way preaching from Jerusalem to Illyricum. Just think, one moment with Christ on the Damascus Road caused a pivotal shift in the next thirty plus years of Paul's life. What can we learn from the way Paul behaved when he was persecuted? What insights can we take to heart from this man who said, "*Pray* on my behalf, that utterance may be given to me in the opening of my mouth, to make known with boldness the mystery of the gospel, for which I am an ambassador in chains; that in *proclaiming it I may speak boldly*, as I ought to speak" (emphasis mine) (**Ephesians 6:19-20**). Even in Paul's imprisonment, he asked for prayers for boldness! We have much to learn from this man.

1. **Read Acts 16:9-40. (Acts 15:40** tells us Paul's companion was Silas. **Acts 16:1-3** tells us Timothy joined Paul and Silas.)

   **Interesting biblical note**: Beginning in **Acts 16:10-40** the pronouns shift from *they* and *them* to *we* and *us*, subtly indicating that Luke, the writer of Acts, joined Paul's missionary journey. Luke, a proselyte (God-fearing Gentile) didn't find it necessary to reveal how he encountered the missionary team. In **Acts 17:1** the pronouns return to they and them, indicating that Luke stayed behind at Philippi, possibly to lead the new church there.[135]

   a. Why did Paul and Silas travel to Macedonia (vv. 9-10)?


   b. To what city did they travel in Macedonia?


Ancient Macedonia is predominantly in modern-day Greece and encompasses the southern tip of Albania and a very small section of modern-day Macedonia. Philippi is in Greece.

   c. Who did Paul and Silas meet? What was the result (vv. 3-15)?


   d. What happened as they went to the place of prayer (vv. 16-18)?


When you first read the account of the slave girl who had a spirit of divination, it would be logical to ask the question, "Why would Paul be annoyed? She was speaking the truth." The NASB, ESV, KJV, and the NKJV versions of the Bible use the phrase "*the* way of salvation" in **Acts 16:17** (emphasis mine). The NIV says, "*the* way to be saved." We as believers would all agree with this statement, yet a more literal translation from the Greek would read *a* way of salvation or *a* way to be saved. This would indicate a pantheistic, (belief in, or worship of many gods) message, she was claiming that Jesus was just one of many ways or many gods—a message Paul would vehemently oppose. This message would be in stark contradiction to what Paul was preaching.

The Greek word for divination is *puthon* from which we get the English word python. *Luke describes her [the slave girl] as having been possessed by a "Python spirit," by which he indicated that she was in the thrall of no ordinary, run-of-the-mill demon. In the ancient Greek world, the "Python spirit" was considered to be the supernatural force behind the famous Oracle of Delphi, whose priestess ("the pythoness") was the "mother of all" fortunetellers."[136] There was even a rite where snakes (i.e. pythons) "would crawl over people as they came to know and affect the future."[137]*

e.   Why were the masters of the slave girl upset when Paul cast out the demon?

f.   What happen to Paul and Silas because of the masters?

g.   What did the masters tell the chief magistrates about Paul and Silas?
   ❖
   ❖

h.   Do you believe the slave girl's masters were truly upset about Paul breaking Roman laws and customs, or were they using this accusation because they were upset about their income stream? Give your reasoning.

The masters asserted Paul and Silas could not make their claims because they were Jews, not Romans. (At this point, they did not know Paul and Silas were Roman citizens.) They did not distinguish between Christianity and being Jewish. *Notice this charge has nothing to do with the slave girl's exorcism. It apparently refers to their preaching of the gospel of Jesus Christ ... It was illegal for Jews to attempt to proselytize Romans, and it was illegal for Paul as well.*[138]

---

### Question to Ponder

Do you hear people or groups in America quoting the Constitution, amendments, or laws to try to stop the spread of the gospel today? Write your examples below. Don't just write yes or no. For example, many people misuse the phrase *separation of church and state* believing it is in our founding documents when in fact it is not.

---

i. How did the crowd react? (v. 22)

j. What was the order of the chief magistrates regarding Paul and Silas? Why were the chief magistrates threatened by their message?

k. Where were Paul and Silas thrown?

l. The inner prison could be compared with maximum security today. What threat did Paul and Silas pose that justified putting them in the inner prison?

m. Why do you think Timothy and Luke were not arrested?

n. What did Paul and Silas do after they were brought before the magistrates, beaten, and thrown in jail?

There are many places in both the Old and New Testaments where people sang praises or were encouraged to sing praises. The Greek word in **Acts 16:25** is *humnĕō meaning to celebrate with song;—sing an hymn (praise unto).*[139] There are only four times *humnĕō* is used in the New Testament. Two occurrences are in **Matthew 26:30** and **Mark 14:26** speak of the event when Jesus and the twelve disciples participated in the last supper. Jesus said, "Truly I say unto you, I shall never again drink of the fruit of the vine until that day when I drink it new in the kingdom of God" (**Mark 14:25**). Then Scripture tells us, "And after singing a hymn, (*humnĕō)* they went out to the Mount of Olives" (**Mark 14:26**). The final use of *humnĕō* is found in **Hebrews 2:12**. The unknown writer of Hebrews quotes **Psalm 22:22**. Also known as the Messianic Psalm, this psalm prophesies the future crucifixion of Christ: "All who see me sneer at me" (v. 7a), "I am poured out like water, and all my bones are out of joint" (v. 14), and "They divide my garments among them, and for my clothing they cast lots" (v. 18). Then verse nineteen begins with, "But Thou, O Lord, be not far off … Deliver my soul … Save me … Thou dost answer me" (v. 19-21). Then we come to the phrase, "I will praise Thee" (**Psalm 22:22b**). The Hebrew word for praise here is *hālal meaning to cause to shine, to make bright, to give light; to deserve praise. At the heart of this root is the idea of radiance. From this came the connotation of the ebullience of rejoicing and praising God.*[140] The writer of Hebrews chose the Greek word *humnĕō* to express the Hebrew word *hālal.*

In three of the four occurrences of this Greek word *humnĕō* is referencing Christ's impending crucifixion. Yet the event is celebrated with exuberant songs of praise. Luke, the writer of Acts, also uses to use the word *humnēō*, to describe celebrating with songs of praise during their imprisonment. Just as Christ understood His need to obey the Father in the seemingly dark hours before His crucifixion, knowing the result of His death and ultimate resurrection would bring salvation to a lost world, Christ could celebrate with praise knowing the final result would bring glory to the Father.

Peter and Silas too were celebrating with song, trusting the final outcome would bring glory to their Father in heaven.

Stop and think of a difficult situation you are presently going through, or have gone through. Did you take Paul and Silas' attitude? Can you sing praises today trusting God, knowing the final outcome will bring God glory? Let's return to our biblical text in **Acts 16:9-40**.

o.  Who paid attention to Paul and Silas (v. 25)?




The Greek word for *listen* is *ēpakrŏaŏmai* meaning *to listen intently*.[141] This is the only time this word is used in the New Testament. This form of the verb implies *they listened continually to Paul and Silas … denotes an intense listening with joyfulness. These down-and-out prisoners eagerly heard and responded to a message of God's love, care, and acceptance!*[142]

p.  Now we have a better understanding of what Luke meant when he said Paul and Silas were "praying and singing," and the prisoners were listening. What does this tell us about Paul and Silas and how the prisoners were receiving their words? What conclusions can you come to?




q.  What happened to the jail and chains when the earthquake began?




r.  What did the jailer suppose had happened to the prisoners? And what was the jailer about to do to himself?




In Roman times, if any prisoners escaped, it was customary for the person in charge of their watch to be executed by government officials. The jailer was choosing death by his own hand rather than the shame of execution.

s.  What was the jailer's immediate response when he found out the prisoners were still there?

t.  Paul and Silas were brought before the magistrates, beaten, put in the inner prison with their feet in stocks, had not slept and they experienced an earthquake. Despite these things, what was their response to the jailer?

u.  What was the result of Paul and Silas' message to the jailer and his household?

v.  When the magistrates sent for Paul and Silas to be released, what did Paul say (v. 37)?

w.  What was the reaction of the police and magistrates?

x.  We will not know the answer to this question until we ask Paul in heaven, but why do you suppose Paul didn't tell them he was a Roman citizen when he first stood before the magistrates?

y.  What did the magistrates beg Paul and Silas to do?

z.  Instead of immediately leaving the city, what did Paul and Silas feel was necessary for them to do?

Wow! The book of Acts is so powerful. It makes one want to be there to experience it personally. As we bring today's lesson to a close we need to apply this message to our lives.

2.  Reminder—Who led Paul and Silas to Philippi, Macedonia? (If you need to refresh your memory read **Acts 16:9-10**.)

Yes, it was the Lord, through a vision to Paul. You might find it difficult to think the Lord would purposefully lead you into a harmful situation. We must remember there are two forces at work in this world—good and evil—and they are constantly at war. Although the Lord's original intent, when He created humanity, did not include persecution, God does not cause persecution, but uses it as a tool to bring about His plans and purpose. To recap what was accomplished, let's look at the chart below.

| Scripture | Event | Results |
|---|---|---|
| **Acts 16:13-15** | Paul and team spoke to the women by the riverside on the Sabbath. | ❖ The Lord opened Lydia's heart.<br>❖ Lydia and her household were baptized.<br>❖ Lydia offered her home to the missionaries.<br>❖ Lydia's home was the probable location of the new church in Philippi (**Acts 16:40**). |
| **Acts 16:16-18** | Paul and team went to the place of prayer and the slave girl who had a spirit of divination was crying out. | ❖ Paul cast out the demon spirit.<br>❖ Paul and Silas were brought before magistrates and thrown in prison. |
| **Acts 16:25-26** | Paul and Silas prayed and sang hymns in jail. | ❖ God's Word was proclaimed to the prisoners.<br>❖ The prisoners listened intently to Paul and Silas. |
| **Acts 16:27-34** | Paul and Silas preached the Word to the jailer and his household. | ❖ The jailer and his household believed in the Lord and were baptized. |

3. Was God glorified in Macedonia?

4. What would NOT have been accomplished if Paul and Silas were not persecuted?

Over the next two days we will take a closer look at the principle **Love your enemies and pray for those who persecute you**. We will look at the Old Testament and make its correlation with the New Testament. We will discover additional insights about how God uses persecution in our lives, and what this shows unbelievers as well. You've worked hard today. Let's close with our application questions and prayer.

5. If you are in or facing a difficult situation, can you sing praises today, trusting God, knowing the outcome will bring glory to God? Explain.

If the answer is no, begin to pray that God would give you the ability to sing praises through the difficult situations in your life.

6. What has the Lord shown you through Paul and Silas to apply to your life? Your church? Your nation?

7. Write your prayer to the Lord. Ask Him to continue to give you insights into this difficult subject.

*"And they overcame him because of the blood of the Lamb and because of the word of their testimony, and they did not love their life even when faced with death."*
**Revelation 12:11**

# WEEK 7—DAY 2

Yesterday we began our study on **loving our enemies and praying for those who persecute** us. Today we will look again at the question, "Was persecution just for the early church?" We will examine the Old Testament to learn about persecution before the time of Christ. It should prove to be an interesting day of study; therefore, we will need the Lord's wisdom. Write your prayer to the Lord.

**Bible study tip of the week:** As you begin to study a book or individual in the Bible, it is important to understand as much as possible about the background of people and events. If you are studying a book of the Bible, try to learn about the history of the time the book was written. If you are studying a person, find out about his or her origin, what was happening during that time period, the culture, etc. Don't feel overwhelmed. God will give you additional insights each time you study a subject. Don't think you have to be an expert to begin.

Today, we will study three prophets. Our principle prophet is Jeremiah; then, we will contrast him with another prophet in the same time period named Uriah. Finally, we will study Micah, a contemporary of Isaiah who is referred to in Jeremiah 26. The Minor Prophet book Micah was named after this same man. Minor prophets books are not less significant than the Major Prophets books, they are just shorter. Micah prophesied about 125 years earlier than Jeremiah during the reign of King Hezekiah (733-701 BC). **Remember**: The BC dates go from larger numbers to smaller numbers as dates get closer to the birth of Christ. AD dates begin at the birth of Christ and move forward from there.

Let's begin by understanding the times in which Jeremiah lived. Jeremiah prophesied from 627-574 BC (53 years) during the reigns of King Josiah, Jehoahaz, Jehoiakim, Jehoiachin, and Zedekiah. Our main text, Jeremiah 26, was written about 609 BC, when King Jehoiakim began to reign.

To fully comprehend the cultural climate of Judah, the Southern Kingdom of Israel, we need a brief history of the time span from King Josiah to King Jehoiakim's reign described in Jeremiah 26. Josiah was only eight years old when he became king of Judah and reigned thirty-one years. When he was about twenty-six years old, the books of the law (Genesis through Deuteronomy) were found in the temple. After they were read to Josiah, he humbled himself before the Lord and understood Judah was sinning against the Lord by following after their own hearts and chasing after idols. Therefore, Josiah made a covenant before the Lord to walk after the Lord, to keep the Lord's commandments, and to carry out the words of the covenant. All the people agreed and entered into the same covenant (**2 Kings 23:3**). King Josiah commanded that all the idols, which were in the land, be torn down. The idols for Baal, Asherah, Molech, along with all their temples were destroyed. Josiah also had mediums, spiritists, and all the abominations that were in the land of Judah destroyed in order to comply with all the words found in the law of Moses. It was said that Josiah was a king like no other who turned to the Lord with all his heart and with all his soul and with all his might (**2 Kings 23:25**). You can learn all the details of the great works that King Josiah did unto the Lord in **2 Kings, chapters 22-23**.

In 609 BC, Pharaoh Neco, the king of Egypt, was on his way to meet with the King of Assyria at the Euphrates River. Along the way, Neco met King Josiah at Megiddo and killed him. Josiah's servants brought the king's body to Jerusalem and buried him. Josiah's son, Jehoahaz became king in his place. Jehoahaz was only allowed to reign three months before Pharaoh Neco imprisoned him, took him to Egypt, and imposed on Judah a fine of one hundred talents of silver and a talent of gold. (Today, this would be equivalent to over $67,000,000.) Then Pharaoh Neco made Jehoiakim, another son of Josiah, king over Judah. In order to pay the money to the pharaoh, Jehoiakim imposed a tax on Judah. You can read about all that transpired in **2 Kings 23:29-37**. This brings us to where Jeremiah 26 opens, which will be our focus of study today.

1. Consider the *times* in which we find Judah. How do you believe the people felt? What might they have said to one another?

2. Do you see similar attitudes today? Give your reasoning.

3. Read **Jeremiah 26**.
   a. Where did the Lord tell Jeremiah to go speak?

   b. What was the problem with the people who were going to the Lord's house to worship?

   c. What was the basic message the Lord wanted Jeremiah to speak to the people?

   d. When Jeremiah spoke the Lord's message what did the people say (v. 8)?

   e. When Jeremiah spoke to the officials, did he back down from his message? Did he try to soften the words to make them more pleasing to their ears (v. 12)?

f.  Did Jeremiah plead for his life (v. 14-15)? Instead, what did he say?

g.  What was the response of the officials (v. 16)?

h.  Who did the officials quote (vv. 18-19)?

i.  Why did the officials quote Micah? What point did they try to communicate?

j.  Who also prophesied in the name of the Lord (v. 20)?

k.  How was Uriah's message compared to Jeremiah?

l.  Was Uriah's message received differently than Jeremiah's?

m.  What did Uriah do when he found out the king wanted to kill him?

n.  How did the king respond to Uriah's flight and what was the end result?

o.  What happened to Jeremiah?

4.  Let's compare and contrast yesterday's and today's studies and how they relate to persecution. Answer the questions within the chart and then we will apply this lesson to our lives.

| Scripture | Individual | Event or Circumstance | Answer |
|---|---|---|---|
| **Acts 16:9-10** | Paul | Paul had a vision from God calling him to preach in Macedonia. | |
| **Jeremiah 26:1-2** | Jeremiah | The Lord told Jeremiah to stand in the Lord's house and speak to the people. He was told, "Do not omit a word!" | |
| **Jeremiah 26:20** | Uriah | Uriah prophesied in the name of the Lord. | |
| **Question:** Who led these men into their circumstances? | | | |
| **Acts 16:13-16** | Paul | Paul went to the place of prayer to minister to those assembled. Lydia and her household received the Word and were baptized. | |
| **Jeremiah 26:3-7** | Jeremiah | Jeremiah entered the temple of the Lord and called for the people to turn from their evil ways so the Lord could repent from the calamity He was to bring upon them. | |
| **Question:** What were the purposes of Paul's and Jeremiah's messages? Were the message themes the same or different? | | | |
| **Acts 16:16-19** | Paul | While Paul ministered, he cast a demon out of a slave girl; her masters dragged Paul before the authorities because they were upset they could no longer profit from the girl's sorcery. | |
| **Jeremiah 26:8-11** | Jeremiah | When Jeremiah was finished speaking, the people cried, "You must die." Then the people took him before the authorities. | |
| **Jeremiah 26:20-21** | Uriah | Uriah prophesied a message similar to Jeremiah's. When King Jehoiakim heard Uriah fled to Egypt, the king sought to put him to death. | |

| Scripture | Individual | Event or Circumstance | Answer |
|---|---|---|---|
| **Question:** Were Paul, Jeremiah, and Uriah being persecuted because they were giving their own messages, or were they being obedient to the Lord? | | | |
| **Acts 16:20, 35-39** | Paul | Paul could have announced his Roman citizenship and possibly prevented his jail sentence, but he didn't. | **Result:** Paul lived to continue the ministry to which God had called him. |
| **Jeremiah 26:14-15** | Jeremiah | Jeremiah did not mince words; he did not try to defend himself. He boldly spoke, "I am in your hands; do with me as is good and right in your sight." | **Result:** Jeremiah lived to continue his ministry for another thirty-five years. |
| **Jeremiah 26:21-23** | Uriah | Uriah fled in fear to Egypt. | **Result:** King Jehoiakim chased after Uriah and slew him with a sword. |
| **Question:** Who did Paul and Jeremiah fear, man or God? Who did Uriah fear, man, or God? | | | |
| **Acts 16:22-34** | Paul | Paul (and Silas) were beaten, thrown into the inner prison, and their feet were placed in stocks, yet they continued to praise the Lord with singing and hymns. Then they experienced an earthquake and the prison doors were opened. Instead of fleeing, they remained and witnessed to the jailer. | **Result:** ❖ Slave girl was healed of a demon. ❖ Prisoners listened intently to them. ❖ Jailer and his household believed and were baptized. |
| **Jeremiah 26:18-19** | Jeremiah compared to Micah | Some of the elders spoke up when the people wanted to put Jeremiah to death. They spoke of Micah, a prophet from the time of King Hezekiah. Micah preached a message similar to Jeremiah's. Unlike the people of Judah, King Hezekiah listened to Micah. The elders remembered this and suggested they should spare Jeremiah thus preventing evil from coming against Judah. | **Result:** Jeremiah's life was spared. **Result:** Both King Hezekiah's and Micah's testimonies were used long after their deaths. They were remembered as men who feared the Lord and served Him. The examples of their lives made others fear the Lord. |
| **Question:** Both Paul and Jeremiah stood strong in the face of death threats. With everything you have studied this week, what does this teach you about how you should react to persecution? | | | |

---

**Questions to Ponder**

Do you see persecution of Christians growing in America? Give reasons for your answer.

If so, what should your response be?

---

It would be very easy to conclude from this lesson, as long as we fear God and not man God will save us from our persecutors. It's a message our flesh can grab and embrace. Yet this is far from scriptural truth. Although God spared both Paul and Jeremiah in these passages, eventually both were martyred for their Messiah. Acts 16 took place during Paul's second missionary journey between AD 49-51. Paul was beheaded in AD 64. Jeremiah is believed to have been sawn in two by evil King Manasseh in 574 BC. As you can see, their journeys as obedient servants to the Lord did not get easier. Their travels were difficult.

In the book of Daniel, three others were spared death because they chose obedience to the Lord instead of man. Their names were Shadrach, Meshach and Abed-nego. When faced with death or bowing down to King Nebuchadnezzar's idol they said, "*Our God whom we serve is able to deliver us* from the furnace of blazing fire; and He will deliver us out of your hand, O king. *But even if He does not,* let it be known to you, O king, that we are not going to serve your gods or worship the golden image that you have set up" (emphasis mine) (**Daniel 3:17-18**). This needs to be our battle cry, "Our God is able to deliver us … but even if He doesn't we won't …."

In 1998, the US Embassy in Kenya was bombed, killing 214 people, twelve of whom were Americans. In 2000, the naval vessel USS Cole was attacked, killing seventeen. Both attacks were by al-Qaeda, Islamic jihadists, whose self-confessed mission is to kill infidels (Jews and Christians). In a Front-page Magazine article shortly after September 11, 2001, Sheikh Ali Gomaa (or Gom'a), Egypt's grand mufti, is quoted from a video which began circulating weeks before the 9/11 massacre. Below is an excerpt from the article.

"While holding that Muslims may coexist with Christians (who, as dhimmis [non-Muslim citizens], have rights), Gomaa categorized Christians as **kuffar [or "kafir"]**— 'infidels' — a word that connotes 'enemies,' 'evil-doers,' and every bad thing to Muslim ears.

After quoting Quran 5:17, 'Infidels are those who declare God is the Christ, [Jesus] son of Mary,' he expounded by saying any association between a human and God (in Arabic, *shirk*) is the greatest sin: 'Whoever thinks the Christ is God, or the Son of God, not symbolically — for we are all sons of God — but attributively, has rejected the faith which God requires for salvation,' thereby becoming an infidel."[143]

During the turbulent times of the late '90s and early 2000s I traveled overseas several times a year for evangelism and discipleship ministry with a church-planting organization. Considering what was happening in the world, my husband and I felt it necessary to sit down and speak about the "what ifs," knowing the time to make a decision on how to respond in such an event would not be in the middle of a crisis, but before the crisis. Then we could trust God would give us the strength and courage to stand for Christ no matter the cost. After much prayer, searching my heart, and weighing the cost, I concluded it is more difficult to live for Christ than it would be to die for Him. I had to take up my cross and become like Paul, Jeremiah, Shadrach, Meshach, and Abed-nego. Indeed my battle cry must be, "My God is able to deliver me, but even if He doesn't, I will not bow down."

In Week 1 I wrote, "As believers we *too* will be called to make difficult decisions. A question we need to ask ourselves is, 'How would I respond if I faced some of the same trials and tribulations?' The time to equip ourselves is not as we are going through the trial, but NOW, before a trial." Now is the time to count the cost and decide. You have a lot to pray and to think about, my friend, so let's close with our application questions and prayer.

5.  What has the Lord shown you today to apply to your life? Your church? Your nation?

6.  Write your prayer to the Lord. Ask Him to give you peace and courage to answer these difficult questions.

*"Do not fear what you are about to suffer. Behold, the devil is about to cast some of you into prison,*
*so that you will be tested, and you will have tribulation for ten days. Be faithful until death,*
*and I will give you the crown of life."*
**Revelation 2:10**

# WEEK 7—DAY 3

You are becoming more knowledgeable about persecution, my friend. But if you're like me it's a subject with which you never planned to become familiar! Today you will discover another *why* or *what* in the equation of **loving your enemies and praying for those who persecute you.** Our focus has been on persecution. Now we turn our attention to loving our enemies and learn why this is crucial to our Christian life and testimony. Write your prayer to the Lord. Ask Him to open your eyes and heart to this difficult subject.

We have studied persecution in the Old Testament through the eyes of Jeremiah and in the New Testament through the eyes of Paul. Why did these men endure such harsh treatment, especially knowing the cost of their actions? While there are many answers to this question, we will concentrate on one that is vitally important—love. As we studied in Week 2, Day 3, the Greek word for *love* which is most frequently used in the New Testament is *agápē: It involves God doing what He knows is best for man and not necessarily what man desires. God gives man what he needs, not what man wants.*[144]

1. Consider the above definition in the context of Paul and Jeremiah's circumstances. Both were persecuted for preaching a message of repentance and obedience to the Lord.

   a. Does this fall under the biblical definition of *agápē*?

   b. What insight does this give you about Paul and Jeremiah?

*Agápē* love is the purest form of love because it's how God loves. It comes with no strings attached and has the other person's interest in mind before one's own. Paul knew the cost when he answered the Lord's call on the Damascus Road. Jeremiah knew the cost, as the Lord clearly forewarned him of the road he would travel (Jeremiah 1). We will discover more about this truth through today's study.

Although we have studied persecution, we've never examined the definition. There are two Greek words used for *persecution* in the New Testament.

*Diókó—to flee … follow (after) [or] given to; (suffer).*[145]

*Thilípsis—symbolically means grievous affliction, or distress (Matt. 13:21; 24:21; John 16:21; Acts 7:10; 11:19; 14:22; 1 Cor. 7:28; James 1:27) pressure or a burden upon the spirit … being crushed.*[146]

Let's see what the Bible says about persecution and loving our enemies.

*Remember* the Bible study tip for Week 3: when studying a subject in the Bible, such as loving your enemies or persecution, try to look up every verse in the Bible related to the subject. This will give you a broader perspective of God's opinion on the subject.

2. Read these verses and note what you learn about loving your enemy. Then answer the questions.

**Proverbs 20:22**

**Matthew 5:10-12**

a. Who are the blessed?

b. How are believers to respond when persecuted for Christ's sake?

**Matthew 5:43-48**

Why did Jesus tell believers to love their enemies, and pray for them?

**Luke 6:27-36**

a. Fill in the blanks:

❖ Believers, love your _____.

❖ Believers, do good to those who _____ you.

❖ Believers, bless those who _____ you.

❖ Believers, pray for those who _____ you.

In contrast:

❖ Sinners love those who _____ them.

❖ Sinners do good to those who do _____ to them.

❖ Sinners lend to _____ in order to receive back the same amount.

b. What sets the believer apart in these Scriptures?

c. Read out loud the first four bullets that refer to believers. Replace the word believers with your own name. Make them proclaiming statements.

Example: I, Marta choose to love my enemies as Jesus does.

**Romans12:17-21**

a. Whose responsibility is it to take vengeance?

b. What are we to do for our enemies?

c. How does one overcome evil?

3. Read **Acts 11:19-21**. The Greek word *thilipsis* is translated as persecution in v. 19. Note how God commingles, love and persecution, and the results for the believer(s) and/or unbeliever(s).

a. Where did they go because of the persecution and what did they do when they arrived?

b. What happened to the gospel because of the persecution?

4. Acts 14 gives us a great education on how Paul and Barnabas reacted to their persecutors and how important proclaiming the gospel message was to them.
    ❖ First, read **Acts 14:21-22**. "That city" in v. 21 refers to Derbe. The Greek word *thilipsis* is translated as *tribulations* in v. 22.
    ❖ Then note how God marries love and persecution, and the results for both the believer(s) and unbeliever(s).
    ❖ Lastly, look at additional Scriptures in Acts 14 to better understand the context surrounding the attitude of Paul and Barnabas under persecution.

a. To what cities did they return?

b. To help us understand the context of **Acts 14:21-22**, read **Acts 14:1-7**. Write a synopsis of the events.

c. What did both Jews and Gentiles attempt to do to Paul and Barnabas? (**Acts 14:1-7**)

d. What did Paul and Barnabas do when they became aware of the plot to stone them?

e. Read **Acts 14:19-20**. What happened while they were in Lystra?

Make sure you notice the order of events and what occurred.

> **Acts 14:1-7**—Paul and Barnabas left Iconium because of a plot to stone them. They traveled from Iconium to Lystra and Derbe.
>
> **Acts 14:19-20**—The Jews were so angry with Paul, that they traveled from Antioch and Iconium to stone him. They supposed him dead, but God saved his life. Instead, Paul rose up and departed with Barnabas to Derbe.
>
> **Acts14:21-22**—After Paul and Barnabas preach the gospel in Derbe they returned to Lystra, Iconium, and Antioch—towns in which people plotted to stone Paul, actually stoned him, or traveled from in order to stone Paul.

To strengthen and encourage the disciples, Paul and Barnabas returned to the place where Paul's life was threatened and he said, "Through many tribulations we must enter the kingdom of God." Although the church in the United States might not consider Paul's statement encouraging, God's Word tells us this was indeed a message of encouragement—for believers then and now!

**Interesting biblical note**—Acts 14 records the third and fourth unsuccessful attempts on Paul's life. The first attempt is found in **Acts 9:23-24**, just days after he met Christ on the Damascus Road. In **Acts 9:29**, Paul had left Damascus by night because the Jews plotted to put him to death; he went to Jerusalem only to find the Hellenistic Jews were also attempting to kill him. Hellenistic Jews were Jewish immigrants who had returned to Israel from territories under Greek influence. They worshiped in Greek-speaking synagogues, unlike native Jews from Israel who worshiped in traditional Hebrew-speaking synagogues. Hellenistic Jews were the ones who stoned Stephen in **Acts 6:1**.

5. Read the verses below and note how God marries love and persecution, and the results for the believer(s) and/or unbeliever(s). Then answer any questions if applicable.

**Acts 20:22-24** - The Greek word *thilípsis* is translated as *afflictions* in v. 23.

**Romans 5:3-5**—The Greek word *thilípsis* is translated as *tribulation* in v. 3. *Love* in v. 5 is *agápē*.

a. What are we to do?

b. What will tribulation bring?

c. What will perseverance bring?

d. What will proven character bring?

e. What does hope NOT do? Why?

f. How does Paul, the writer of Romans, marry *thilípsis* and *agápē* again in these verses? What conclusions can you reach?

**Romans 8:28-39**—Many of you are familiar with this passage. Please don't skim these verses ... meditate on them. The Greek word *thilípsis* is translated as *persecution* in v. 35. The word *love* in **Romans 8:28, 35, 37** and **39** are all the Greek word *agápē*.

a. What does God cause?

b. For whom does God cause ALL things to work together for good?

c. What are we predestined to become (v. 29)?

d. If we are predestined, we are also _____.

e. If we are called, we are also _____.

f. Those He justified He also _____.

The Greek word for *called kaléo* is used in **Romans 8:30** as *the divine invitation to participate in the blessings of redemption.*[147] *The Greek word for justified, dikalóō, means either to bring out the fact that a person is righteous, or if he is not, to make him righteous … The NT tells how being justified by God and declared just before Him are achieved in the lives of men. We are justified before God by Christ through grace (Gal. 2:16, 3:11; Titus 3:6,7). When one receives Christ, he recognizes God's right over him. His justification simultaneously performs a miracle in him and changes his character. He does not then obey God because he is afraid of the consequences of his disobedience, but because of His [sic] grace in Christ which has changed his character and made him just. When one becomes a child of God, he exercises rights toward God and acts as His child. He is thus liberated from the guilt and power of sin, but not from the presence of it.*[148]

g.  Who will bring a _____ against God's elect (v. 33)?

h.  God is the one who justifies. Who is the one who _____ (v. 34)?

i.  Make a list of what v. 35 teaches about what cannot separate us from the love of Christ.

   ❖

   ❖

   ❖

   ❖  *thilípsis* = _____

   ❖

   ❖

   ❖

j.  For whose sake are we being put to death?

k.  How are we to be considered?

I have written in my Bible next to this verse, "when you slaughter a pig they squeal like a pig but when you slaughter a lamb they never do a thing." This gives us a vivid image.

l.  How does v. 36 apply to you?

m.  To what do all *these things* we conquer refer (v. 37)?

n.  How are we to conquer all *these* things?


o.  We all have our own *these things*. Fill in the blank: I will overwhelmingly conquer _____

_____through Christ who loves me.


p.  What cannot separate us from the love of God?

    ❖

    ❖

    ❖

    ❖

    ❖

    ❖

    ❖

    ❖

    ❖

    ❖


q.  We each have our own obstacles. Fill in the blank: _____

_____ is not able to separate me from the love of God.


r.  How does Paul commingle *thilípsis* and *agápē* in these verses? What conclusions can you reach?



Romans 8 contrasts: *setting your mind on the flesh, which equals death*, with *setting your mind on the spirit, which equals life*. **Romans 8:13** says, "For if you are living according to the flesh, you must die; but if by the Spirit you are putting to death the deeds of the body, you will live."

6.  **Romans 8:17-19** says:

"And if children, heirs also, heirs of God and fellow heirs with Christ, if indeed we suffer with Him so that we may also be glorified with Him. For I consider that the sufferings of this present time are not worthy to be compared with the glory that is to be revealed to us. For the anxious longing of the creation waits eagerly for the revealing of the sons of God."

a. Because we are heirs of God, in what will we participate? Why?

b. How did Paul consider his sufferings?

---

### Questions to Ponder

After studying **Romans 8:28-39** and other verses in Romans 8, do you understand them better or differently? Explain your answer.

Do you see persecution in a different light?

---

When I first heard a pastor preach from **Romans 8:28-39** the verses were presented as victory verses for believers. And let me be the first to give a hearty AMEN to this analogy. But I realize now, I overlooked the context of the chapter that spoke of suffering and persecution, and focused only on God working everything out to accomplish His perfect plan in my life. Although there is "victory" in the verses, my idea of a perfect plan didn't include peril or persecution and I certainly couldn't believe this was in God's plan either. The more I have studied the Bible and walked the Christian life, the more I have learned peril and persecution are tools, which the Lord uses BECAUSE He loves me. And through difficult circumstances I draw closer to Him, and I am comforted.

We *must* learn from this Scripture, through tribulation, distress, persecution, peril, etc., we become more Christ-like (conformed to the image of His Son). It's easy to conclude, in our human mind, during these trials and tribulations God is far off and not concerned about us. Yet Scripture assures us this is not true. We need to settle in our hearts *nothing* can separate us from His love or His presence. God never stands at a distance. He is ever-present in our lives and our circumstances are ever-present on His mind. He is the Sovereign God who is in control of the universe and His creation.

The Greek word for *glorify* is *doxázō—to recognize, honor, praise ... the dóxa of God is the revelation and manifestation of all that He has and is. It is His revelation in which He manifests all the goodness that He is.*[149] When we are conformed to Christ's image, He glorifies us (**Romans 8:30**). When we love our enemies, this glorifies God because we are representing the image of Christ, His *dóxa* (all that He has and is) to those enemies. Christ is revealed to them. There could be no greater love than this. **Romans 5:8** teaches, "While we were yet sinners Christ died for us." When Saul was an enemy of God, Christ died for him. When I, Marta, was an enemy of God, Christ died for me. When you, _____ (fill in your name) were an enemy of God, Christ died for you. Your enemy of God, Christ died for them. An enemy of God, Christ died for them. Saul—transformed. Marta—transformed. You—transformed. Your enemies' transformation may not have occurred yet, but until they receive a revelation of who Jesus is and His goodness is revealed to them, transformation is not possible. Therefore, we must **Love our enemies and pray for those who persecute us.**

Let's close with our application questions and prayer.

7.  What has the Lord shown you today through our lesson that you will apply to your life? Your church? Your nation?

8.  Write your closing prayer to the Lord. Thank Him for loving humanity with an *agápē* love and giving us what we need, NOT what we want.

*"If the world hates you, you know that it has hated Me before it hated you. If you were of the world, the world would love its own; but because you are not of the world, but I chose you out of the world, because of this the world hates you. Remember the word that I said to you, 'A slave is not greater than his master.' If they persecuted Me, they will also persecute you; if they kept My word, they will keep yours also."*
**John 15:18-20**

# WEEK 7—DAY 4

Welcome to Day 4, my friend! Are you enjoying the biography of William Tyndale? This man from the sixteenth century is a wonderful example of a faithful servant of the Lord. Begin your time today asking the Lord to give you a passion to fulfill the call He placed on your life. Thank Him for the testimonies of leadership He gave us in His Word and throughout the centuries. Finally, ask Him to give you the strength to finish strong so you can be a model for future generations.

God was working during the 1500s. He wanted His Word translated into languages His people could understand. This was the work God *was* accomplishing as He raised up people to fulfill this purpose. He selected Martin Luther and William Tyndale, two godly men with the God-given intellect, creativity, and passion to carry out His plan. Listed are other Bibles published during the same time period as Luther's and Tyndale's translations. God used other obedient men to accomplish His work during this time.

1454 - Gutenberg Vulgate Bible printed.

1506 - First edition of the Latin Bible printed in France.

1516 - Desiderius Erasmus published first Greek New Testament; said to have had a greater influence on Tyndale than either the Vulgate [Latin version of Bible] or Luther [Bible].

1522 - First German New Testament translated by Martin Luther (Wittenberg).

1524 - First Danish New Testament published.

1526 - William Tyndale's English translation of the New Testament printed.

1526 - First edition of the complete Swedish translation.

1526 - First complete Dutch Bible.

1528 - Robert Stephen's first Latin Bible.

1529 - The Zurich Bible, first Swiss-German Bible.[150]

This is not an exhaustive list, just a sample of those God used to accomplish His purpose in the 1500s. Our chart is beginning to be filled with details on both Martin Luther and William Tyndale. Let's review what we've studied. We will add additional details at the end of today's lesson.

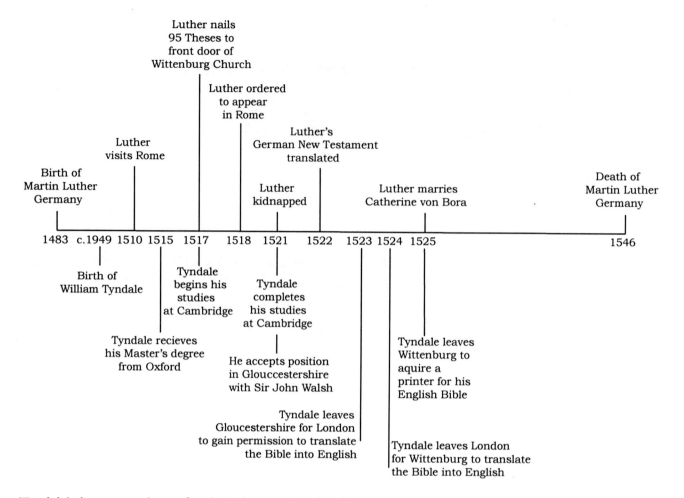

Tyndale's heart was always for the "plowman" to be able to read, understand, and know God's Word. How copies of Tyndale's Bible arrived in London is a great demonstration of the sovereignty and providence of God. Because of a drought in 1525, England was in crisis; food was scarce and people were in danger of starving. The problem was resolved by allowing merchants from northern Europe to export grain to England. Buried in the sacks of grain were copies of Tyndale's New Testament. "Smugglers also secretly marked bales of cloth, inside of which were hidden flat, printed sheets. Once delivered, those sheets would be folded, stitched, cut, and bound into books."[151] And by early 1526 copies of Tyndale's Worms New Testament were being sold openly in England.

This was not the first time God used nature's events to bring about His purposes. In the first chapter of the book of Jonah, we find the prophet Jonah fleeing on a ship from the mission assigned to him by the Lord. To get his attention, the Lord sent a great storm on the sea. The sailors became afraid and sought their own gods to determine whose sinful action caused the storm. Finally, Jonah confessed he was a Hebrew and feared only the Lord Jehovah. The sailors understood he was fleeing from the presence of the Lord and became even more frightened. They knew the storm had come upon them because of Jonah's sin. Once they threw Jonah overboard, the seas calmed, and a great fish swallowed him.

Today, God still works through natural disasters. The reason we do not recognize this is because we are not looking for God to work in this way. We must not be blind to when and where God is at work.

To obtain Tyndale's New Testament, the plowman would have to pay *half his week's* wages for a copy, unlike the minimum wage worker today who would now pay only 20 percent of *one hour's* wage to buy a Bible. In the United

States, we can even purchase a New Testament for as little as $1.50! People bought this banned book collectively, regardless of the cost. Desperate to hear God's Word in a language they understood, they came together and heard the Word read for the first time in their own language. God's Word was precious, life-giving power to the people.

Within a matter of months, Tyndale's New Testaments were flooding London and Bishop Cuthbert Tunstall acquired a copy of Tyndale's work. Tunstall was the same man who in 1523 had denied Tyndale permission to translate the Bible into English. Tunstall attacked Tyndale's English translation with a vengeance. He threatened the church, burned copies of Tyndale's New Testament, and all imports were closely monitored for contraband. Buying and selling Tyndale's or Martin Luther's material became a serious offense. "In spite of Tunstall's effort to destroy Tyndale's work, the supply of New Testaments in England increased. About six thousand English New Testaments were in circulation. This represented a huge number of copies at the time. Most print runs in Europe at the beginning of the sixteenth century numbered between one-thousand and fifteen-hundred copies . . . [Tyndale] understood quite well what a demand existed among the people in England for possessing any part of the Bible written in their own language."[152]

March 1527 found the prisons overflowing with those persecuted for reading Tyndale's New Testament and other offences against the church. When Tyndale received word of the persecutions and imprisonments in England he was working on the promised revisions of his New Testament and likely beginning the translation of the Old Testament.

Tyndale's second book, *The Obedience of the Christian Man,* was printed by October 1528. This would become his most popular book other than his biblical translations. It was written in response to the Peasants' War in Europe.

He wanted to make clear that subjects must obey their kings and that the reformers were not teaching people to revolt. . . The book quickly made its way to England, and John Foxe recorded that Anne Boleyn [Henry VIII's future second wife] received a copy."[153] "[T]he king decided to read it for himself. He reportedly liked the book, probably because it asserted that God did not intend kings to be subservient to popes. . . Wolsey and other members of the church establishment were unanimous in their hatred of *The Obedience of the Christian Man*. Possession of the book became one of the primary "proofs" that a person was a heretic.

In January 1529, Tyndale's name was mentioned during open court in England in connection with heresy and rebellion. By February, a renewed search for him on the Continent had begun. . . Tyndale had been translating the Pentateuch, the first five books of the Old Testament, while he was [also] working . . . [on] *The Obedience of the Christian Man*. . . . Not wanting to draw attention to himself in Antwerp, Tyndale took his completed Pentateuch, along with all his books, papers, and money and caught a ship to Hamburg, . . . German[y].[154]

Tragedy struck as Tyndale lost everything when the ship wrecked. All his translations, reference books, and Hebrew documents were gone, lost in the depth of the sea. Tyndale simply began again after finding new copies of the books from which he worked, which was not an easy task. Political distractions in England allowed Tyndale to redo his work on the Pentateuch in relative safety.

When Henry VIII named Sir Thomas More (a vehement defender of the Roman Catholic Church) as the new lord chancellor, concerns increased for those not aligned with every aspect of the Catholic Church. More had published his *Dialogue Concerning Heresies*, a four-volume set attacking Luther, Tyndale, and the English Bible in scathing terms. Tyndale boldly took his second translation of the Pentateuch to Antwerp for printing. The first book of the Bible, Genesis, came off the press in January 1530.

> The Pentateuch made its way to England later that year and was distributed as five individual books. . . . At the same time . . . a priest named Thomas Hitton [who knew Tyndale] was arrested in Kent, England, and charged with heresy. . . . During his hearing, he confessed that he had smuggled a New Testament into England. He was convicted [and] . . . On February 23, 1530, Thomas Hitton was burned alive at the stake, becoming the reformer's first English martyr.
>
> When the Pentateuch arrived on England's shores, some of Tyndale's marginal notes gave his opponents more ammunition. At the end of Exodus eighteen, where Moses' father-in-law gives advice about the qualities to look for in leaders, Tyndale's translation reads, 'Moreover seek out among all the people, men of activity which fear God, and men that are true and hate covetousness; and make them heads over the people' (v. 21). In the margin, Tyndale noted, 'Our prelates neither fear God, for they preach not [H]is word truly: nor are less covetous than Judas: for they have received of the devil the kingdoms of the earth and the glory thereof which Christ refused. Mat. 4.'
>
> Little hard evidence was needed for a person to be investigated. John and Cecily Eaton were persecuted for being noticed by unnamed persons of their parish holding down their heads in church and not looking at the sacrament during mass. In August 1530, a man was arrested for believing that the church service in England should be spoken in English rather than Latin. His wife, sister, and father testified against him."[155]

There was no place in England where Tyndale could safely stay; therefore, he probably stayed in Germany for the next four years. On December 7, 1529, an edict was issued making it unlawful to write or print any book without obtaining a license. Any person found violating this edict could be executed without mercy.

Wherever Tyndale turned he seemed to be in a terrible predicament, all for the sake of Christ. Tyndale was not the first to suffer for Christ and he certainly will not be the last. Tyndale had learned the cost of discipleship and following Christ. "Jesus said to His disciples, 'If anyone wishes to come after Me, he must deny himself, and take up his cross and follow Me'" (**Matthew 16:24**). Tyndale denied his life, comforts, and security to passionately accomplish the task God gave him. Like the biblical men and women who had gone before him, Tyndale lived his life pursuing God's call and poured his life into these translations.

Let's review some of the lives Tyndale knew so well through his studies of the Bible.

1.  Read the following verses. In the space provided note how Tyndale's life paralleled the lives of biblical heroes of the faith. Write what application we learn from these people for our lives. These Scriptures are a review, we have studied them previously.

| Scriptures and synopsis | Comparison with biblical figure(s) and Tyndale. Then application for your life. |
|---|---|
| **Read Acts 4**—Peter and John stood before the Sanhedrin the first time. They are asked to stop speaking about Jesus' resurrection. Their response, "For we cannot stop speaking about what we have seen and heard." | |
| **Read Acts 5:14-42**—Apostles seized and jailed. The Lord opened the gates of the prison. The next day the apostles were found in the temple preaching Jesus' resurrection. | |
| **Read Acts 12:1-17**—James had just been martyred. Peter was in prison awaiting certain death. The Lord loosed Peter's chains, and led him out of the prison. Then Peter reported to those praying for him. | |
| **Read Acts 13:42-14:22**—Paul and Barnabas spoke boldly about Christ. The Jews were filled with jealousy and began contradicting them. Paul and Barnabas turned to the Gentiles. Several attempts were made on their lives, but the Lord sustained them. | |
| **Read Nehemiah Chapters 4-6**—Nehemiah began to rebuild the wall. Sanballat and others began to undermine Nehemiah's plans. Sanballat began with verbal assaults; he eventually devised a plot to assassinate Nehemiah's character. | |

---

**Questions to Ponder**

❖ Do you believe persecution only occurred in the past, or is it happening today? If so, where?

❖ Do you see any evidence persecution exists in the US? Give evidence to support your view.

❖ Are you prepared to be persecuted for Jesus Christ?

❖ If your answer is no, what steps do you need to take today to be prepared for tomorrow?

---

While we can never be fully prepared for the unknowns in life, especially something as difficult as persecution, there are steps we can take to better equip ourselves for life. Stop right now and give yourself a gold star. The number one tactic for equipping yourself is immersion in God's Word. Studies like *ACTs420NOW* are great weapons of war for life's difficult trials.

2. Add the following dates to our timeline on page 236

❖ October 1528—Tyndale's *Obedience of the Christian Man* was published.
❖ January 1529—Tyndale's name was mentioned in open court associated with heresy.
❖ January 1530—Tyndale's translation of the book of Genesis rolled off the press.

Let's close today with our application questions and prayer.

3. What have you learned today to apply to your life? Your church? Your nation?

4. Close with prayer. Ask the Lord to help you to be faithful during the difficult seasons of your life. It has been said that you are either going into a trial, in the midst of a trial, or coming out of a trial. Wherever you find yourself, asking the Lord to strengthen you is always prudent.

*"But the Lord stood with me and strengthened me, so that through me the proclamation might be fully accomplished, and that all the Gentiles might hear; and I was rescued out of the lion's mouth."*
**2 Timothy 4:17**

# Week 7—Day 5

Have you been challenged this week? Isn't it good to immerse yourself in His Word? God's Word is truth and brings healing to your soul. Loving our enemies and praying for those who persecute you is not an easy assignment, yet this is what we are called to do through Christ Jesus. Let us begin with prayer. Thank Him for His truth and ask Him to give us the discipline to tackle these difficult tasks, so we can be a light in a world of darkness.

In Week 5 we began studying the Great Awakening. Let's review what we have studied for the previous two weeks.

❖ About 100 years after the Pilgrims landed in America pastors began to pray for the Holy Spirit to energize their churches.

❖ The church prayed fourteen years for this Holy Spirit energy.

❖ In 1734, at Jonathan Edwards' Northhampton Church, passion for God began to grow in the youth.

❖ This passion quickly spread throughout the city.

❖ George Whitefield was one of the most well-known evangelists during the Great Awakening.

❖ Whitefield used many new and innovative techniques to draw large crowds such as tent revivals, and sending messengers door-to-door to announce these events.

❖ Whitfield's messages focused on the *new birth*.

❖ Great Awakening converts gave testimonies as had the first-century church focusing on the Holy Spirit's work in transforming lives.

❖ Anti-revivalists were critical of the movement and began persecuting those in the awakening calling them radical evangelicals or dissenters.

❖ As radical evangelicals began to break away from the Church of England they faced heavy fines and harassment even while their taxes continued to fund the state church (Church of England).

❖ Because of the persecution, the radical evangelicals began to move south in proclaiming the gospel.

❖ By mid-1750s African slaves in the south had experienced the new birth.

❖ Today the south is known as the *Bible Belt*—a direct result of migration of dissenters in the Great Awakening.

The political climate in the colonies was beginning to change. By 1756, the French and Indian War, also known as the Seven Years War, began. The British and French battled for control over North America, the Caribbean, and India.

The Ohio Valley was an area of conflict for France and Britain. Whoever could control the Ohio Valley had access to the rivers that flowed into the mighty Mississippi River. And if you had control of the Mississippi River, you had control over all the trade traveling on the river. Great wealth was at stake for both Britain and France. France also wanted to block expansion of the colonies. Control of the Ohio Valley would render future growth of the British colonies an impossibility.

Lieutenant Governor Robert Dinwiddie of Virginia sent twenty-one year old George Washington and his troops on a mission to confront French forces. Washington's job was to send the French packing from territory they had already claimed. The French laid siege to Fort Necessity and easily defeated George Washington and the Virginians.

The British blamed the colonists for the defeat. "General Lord Albemarle, the British Ambassador to France, wrote the Duke of Newcastle in September of 1754 stating his opinion on the lack of knowledge and experience Washington and other colonial officers possessed, and pressing for the dispatch of good regular officers to be sent to North America to discipline and lead the colonial militias. Newcastle sent not only officers to the American continent, but also two regiments of British regulars under the command of General Edward Braddock, which arrived in February of 1755."[156]

Before the war the colonists were self-sufficient, having been left to care for themselves. Problems began to arise with the arrival of British troops. British officers considered themselves superior to colonial officers of equal rank. The British solution was to restructure the system, giving British officers more authority.

Many colonists were insulted over this revision and resigned from the military. This included George Washington. "Washington wrote to William Fitzhugh after learning of the new edict: 'You make mention in your letter of my continuing in the Service, and retaining my Colo.'s [Colonel's] Commission. This idea has filled me with surprise: for if you think me capable of holding a Commission that has neither rank nor emolument annexed to it; you must entertain a very contemptible opinion of my weakness, and believe me to be more empty than the Commission itself.'

"Washington left the service and returned to his home at Mount Vernon. He would return to the military as the aide-de-camp for General Braddock solely as a volunteer. He received no pay, but took orders only directly from the General himself, which appealed greatly to the young Virginian. He could suffer enemy fire, but not the sense of shame that serving under British captains would have instilled in him."[157]

Little did Washington know the providence of God was orchestrating his present predicament for America's future benefit! The skills Washington learned under Braddock prepared him to become General George Washington in the American Revolution. Washington learned everything from organizing supplies, negotiating, administering military justice, and managing troops.

Over time, Washington's journal of the war was published in newspapers in both America and Britain. In General Braddock's final battle, the French surprised Braddock surrounding him at the Monongahela River and a costly, bloody battle raged. Braddock received a fatal wound, and without Washington taking charge, chaos would have ensued. By the end of the French and Indian War, Washington had become a hero, both in the colonies and in Britain.

By 1763, the British were victorious but the cost of the war was astronomical and nearly destroyed the English government. Parliament's solution to recover war costs was to tax the colonies for their portion of the defense. This solution caused growing tensions between the colonist and their homeland, England. Britain may have won the war but they lost the respect of the colonist and would soon lose much more.

The colonists were bitter against Britain for several reasons:

- ❖ British mistreatment of the colonists during the war
- ❖ British Proclamation of 1763 stated that no colonists could inhabit land west of the Appalachian Mountains (The colonists had just fought side-by-side with the British in the French and Indian War for this very land.)
- ❖ Realization that their independence could be stripped from them at any time
- ❖ Excessive taxation after the war.

There was also the issue of freedom of religion. This was of course the driving force that brought the Pilgrims to American soil a century before. Today there is considerable debate over the role of religion or the lack thereof in America's foundation. This debate includes the American Revolution. Just as an investigator would do, we will examine the facts. Then you will judge for yourself their relevance to American history.

On the Library of Congress website under Religion and the Founding of the American Republic—Religion and the American Revolution, "Joseph Galloway a former speaker of the Pennsylvania Assembly and close friend of Benjamin Franklin . . . asserted in this pamphlet, the Revolution was, to a considerable extent, a religious quarrel, caused by Presbyterians and Congregationalists whose 'principles of religion and polity [were] equally averse to those of the established Church and Government.'"[158]

Today, many point to people like Thomas Jefferson as evidence to why this country was not founded on Judeo-Christian values. Jefferson, after all, was a deist and "did not believe that Jesus ever claimed to be the Son of God. He similarly thought the doctrine of the Trinity was nonsense. . . . [Yet] at the founding of the United States, deists and evangelicals (and the range of believers in between) united around principles of religious freedom that were key to the success of the Revolution and that aided in the institution of a nation."[159]

In Thomas S. Kidd's book *God of Liberty: A Religious History of the American Revolution*, he outlines five points or precepts as to why these unlikely fellows united to create the Judeo-Christian foundation of the United States of America.

**Principle One:** *The necessity to disestablishment of the state churches*[160]

**Principle Two:** *God is the creator and guarantor of fundamental human rights.*[161]

**Principle Three:** *Human sinfulness posed a threat to the polity (society).*[162]

**Principle Four:** *A republic would be sustained by virtue.*[163]

**Principle Five:** *The belief that God—or Providence, as deists and others might prefer to deem it—moved in and through nations.*[164]

Although the Separatists fled England for religious freedom, the Church of England was still the state church of the British colonies. The colonists' taxes went to fund the church. The King of England not only had absolute rule over the country, he had absolute rule over the church. The false belief in the Divine Right of Kings, instituted by King James I in the early 1600s, held that if the king spoke, it was as if God Himself were speaking. This resulted in absolute power over church and state.

Radical evangelicals and dissenters firmly believed there was no king but King Jesus. This view immediately placed them at odds with the England. Until the mid-1700s the colonists were unhindered in their worship, but harassment had begun and the disestablishment of the state church would bring unrestricted freedom to these persecuted believers.

If Thomas Jefferson, a deist, believed the Trinity was nonsense and that Jesus never claimed to be God, then how could he align himself with these principles? Deism is the "Belief in the existence of a supreme being, specifically of a creator who does not intervene in the universe."[165]

As you can see, Jefferson could agree with *the disestablishment of the state church* without agreeing with radical evangelicals. He, too, would have wanted to separate from the state church to be free to believe things contrary to a king who believed his words were from God Himself.

How did our Founding Fathers' desire for the precepts outlined above align with God's Word? What does God say on the subject? Let's take a look.

1. Look up the following Scriptures and note what you learn for each principle.

   **Principle One:** *The disestablishment of the state churches.*

   a. **Exodus 20:1-6**

   1st Commandment –

   2nd Commandment –

   How does the Divine Right of Kings contradict these commandments?

   Do the commandments conflict with the Divine Right of Kings' philosophy? Why or why not?

   b. **Deuteronomy 29:14-18.**

   c. **1 Chronicles 16:25-26.**

Many years ago when my husband and I were helping to establish a church in Romania, one of the "attacks" we encountered was our church was not under the state (government). Having an American mentality, I could not understand why this was such an issue. Although Romania is a free country today, they still have a state church, Romanian Orthodox. Like the church in England, the Romanian churches approved by the state receive tax money. Yes, this provides income to run the necessary daily functions of the church, but the state also grants or denies money on the basis of the church falling in line with government protocol.

One of the freedoms we hold dear in America is our freedom to worship or not worship, as we choose. The 1st Amendment undoubtedly deals with religion. The state (government) cannot establish religion or deny the establishment of religion. By *not* allowing the state to establish religion this secured the freedom the colonists had desired for over 100 years. The pilgrims dreamed of this freedom, our Founding Fathers would fight for this freedom, and some would give their lives for religious freedom, in order for American citizens (like you and me) to establishing religious freedom apart from governmental control.

Our Founding Fathers wanted deists and radical evangelicals to worship as they wished, without the fear of governmental involvement. Today, people of all faiths—Christian, Hindu, Buddhist, Mormon, Jews, Muslim, and more—have the freedom to worship because of the sacrifices of our Founding Fathers. I don't have to agree with their beliefs, to appreciate we should all have freedom to worship as our Founding Fathers desired.

**Principle Two:** *The idea of a creator God as the guarantor of fundamental human rights.*

   d. **Genesis 1:26-27**

   e. **Acts 10:34-35** (You may want to read all of Acts 10 for context.)

   f. **Acts 15:7-9**

   g. **Galatians 3:28**

We can see the thread of principles in Thomas Jefferson's revolutionary wording in the Declaration of Independence which states, "We hold these truths to be self-evident, that all men are created equal, that they are endowed by their Creator with certain unalienable Rights, that among these are Life, Liberty and the pursuit of Happiness."[166] This "doctrine of the common creation of all people would also prove to be one of the most cogent arguments against slavery . . . If, as the Bible taught, all humans descended from a single, God-initiated origin, then what principle could justify racial slavery? . . . The doctrine of rights guaranteed by creation, widely shared among deists and evangelicals, would set American slavery on a path to extinction."[167] Even though this path took the next fifty-seven years.

**Principle Three:** *The threat to the polity (society) posed by human sinfulness.*

    h. **Jeremiah 17:9**

    i. **Romans 5:12**

    j. **James 1:13-16**

    k. **Genesis 37**—As you read the chapter answer the following questions.

    List any sins you see that people commit during this chapter.

    Did the brothers influence one another to sin against their brother Joseph? Explain.

    How does this story relate to our Founding Fathers' concern over *"the threat to the polity (society) posed by human sinfulness?"*

From this principle our Founding Fathers set up the checks and balances of our government. We know these to be the three branches of government—executive Branch, legislative Branch, and the judicial Branch. The Founders believed each branch had to be accountable to one another. The executive branch would carry out the laws; the legislative branch would make the laws; the judicial branch would review the laws. This would make the tyranny they were enduring under King George III an impossibility in the new system of government. The Founders believed if one branch overstepped its authority, the other two branches had the authority to intervene and correct the imbalance.

## Questions to Ponder

Do you see our three branches of government being operating today as our Founding Fathers' intended? Why or why not?

**Principle Four:** *A republic needed to be sustained by virtue.*

l. **Proverbs 27:17**

m. **Ecclesiastes 4:9-12**

n. **Luke 17:3**

In 1749 Samuel Adams said, "Neither the wisest constitution nor the wisest laws will secure the liberty and happiness of a people whose manners are universally corrupt."[168] If our Founding Fathers believed a threat to society was sinfulness, and morality was the key to liberty and happiness, from where would morality come? We get the answer from the Father of our Country, George Washington, who said, "It is impossible to govern the world without God and the Bible. Of all the dispositions and habits that lead to political prosperity, our religion and morality are the indispensable supporters. Let us with caution indulge the supposition that morality can be maintained without religion. Reason and experience both forbid us to expect that our national morality can prevail in exclusion of religious principle."[169] If one is seeking to find the foundation of the United States, it is impossible to dismiss its biblical foundation. It is also impossible to find if one chooses not to search.

**Principle Five:** *The belief that God—or Providence, as deists and others might prefer to deem it—moved in and through nations.*

o. **Ezra 6:22**

p. **Daniel 2:20-21**

q. **Proverbs 21:1**

From the Great Awakening to the American Revolution, the providential hand of God moved through His people to bring forth His purpose for the United States. God's providence is not limited to America. He works throughout all the nations of the earth. His Word tells us "For the eyes of the Lord move to and fro throughout the earth that He may strongly support those whose heart is completely His" (**2 Chronicles 16:9**).

When we say yes to Jesus, we should expect to ruffle a few feathers. We are the defenders of the gospel and the lovers of those who are weak and helpless. We are those who are in charge of presenting godly thoughts, principles and standards, which are in sharp contrast to the world's beliefs. Remember what was said about Paul, Silas, and Timothy when they were dragged before the city authorities in **Acts 17:6b**, "These men who have upset the world have come here also." Are you the man or woman of God who will be used to turn the world upside down in this generation? Our Lord is not partial to a gender, color, economic, or social ranking. He is only partial to those whose heart is completely His.

2. Let's close with our application question. What has our Lord been showing you today? Write what you are going to apply to your life. Your church. Your nation.

3. Write your prayer to the Lord. Thank Him for the men and women who have gone before you to lead the way. Picture these heroes of the faith surrounding you as described in **Hebrews 12:1**. Ask for courage to lay aside every encumbrance and sin so that you can run the race that God has prepared for you.

*"Blessed is the nation whose God is the Lord, the people whom He has chosen for His own inheritance."*
***Psalm 33:12***

We want to know what God has done in your life!

Write your testimony here or send an e-mail to info@wogt.org

_____ Become a Words of Grace & Truth Supporter _____

_____ Yes, I want to become a member of the prayer warrior team!
(You'll receive a daily e-mail.)

_____ Yes, I would like to become a faithful friend of Words of Grace & Truth and support the ministry financially. I want to help spread His truth to the nations.

_____ Expect a monthly check for $ (e.g., $25, $50, $100, or more). Please make all checks payable to Words of Grace & Truth. You may also make a one-time or recurring donation online at www.wogt. org.

_____ Please charge my credit/debit card on the 1st or 15th of each month in the amount of $ (e.g., $25, $50, $100, or more).

_____ Enclosed is my one-time gift to help spread His truth through Words of Grace & Truth.

Visa/MasterCard/AMEX/Discover Card # _____

Name: _____

Address: _____

Email Address: _____

Phone Number: (_____) _____ - _____

"And blessed be His glorious name forever; and may the whole earth be filled
with His glory. Amen, and Amen."
**Psalm 72:19**

Words of Grace & Truth
PO Box 860223
Plano, TX 75086-0223
469-854-3574 or 800-257-1626

# Week 8 Overview

*Never compromise your faith even unto death.*
**(Philippians 1:20-21)**

As you read the final step this week many of you might be ready to run out of the room or shut the book. But I promise, you will be blessed by your study. Yes, it will challenge you, but you will be more equipped at the end of this week's study. God's Word promises, "So will My word be which goes forth from My mouth; it will not return to Me empty, without accomplishing what I desire, and without succeeding in the matter for which I sent it" **(Isaiah 55:11)**. Persevere, my friend, persevere.

This week we will:
* ❖ Study Stephen, the first martyr.
* ❖ Investigate Stephen's message to the Sanhedrin.
* ❖ Examine Stephen's message through Jewish eyes.

This week's applications include:
* ❖ Determining to be faithful to the Lord.
* ❖ Equipping yourself in God's Word.
* ❖ Equipping ourselves in how we should *act* and *react* to those who persecute us.

This week's verse to memorize:

*". . . I will not be put to shame in anything, but that with all boldness, Christ will even now, as always, be exalted in my body, whether by life or by death. For to me, to live is Christ and to die is gain."*
**Philippians 1:20b-21**

Fill in the blanks where appropriate.

**Foundational Step:** _____ there is _____ in none other than

_____ _____ **(Acts ____)**.

**Step 2:** _____ you will begin to _____ the Word of God with _____ **(Acts ____)**.

**Step 3:** _____ the _____ is "_____" to a lost and dying _____ **(2 Corinthians ____)**.

**Step 4:** _____ yourself, _____, seek, and _____ to God for _____ in our land **(2 Chronicles ____)**.

**Step 5:** _____ by _____ and _____ America and the world until our land is _____ **(Isaiah ____)**.

**Step 6:** _____ your _____ and _____ for those who _____ you **(Matthew 5:44)**.

**Step 7:** Never compromise your faith even unto death **(Philippians 1:20-21)**.

# WEEK 8

Never compromise your faith even unto death.
—Philippians 1:20-21

## WEEK 8—DAY 1

This is our final week of study my friend, I will miss spending this time with you and pray you will continue to spend time daily with our Savior, Jesus. Write your prayer to the Lord. Ask Him to continue to give you a hunger for His Word and perseverance to come to Him daily for bread.

Our final principle is **Never compromise your faith even unto death**. You may be screaming on the inside, NO! I don't want to go down that road. I don't want to even think about it. This is not an easy subject matter but we must discuss what the Bible says on the subject. We must also understand that just because we study the subject doesn't mean we will be called to lay down our lives. We all want the Christian life described in Hebrews 11—one that conquers kingdoms, shuts the mouths of lions, becomes mighty in war, and receives back their dead, but we would rather not be destitute, stoned, or sawed in two. But we are not the ones who get to choose. However, we can take comfort in what God's Word teaches.

1. Read **Psalms 139:16**.

   a. When were the number of our days ordained?

   b. Therefore, who is in control of your life and death?

2. Read **Job 14:1-6**.

    a. Who determines the number of our days?

    b. What comparison is given in v. 6?

       He fulfills his day like _____.

We can study this difficult subject without fear because we rest in the Lord. As believers, we are invincible until the day we see Christ Jesus face-to-face. But this fact does not give us a free pass to live dangerously. We are to be wise as serpents. "Behold, I am sending you out as sheep in the midst of wolves, so be wise as serpents and innocent as doves" (**Matthew 10:16** ESV).

The truth we will study this week is *not about* what we can or cannot do. It is about how we *act and react* to those who persecute us. We need *not* be concerned about their threats or attempts to intimidate us. We are solely in the hands of the Sovereign God for whom nothing is a surprise or out of His control. Our life or death is for the glory of God. We must have the attitude of Paul.

3. Write **Philippians 1:20-21**.

    a. What was Paul's hope?

    b. How did Paul want Christ to be exalted in his body?

    c. What can you learn from Paul?

    d. Read **Philippians 1:22-24**.

When we share Paul's attitude, to live is Christ and to die is gain, we have a winning combination. Yet, we should be hard pressed in both directions…longing to be with Christ, but knowing there are the lost who need to be shown the light, believers in need of discipleship, and a world in need of a love like Jesus' love.

In this lesson we will study the first recorded martyr for Christ. Everything we know about Stephen, a true hero of the faith, is found in **Acts 6** and **7**. What we can learn from him is immeasurable. Luke, who penned the book of Acts, recounts the acts of the first church to Theophilus. Luke wanted Theophilus to have an accurate account of what happened in the early days of the first church. Many people are surprised to learn that the book of Acts spans from AD 32 or 33 to about AD 62 (some biblical theologians date it as late as AD 67). This gives us over thirty years of extraordinary information on how our first church loved God, fellowshipped with one another, shared the gospel, made disciples, and even how they resolved conflicts.

Although Luke wrote Acts, he did not have a firsthand account of the events until Acts 16. How did Luke have the intimate details of Stephen's death? How would Luke know Stephen said, "Lord do not hold this sin against them!" as the mob began to throw stones (**Acts 7:60**)?

4.  How do you think Luke knew the details of Stephen's death?

Ultimately the Holy Spirit led Luke to write not only about Stephen but also the entire book of Acts (**2 Peter 1:20-21**). Yet there are some interesting details that we would be remiss not to notice. Luke joined Paul, Silas, and Timothy either on their way to Macedonia or once they arrived in Macedonia (**Acts 16:10**). **Remember:** Paul, was the man who held the robes of the men who killed Stephen (**Acts 7:58-59**), and he also recounted his testimony to Luke. We will never know what Paul told Luke, but we can imagine Luke listening intently to Paul's description of his life before Christ. Paul's life was never the same once he surrendered it to the risen Christ on the Damascus road. Stephens's words, "Lord, do not hold this sin against them" must have been words Paul treasured. Yes, Paul knew only Christ could forgive sin, but to comprehend this Stephen's forgiveness also dramatically impacted Paul's life. Forgiveness is powerful, especially when you are on the receiving end!

We don't have the exact date of Stephen's martyrdom but we can narrow the window. Most biblical historians place Paul's conversion on the road to Damascus within the first two years after Christ's ascension. Stephen's death took place before Paul's conversion; therefore Stephen's murder was within the first two years of the birth of the church. As we can surmise, these believers were young in the faith and had to grow up quickly.

5.  After you became a believer in Christ, think about the first difficult situation you encountered.

    a.  How did the situation affect your spiritual life?

    b.  What factor(s) do you believe led to your spiritual growth or setback?

Let's read Stephen's story. As you read, consider Stephen's character, what is said about him, and how he acts and responds to the Sanhedrin.

6. Read **Acts 6:1-7:60**.

   a. Write your first thoughts about Stephen.

   b. How is Stephen described in **Acts 6:3-5, 8**?

   c. Why did the men rise up against Stephen (6:10)?

We have established a good foundation for our study this week and we will learn more about Stephen tomorrow, but before we close with our application questions and prayer read the testimony of Ezzat Habib, from Cairo (2005). Most Americans assume persecution, suffering, and martyrdom were restricted to the first century church, but persecution has been and always will be a part of the life of a Christ follower. For this reason, we will read about ordinary believers who gave everything to stand for Christ. These testimonies put our Christian lives in perspective; we understand no matter how difficult our paths are we have never been asked to give up our lives. We can be encouraged to stand strong in difficult moments by believers who stood strong before us.

7. As you read, consider the principles we have studied over the past eight weeks. How many of these principles did Pastor Ezzat Habib live out in his testimony?

   "The taxi's tires screeched as it careened into the street and hit Pastor Ezzat Habib, his son Ibram Habib, and a friend as they were crossing the street in Cairo. The men were thrown across the street as the taxi raced away.

   "People hurried to the scene and Ezzat was rushed to the hospital, suffering from internal bleeding and a broken skull. He underwent surgery, but it didn't help; he died the next day. The friend suffered a broken leg, and Ibram had severe bruising in his legs and persistent lower back pain.

   "While he was still stunned and in shock, the hospital had Ibram sign an incident report after his father was delivered to the hospital. He signed the report even though he was unable to read it clearly at the time. Later he saw the report was completely different than what had actually happened. The taxi driver went unpunished.

   "This was no accident. The Habib family was frequently threatened, and faced physical abuse from neighbors and from Egypt's national security police. In June 2003, Pastor Ezzat was arrested for supposedly 'disturbing the neighborhood.' He was put in an underground cell so narrow he couldn't sit down. He was physically and sexually abused by the police officers; yet he never rejected his Lord Jesus Christ.

"After being in prison for five days, an officer bandaged his eyes, chained his hands, and interrogated him. There was a police officer on each side that hit him, kicked him, and insulted his wife. He was warned to stop his Christian meetings and to forbid non-Christians from attending. The source of the abuse was clear; police knew that Pastor Habib had been sharing the gospel with Muslims; he'd been encouraging them to leave Islam and follow Jesus Christ. This could not be tolerated.

"In spite of repeated threats, Habib's congregation continued meeting. Later, two trees smashed through the windows of the Habib's apartment building. There was a man in the front yard chopping the trees with an axe. The phone line was cut, and the front door was blocked from the outside. The man claimed a police officer told him to cut down the trees.

"'Didn't I tell you to stop doing your meetings?' the officer told Habib. 'Look what is happening to you.'"[170]

Persecution led to Pastor Habib's death. His perseverance strengthened his church family and their resolve to stand firm. Habib's church can strengthen and encourage us to stand strong. Read what has been said about his church since his death:

"In spite of harassment and continued threats from police and neighbors, Ibram and the family resolved to continue the house fellowship. They had seen Pastor Habib stand firm in his faith, even unto death; they were determined to do the same."[171]

Before we close with our application questions and prayer, let's evaluate how Pastor Habib used the principles studied in *ACTs420NOW*. I know we only have a snapshot but you will still be able to see some similarities. If Pastor Habib lived out a principle in the last moments of his life under difficult circumstances, he surely lived them out in other times.

8.  As you read the principles, make a check mark by each one Pastor Ezzat Habib lived out in his life.

| Foundation or Principle | Applied or lived out |
|---|---|
| I.  *Believe* there is salvation in none other than Jesus Christ (**Acts 4:12**). | |
| II.  *Pray* you will begin to speak the Word of God with boldness (**Acts 4:31**). | |
| III.  *Pray* the gospel is "unveiled" to a lost and dying America, and world (**2 Corinthians 4:3-4**). | |
| IV.  *Humble yourself,* pray, seek, and repent to God for healing in our land (**2 Chronicles 7:14**). | |
| V.  *Persevere* by going and telling America and the world until our land is healed (**Isaiah 6:8-11**). | |
| VI.  *Love* your enemies and pray for those who persecute you (**Matthew 5:44-46**). | |
| VII. *Never compromise* your faith, even unto death (**Philippians 1:21**). | |

9.  What did you learn today that you can apply to your life? Your church? Your nation?

10. Write your prayer to the Lord. Ask Him for perseverance to finish strong. We live in difficult days and we need His divine power to be lights in a perverse generation.

*"The Lord will rescue me from every evil deed, and will bring me safely to His heavenly kingdom; to Him be the glory forever and ever. Amen."*
**2 Timothy 4:18**

# WEEK 8—DAY 2

In Day 1 we studied our concluding principle **Never compromise your faith even unto death.** Our Lord and biblical fathers have taught us we can live in victory, not fear, as our lives are in His hands. Write your prayer to the Lord. Thank Him for being the Sovereign God who is in control. Ask Him to open your heart to the truth of His Word and to help you not only to hear, but act upon the truths He has taught you throughout this study.

Yesterday we read Acts 6 and 7, the story of Stephen and his martyrdom. Now we will dig into these Scriptures to learn from Stephen, a first-century Christian, about how we should live and act as twenty-first century Christians. We will begin in **Acts 6:7**. Therefore, let us do a brief review of the first-century church to this point.

**Acts 1**—Jesus ascended to heaven and commanded the disciples to wait until the Helper, the Holy Spirit, came.

**Acts 2**—The day of Pentecost arrived, and the believers received the Holy Spirit. The multitudes heard the gospel in their own languages, and three thousand souls were added to the kingdom that day.

**Acts 3**—Peter and John, through the power of the Holy Spirit, healed a lame man by the temple. The people were amazed and Peter preached a gospel message.

**Acts 4**—Peter and John were arrested for teaching and proclaiming their power to heal came from Jesus, the Son of the Living God. The Sanhedrin warned Peter and John not to teach in Jesus' name. Their reply was, "For we cannot stop speaking about what we have seen and heard" (**Acts 4:20**). Peter and John were released and reported to their companions all that had been said. Their gathering place shook when the congregation, with Peter and John, prayed that they would speak the Word of God with boldness (**Acts 4:31**).

**Acts 5**—Again the Sanhedrin arrested Peter and the apostles and put them in the jail. The angel of the Lord opened the jail and Peter and the apostles were told to go to the temple to preach. The apostles were reprimanded before the council, "We gave you strict orders not to continue teaching in this name, and behold you have filled Jerusalem with your teaching and intend to bring this man's blood upon us" (v.28). Peter responded, "We must obey God rather than men" (v. 29). After the council flogged them, Peter and the apostles went their way rejoicing because they were considered worthy to suffer shame for Christ's name (v. 41). The apostles continued to teach daily in the temple and from house to house (v. 42).

**Acts 6**—In **Acts 6:1-6** a conflict arose within the congregation about neglecting the daily serving of food for the Hellenistic Jewish widows. Seven men were chosen to oversee the task in order for the apostles to devote themselves to prayer and ministry of the Word of God. Stephen, a man full of faith and the Holy Spirit, was one of the seven chosen.

11. Read **Acts 6:7-15.**

    a.  What was happening in Jerusalem during this time (v. 7)?

        ❖

        ❖

        ❖

    b.  What was Stephen doing during this time?

    c.  Who rose up and argued with Stephen?

    d.  Where were the Freedmen from?

        ❖

        ❖

        ❖

        ❖

**Note:** The Synagogue of Freedmen members were "composed of Jews who were either formerly Roman slaves or the free children of Jewish slaves."[172] Although speculation, many believe Saul of Tarsus worshiped in the Synagogue of Freedmen, since the Synagogue of Freedmen included those from Asia-Minor (modern-day Turkey). This would be a logical conclusion since Tarsus was/is located in Asia-Minor.

Another interesting side note: Mark Antony and Cleopatra met in Tarsus, then committed suicide there in August, 30 BC after being defeated by Octavian's forces at the Battle of Actium. Octavian was then considered ruler of Rome. Some years later, Octavian was awarded the title Augustus, meaning *revered*. Octavian, Caesar Augustus was the same Caesar mentioned in Luke 2 who was emperor of Rome when Jesus was born. Caesar Augustus reigned until his death in AD 14. Information intertwining biblical history with ancient world history can be so interesting. Many people who never question ancient world history try to present biblical history as a myth or fable. When the two histories intertwine it gives authenticity to biblical history doubters have difficulty refuting. It also gives believers time references for the events we read about in God's Word. This helps us put the pieces together so we can see God's masterpiece.

Before we travel too far from our study let's return to Acts 6.

    e.  With what were the men in the Synagogue of Freedmen unable to cope from Stephen (v. 10)?

Stephen's name was Greek (as were the other six who were chosen to look after the widows); therefore, he was probably a Hellenistic Jew. Since the Synagogue of Freedmen was a Hellenistic synagogue, these men were most likely well acquainted with Stephen.[173]

    f.   What did those in the Freedmen synagogue do (v. 11)?

    g.   Where was Stephen dragged?

Jesus stood in front of this same council days before He was crucified, and we know Peter and John stood before them in **Acts 4:15** and **Acts 5:27-28**. Stephen clearly understood the ramifications of what could happen.

    h.   What were the accusations that were brought before Stephen?
- ❖ (v. 11)
- ❖ (v. 11)
- ❖ (v. 13)
- ❖ (v. 13)

    i.   How did Stephen appear to the council?

As we move into Acts 7, we need to consider these Scriptures through Jewish eyes. Most of us are Gentiles; therefore, this might be a challenge! We will do an overview and a brief outline of the verses. Then tomorrow we will study probing questions to learn the importance of what Stephen was communicating. As you read the verses, think about what is being said to the council. Ask yourself questions such as, "Why did Stephen choose to speak about these particular patriarchs?" Ask the Lord for wisdom which only He can give. By the time we finish our study on Acts 7 you will be amazed at Stephen's ability to masterfully communicate his message.

12. Read Acts 7, as you work through the sections, write a synopsis in the *Notes* space. We will use the additional space in question 3.

| Section and Notes | Question 3 Section |
|---|---|
| Acts 7:1-8 | |
| Acts 7:9-18 | |
| Acts 7:19-44 | |
| Acts 7:45 | |
| Acts 7:46 | |
| Acts 7:47 | |
| Acts 7:48-50 | |
| Acts 7:51-54 | |

| Section and Notes | Question 3 Section |
|---|---|
| Acts 7:55-60 | |

13. This is where we need to put on our Jewish thinking caps! In the **Question 3 section** above, write the name of the main character mentioned in the verses.

    a. After each name, write why you believe Stephen spoke about that particular patriarch.

    b. Review each segment. What message was Stephen communicating about God's relationship with the patriarch?

If you're having trouble with your Jewish thinking cap, don't worry, there is more to discover about Stephen's message to the Sanhedrin. We will study in Acts 7 again tomorrow. Before we close with our application questions and prayer, read about William Swinderby (1401) from *Foxe: Voices of the Martyrs*. As you read, consider the principles we have studied over the past eight weeks. How many of these principles does William Swinderby live out in his testimony?

John Wycliffe began the trouble. He claimed the Bible taught what the church did not, and the church taught what the Bible did not. In 1380, Wycliffe translated the first Bible from Latin into English. Others followed who called themselves Lollards. They read, studied, and preached a faith that sought genuine conversion and renewal from old forms and rituals, deposits from the past encrusted with residue of power and privilege. A stroke took Wycliffe's life in 1384. Forty-four years after John Wycliffe died, the Pope ordered his bones to be exhumed and burned.

But other Lollards carried on. William Swinderby was reputed to be among their ablest preachers, thus also one of Wycliffe's most dangerous protégés. Of his work little is known, except that his effectiveness and lack of conformity drew the attention of church officials five years after Wycliffe's death. Swinderby was a priest in the Lincoln diocese when a board of examiners found his teaching outrageous and ordered him to never speak again, lest the dry wood they had carried to the examination be used to reduce his body to ashes.

Such threats would quickly silence most men, but Swinderby kept talking and teaching. In 1392 another order was issued against this persistent priest, this time by King Richard II. Swinderby was apprehended, questioned, and found wrong on matters of baptism, church policy, governance, salvation and the sacraments.

Records indicate that nine years passed between this second arrest and Swinderby's torturous death at the stake in London in 1401. What happened during those years one cannot tell, but the final chapter of his life shows that Swinderby's heart and mind were convinced that the Bible was intended to be the Christian's foundational document, that its way of salvation—God's mercy expressed in personal faith—was the Christian's hope. He surrendered neither that hope nor his integrity nor conscience during his long testing and confinement. And when his day of pain came, it was a small price for the reward of a faithful life and the sure hope of life to come.[174]

Let's evaluate how William Swinderby used the principles studied in *ACTs420NOW*. Again we only have a snapshot but you will still be able to see some similarities.

14. As you read the principles, make a check mark by each one William Swinderby lived out in his life.

| Foundation or Principle | Applied or lived out |
|---|---|
| I. *Believe* there is salvation in none other than Jesus Christ (**Acts 4:12**). | |
| II. *Pray* you will begin to speak the Word of God with boldness (**Acts 4:31**). | |
| III. *Pray* the gospel is "unveiled" to a lost and dying America, and world (**2 Corinthians 4:3-4**). | |
| IV. *Humble yourself*, pray, seek, and repent to God for healing in our land (**2 Chronicles 7:14**). | |
| V. *Persevere* by going and telling America and the world until our land is healed (**Isaiah 6:8-11**). | |
| VI. *Love* your enemies and pray for those who persecute you (**Matthew 5:44-46**). | |
| VII. ***Never** compromise* your faith, even unto death (**Philippians 1:21**). | |

15. What did you learn today that you can apply to your life? Your church? Your nation?

16. Write your prayer to the Lord. Ask Him for perseverance to finish strong. We live in difficult days and we have His divine power to be lights in a perverse generation.

*"Now to Him who is able to keep you from stumbling, and to make you stand in the presence of His glory blameless with great joy, to the only God our Savior, through Jesus Christ our Lord, be glory, majesty, dominion and authority, before all time and now and forever. Amen."*

***Jude 1:24-25***

# WEEK 8—DAY 3

Today, we will conclude our study on Stephen. We have seen this man, who was chosen to make sure the widows weren't overlooked in the daily serving of food, was a bold witness for Christ. After all, why would the council have been upset at feeding the elderly? The accusations against Stephen were "speaking blasphemous words against Moses and against God" (**Acts 6:11**) and bringing false witness against the holy place and the law (**Acts 6:13**). In today's culture Stephen's words would be called hate speech. Stephen teaches us no matter what our *job* might be we can passionately present a powerful case for Christ. As you write your prayer, thank the Lord for placing you in a position to proclaim His message. Thank Him for the opportunity to make an impact in this fallen world.

Yesterday we studied Stephen's message through Jewish eyes. Today we will discover what Stephen, a Jewish believer in Christ as Messiah, taught to the non-believing, non-Christ-following Sanhedrin. Reading Stephen's oration, one might assume he was giving a history lesson to the Sanhedrin to convince them that the accusations of blasphemy made against him were false. But what core message was Stephen trying to communicate? Let's find out.

1. Read **Acts 7:1-8**.

   a. How did Stephen address the council (v. 2)?

Note: *Brethren* was a common reference given to fellow Israelites, and *fathers* was a term of respect for the older members of the council. Stephen was setting the tone with a respectful greeting.

   b. Where was Abraham living when God appeared to him (v. 2)?

   c. If the Israelites (Jews) spoke of someone who came from Mesopotamia, how would a Jewish person contrast this foreigner with himself?

If you weren't able to answer the question, don't worry; most of us are not trained in Jewish thinking. In biblical times, the Greeks categorized people into two groups: Greeks and barbarians. Regardless of where you lived, if you were not born a Greek, you were a barbarian. This was also the mindset of the Israelites—people were either Jews or Gentiles. Stephen was emphasizing to the Sanhedrin that Abraham was a Gentile when God called him out of his circumstance.

d. How would one describe the birth of Isaac to a 100-year-old father and a 90-year-old mother?

e. When God rescued Abraham's people from bondage what did they do (v. 7)?

f. Think about the message Stephen was communicating to the Sanhedrin. To whom might Stephen have been comparing Abraham?

Once Stephen greeted his *brethren*, he immediately pointed out God's call to Abraham—the divine God with a divine invitation to a Gentile in a foreign land.[175] This invitation included a promise from a gracious and loving God of an inheritance based on a miracle birth for a people who were called out of a pagan culture. If you didn't know we were talking about Abraham, one might think we were talking about Jesus! This is the exact message Stephen was communicating to the Sanhedrin. He wanted them to see the pictures God had painted for them throughout their Jewish history. Each example Stephen presented points to similarities between the Jewish patriarch (Abraham), Jesus Christ, and the gospel.

One principle I have learned over my years of teaching the Bible is a teacher needs to communicate in a language the students can understand. This was how Stephen was speaking. His audience of scholarly Jewish men were trained in the *Tanak*, or *Masoretic Text*. The **TaNaK** stands for:

- ❖ *Torah*—the first five books of the Bible—Genesis through Deuteronomy

- ❖ *Nabiy'*—the Hebrew word for prophets—books like Isaiah, Jeremiah, and Daniel

- ❖ *Ketuvim*—the Hebrew word for writings—books like Psalms, Proverbs, and Esther.

This is how the Jewish manuscript is organized. Even though the books are not in the exact order as the Jewish text, Christians know these same books as the Old Testament. Stephen's speech in Acts 7 is one of the longest presentations given in the New Testament. His speech is longer than any Paul gave to kings or common people. Although Stephen presented a masterful argument, he had to have intricate knowledge of the *Tanak* himself.

**Bible study tip of the week**: When you are studying a message addressed to a particular audience, try to learn everything you can about that audience. This will help you understand the message being communicated. Examples: Think about whether the message is to a Jewish audience, a Gentile audience, a believer or unbeliever. Is the audience receptive or resistant to the message?

Now that you are better skilled at wearing your Jewish thinking cap, it might be easier to discern Stephen's message regarding Joseph, our next biblical figure.

2. Read **Acts 7:9-19**.

   a. Think about the time Joseph's brothers sold him into slavery. Write one word to describe what Joseph's brothers did to him.

You may have used a different word but the meaning would be similar. The word which first comes to my mind is rejected.

   b. In contrast, after Joseph's brothers rejected him, he found favor in the sight of Pharaoh. What word would you use to describe the favor of Pharaoh that contrasts with rejected?

   c. When Joseph's brothers came to Egypt for grain, at what point did they recognize Joseph (7:13)?

   d. How would you compare Joseph's events with those of Jesus?

Steven Ger writes in *The Book of ACTS: Witnesses To The World*:

> "Although Joseph had been rejected by his own family, he had been accepted by foreigners in a foreign land and exalted by God's hand … [T]he rejected one, now exalted, becomes the savior of those who had rejected him … [T]he patriarchs did not recognize their brother the first time that they saw him. The sons of Israel only perceived that their own brother was their savior on his second appearance before them. The parallel Stephen drew is clearly seen. The first time the descendants of the sons of Israel saw Jesus, they likewise did not recognize Him. Unfortunately, the vast majority of the Jewish people will not perceive that Jesus is their Messiah until His glory is eminently manifest upon His return."[176]

**Note:** Like Jesus, Joseph found acceptance from foreigners (Gentiles).

3. Read **Acts 7:20-40**.

   a. What did the Israelites say to Moses when he tried to reconcile the two men fighting (v. 27)?

   b. What did Moses believe the Israelites understood (v. 25)?

   c. Did the children of Israel understand Moses was to be their deliverer (v. 25)?

d. What does verse 35 tell us about how Israel treated Moses?

e. God sent Moses to be both _____ and _____ over Israel (v. 35).

f. What did Moses perform in Egypt (v. 36)?

g. What did Moses tell the Israelites in verse 37?

h. Who do you believe the prophet from verse 37 to be?

i. What theme did Stephen repeat to the Sanhedrin? When was Moses recognized as deliverer and judge?

j. Compare the events that happened to Moses with Jesus.

k. Place a check mark next to the statements you believe are true of both Moses and Jesus.

| Comparison of Moses with Jesus | | |
| --- | --- | --- |
| Statement | Moses | Jesus |
| ❖ Raised to be prince (Prince of Egypt) (Prince of Peace)<br>❖ Mission was to be redeemer<br>❖ Went to his own people<br>❖ Was not recognized the first time by his people<br>❖ Rejected by his own people<br>❖ Went away for a time<br>❖ Returned/returning a second time to be deliverer | | |

Let's read what Steven Ger has to say about Stephen's statements about Moses:

"As in the account of Joseph and his brothers, it was not until Moses' second appearance to the Jewish people that they finally recognized Moses' authority as God's agent of redemption. The rejected one, now exalted, had become the deliverer of those who had rejected him.

Stephen's insinuation was that history was once again repeating itself. Israel had held true to the established pattern of not immediately recognizing their own [S]avior, Jesus, too, was disowned by [H]is people (Acts 3:13) although He was appointed by God to be the ultimate "ruler and judge," not just of Israel, but of the world (Acts 10:42;17:31). As with Joseph and Moses, when

Israel sees Jesus at His second appearing, the rejected one, now exalted, will become the deliverer of those who had rejected [H]im."[177]

Isn't God's Word fascinating! When one starts to truly understand the message God presented through His Word, one must stand in awe at the masterpiece He gave us, the Holy Bible. The sixty-six books of the Bible took 1400 to 1800 years to write, with 66 books by more than 40 authors; and every word is inspired by God (**2 Timothy 3:16, 2 Peter 1:20-21**). The message is the same from Genesis to Revelation. God sent His Son, Jesus, to redeem people for Himself. Jesus appeared once for salvation (deliverer) and will return one day to reign (judge).

4.  Read **Acts 7:41-44**.

    a.  What did the Israelites in Moses' time choose to worship?

    b.  How did the reminder of idol worship relate to Stephen's overall message to the Sanhedrin?

5.  Read **Acts 7:45-50**.

    a.  Where did Stephen say God, the Most High, dwells?

    b.  Knowing that God "does not dwell in a temple made with human hands" (**Acts 7:48**), how do you think Stephen was defending himself against the accusation that he was blaspheming against the holy place (temple) (**Acts 6:13**)?

    c.  How does this relate to Stephen's gospel presentation?

6.  Reread **Acts 6:11-13**.

    a.  List the four targets of Stephen's "blasphemous" statements.

        ❖

        ❖

        ❖

        ❖

b.   Make a check mark next to the topic(s) Stephen addressed in **Acts 7:1-50**.


The Greek word for *blasphemous* in **Acts 6:11** is *blasph mía,* meaning *blasphemy, abuse against someone. Denotes the very worst type of slander, mentioned in Matthew 15:19 with false witness; wounding one's reputation, by evil reports, evil speaking.*[178] The Lord spoke to Moses in **Leviticus 24:16** saying, "Moreover, the one who blasphemes the name of the Lord shall surely be put to death; all the congregations shall certainly stone him." The accusations that were brought before the Sanhedrin against Stephen were a death sentence and he understood what was at stake.


c.   From the facts you have read and studied in Acts 7, did Stephen bring false witness against Moses or God?


d.   Did Stephen wound Moses' or God's reputation?


e.   Returning to question 6a, beside each bullet, write a short synopsis what Stephen's testimony in each category.


Let's read what Steven Ger writes about Stephen's remarks on the temple.

> In no way does Stephen's sermon provide support for the false accusation of his having threatened the Temple. Stephen did not reject Temple worship but simply argued that the Temple must be held in proper perspective. Just as Tabernacle worship had been divinely instituted and yet replaced, with God's sanction, by Temple worship, the possibility existed that the Temple might also be an impermanent institution. Since the biblical record teaches that God's program changes and develops over time, at some point God might have other plans. The uncomfortable question Stephen raised was whether or not the nation of Israel would be alert when God instituted those plans.[179]

When God instructed Moses to build the tent of meeting in the wilderness, God used it as a foreshadowing of a future truth. Stephen was trying to open the eyes of the Sanhedrin by showing them just as God took the Jewish people from meeting in a tent in the wilderness to meeting in a tabernacle, God just might have a better plan. Everything God did in the Old Testament pointed to the coming Messiah and the tent of meetings/tabernacle was not any different.

7. Look at the chart. Notice how the tabernacle itself was built to show Jesus as the Messiah and read the scriptures which were used.

| Tabernacle | Jesus |
|---|---|
| Entrance—There was only one entrance into the tent of meetings. | "Truly, truly, I say to you, he who does not enter by the door into the fold of the sheep, but climbs up some other way, he is a thief and a robber" (**John 10:1**).<br><br>"So Jesus said to them again, 'Truly, truly, I say to you, I am the door of the sheep'"(**John 10:7**).<br><br>"I am the door; if anyone enters through Me, he will be saved . . ." (**John 10:9**). |
| **Bronze Altar**—The bronze altar was located in the front courtyard. Animal scarifies were burnt on the altar and showed Israelites for sinful man to approach a holy God they needed to be cleansed by the blood of an innocent animal. For a sin offering, a person had to bring an animal—a male one without blemish or defect—to the priest at the tabernacle gate. The Hebrew root for altar means *to slaughter. This verb is used primarily to describe the killing of animals for sacrifices.*[180] | ". . . knowing that you were not redeemed with perishable things like silver or gold from your futile way of life inherited from your forefathers, but with precious blood, as of a lamb unblemished and spotless, the blood of Christ" (**1 Peter 1:18-19**).<br><br>"For God so loved the world, that He gave His only begotten Son, that whoever believes in Him shall not perish, but have eternal life" (**John 3:16**). |
| **Bronze Laver**—The laver was a large bowl filled with water located halfway between the brazen altar and the Holy Place. The priests were to wash their hands and their feet in it before entering the Holy Place. The laver reminded the people they needed cleansing before approaching God. | "Christ also loved the church and gave Himself up for her, so that He might sanctify her, having cleansed her by the washing of water with the word, that He might present to Himself the church in all her glory, having no spot or wrinkle or any such thing; but that she would be holy and blameless" (**Ephesians 5:25b-27**).<br><br>"Let us draw near with a sincere heart in full assurance of faith, having our hearts sprinkled *clean* from an evil conscience and our bodies washed with pure water" (**Hebrews 10:22**). |
| **The Lampstand**—The lampstand was placed at the left side of the Holy Place. The lampstand had a central branch from which three branches extended from each side, forming a total of seven branches. Each branch looked like that of an almond tree, containing buds, blossoms and flowers. The lamp was to burn continuously and was the only light in the Holy Place. The lampstand illuminated the Holy Place and allowed the priests to fellowship with God and intercedes on behalf of Israel. | "In Him was life, and the life was the Light of men. The Light shines in the darkness, and the darkness did not comprehend it" (**John 1:4-5**).<br><br>"There was the true Light which, coming into the world, enlightens every man" (**John1:9**).<br><br>"Then Jesus again spoke to them, saying, "I am the Light of the world; he who follows Me will not walk in the darkness, but will have the Light of life" (**John 8:12**). |

| Tabernacle | Jesus |
|---|---|
| **Table of Showbread**—Each week the priest would bake twelve loaves of bread, which represented the twelve tribes of Israel. The table symbolized a place where God could "break bread" or fellowship with man, expressing God's willingness to enter into fellowship (a relationship) with man. The fact that the priest would place twelve new loaves each week illustrated God's open hand and never ending grace to extend fellowship to man. | "I am the bread of life. Your fathers ate the manna in the wilderness, and they died. This is the bread which comes down out of heaven, so that one may eat of it and not die" (**John 6:48-50**). |
| **Altar of Incense**—This altar sat in front of the curtain that separated the Holy Place from the Holy of Holies. God commanded the priests to burn incense on the golden altar every morning and evening. The incense was to be left burning continually throughout the day and night as a pleasing aroma to the Lord.<br>The incense was a symbol of the prayers and intercession of the people going up to God as a sweet fragrance. God wanted His dwelling to be a place where people could approach Him and pray to Him. | "Therefore He is able also to save forever those who draw near to God through Him, since He always lives to make intercession for them" (**Hebrews 7:25**).<br><br>"Another angel came and stood at the altar, holding a golden censer; and much incense was given to him, so that he might add it to the prayers of all the saints on the golden altar which was before the throne. And the smoke of the incense, with the prayers of the saints, went up before God out of the angel's hand" (**Revelation 8:3-4**). |
| **Veil**—The veil was a curtain between the Holy Place and the Holy of Holies. The high priest could only enter the Holy of Holies once a year on the Day of Atonement. Once inside the priest would enter into the very presence of God. The veil was placed there to remind Israel that there was a barrier between man and God and they needed a High Priest to make intercession for them. | "And behold, the veil of the temple was torn in two from top to bottom; and the earth shook and the rocks were split" (**Matthew 27:51**). |
| **Holy Place** - Within the Holy Place of the tabernacle, there was an inner room called the Holy of Holies, or the Most Holy Place. No ordinary person could enter this place. It was God's special dwelling place in the midst of His people. During the Israelites' wanderings in the wilderness, God appeared as a pillar of cloud or fire in and above the Holy of Holies.<br>Even as the high priest entered the Holy of Holies on the Day of Atonement, he had to make some meticulous preparations: he had to wash himself, put on special clothing, bring burning incense to let the smoke cover his eyes from a direct view of God, and bring blood with him to make atonement for sins. | "For Christ did not enter a holy place made with hands, a mere copy of the true one, but into heaven itself, now to appear in the presence of God for us; nor was it that He would offer Himself often, as the high priest enters the holy place year by year with blood that is not his own. Otherwise, He would have needed to suffer often since the foundation of the world; but now once at the consummation of the ages He has been manifested to put away sin by the sacrifice of Himself" (**Hebrews 9:24-26**).<br><br>"Therefore, brethren, since we have confidence to enter the holy place by the blood of Jesus, by a new and living way which He inaugurated for us through the veil, that is, His flesh, and since we have a great priest over the house of God . . ." (**Hebrews 10:19-21**). |

| Tabernacle | Jesus |
|---|---|
| **Ark of the Covenant**—Behind the veil in the Holy of Holies, shielded from the eye of the common man, was the Ark of the Covenant and "mercy seat" on top of it. God commanded Moses to put in the ark three items: a golden pot of manna, Aaron's staff that had budded, and the two stone tablets on which the Ten Commandments were written.<br><br>The atonement cover was the lid for the ark. On top of it stood two cherubim at the two ends, facing each other. The cherubim, symbols of God's divine presence and power, were facing downward toward the ark with outstretched wings that covered the atonement cover. This is where God dwelled in the tabernacle. It was His throne. | "So Jesus was saying to those Jews who had believed Him, 'If you continue in My word, then you are truly disciples of Mine; and you will know the truth, and the truth will make you free.' They answered Him, 'We are Abraham's descendants and have never yet been enslaved to anyone; how is it that You say, 'You will become free?'" (**John 8:30-33**).<br><br>"Therefore I said to you that you will die in your sins; for unless you believe that I am He, you will die in your sins" (**John 8:24**).<br><br>"Jesus said to them, 'Truly, truly, I say to you, before Abraham was born, I am'" (**John 8:58**).<br><br>"By this will we have been sanctified through the offering of the body of Jesus Christ once for all. Every priest stands daily ministering and offering time after time the same sacrifices, which can never take away sins; but He, having offered one sacrifice for sins for all time, sat down at the right hand of God, waiting from that time onward until His enemies be made a footstool for His feet. For by one offering He has perfected for all time those who are sanctified" (**Hebrews 10:10-14**). |

There are no accidents in God's Word. His Word amazes me because Genesis connects to Revelation and every book in between. His Word is living and breathing, intricately prepared and crafted over 1400 years to perfectly fit together to tell God's story of love, grace, and redemption.

Let's return to Stephen and Acts 6 and 7.

8. Fill in the chart with how Stephen is described in each verse. Then we will finish the remainder of Acts 7.

| | |
|---|---|
| **Acts 6:3** | |
| **Acts 6:5** | |
| **Acts 6:8** | |
| **Acts 6:10** | |
| **Acts 6:15** | |
| **Acts 7:55** | |

9.  Read **Acts 7:51-60**.

    a.  How did Stephen describe the council (v. 51)?

        ❖

        ❖

        ❖

    b.  Who did Stephen say they had become (v. 52)?

    c.  What did the fathers do? What action did they take?

    d.  How did the fathers receive the law (v. 53)?

    e.  How did the fathers treat the law (v. 53)?

    f.  How did the council/crowd react to Stephens's presentation (v. 54)?

    g.  What did Stephen see (v. 55)?

    h.  What did Stephen say to the crowd (v. 56)?

    i.  How did the crowd respond to Stephens's statement (vv. 57-58)?

---

### Question to Ponder

How is the crowd's response to Stephen any different from our culture's response to a Christian worldview today?

---

I wonder if Stephen knew what was to happen when he saw heaven open up and Jesus standing at the right hand of God. Did he did comprehend the impending events; did he care? **Acts 7:55** tells us Stephen saw the glory of God! Then Stephen called upon the Lord and asked Him to, "Receive my spirit!" (**Acts 7:59**). Stephen could have asked the Lord to stop the attackers, or prevent his death, yet we learn he did neither.

10. Write Stephen's final two statements from **Acts 7:59-60**.

These are powerful words from a man who was moments from his earthly death. In Day 1 this week the statement was made, "This week is not about what we can or cannot do. It is about how we act and react to those who are persecuting us." What did you learn from Stephen about how to act and react to those who are persecuting us?

*ACTs420NOW* is a study on how we as believers of Jesus Christ need to act/react to a world that is increasingly intolerant to Christian's and our beliefs. Our faith is grounded on the principle *believe there is salvation in none other than Jesus Christ.* Over the past seven weeks we have studied one principle each week, each built upon the previous week. Before we close with our application questions and prayer, let's evaluate how closely Stephen used the principles studied in *ACTs420NOW*.

11. As you read the principles, make a check mark by each one Stephen lived out in his life.

| Foundation or Principle | Stephen applied or lived out |
|---|---|
| I. *Believe* there is salvation in none other than Jesus Christ (**Acts 4:12**). | |
| II. *Pray* you will begin to speak the Word of God with boldness (**Acts 4:31**). | |
| III. *Pray* the gospel is "unveiled" to a lost and dying America, and world (**2 Corinthians 4:3-4**). | |
| IV. *Humble yourself*, pray, seek, and repent to God for healing in our land (**2 Chronicles 7:14**). | |
| V. *Persevere* by going and telling America and the world until our land is healed (**Isaiah 6:8-11**). | |
| VI. *Love* your enemies and pray for those who persecute you (**Matthew 5:44-46**). | |
| VII. *Never compromise* your faith, even unto death (**Philippians 1:21**). | |

**Remember:** We only have a very small snapshot of Stephen's life. Yet, by this brief testimony God has allowed us to witness, we can see these principles were an important part of his spiritual tenets as a believer.

We, like Stephen, must not only read and understand the principles God outlines in His Word for a *successful* life as a believer, we **must choose** to live them out. Success in God's eyes is determined very differently than in the world's eyes. As Stephen entered into the gates of heaven, I'm sure he was welcomed by the words, "Welcome home, My good and faithful servant, you have labored hard, enter into your eternal rest" (**Matthew 25:23**). This too must be our life's desire. We must push away the voices of the world and choose to live for eternity,

ACTs420NOW

knowing that only the Master knows when we will enter into our eternal rest.

Read Lizzie Atwater's (1900) personal account just before she saw her Lord face-to-face.

> "In June 1900, a fierce nationalist reaction in China against Christian missionaries and churches claimed more than 32,000 lives. The worst massacres occurred in the northern province of Shanxi. The pregnant Lizzie Atwater wrote a memorable letter home before she and six others were martyred.
>
> > Dear ones. I long for a sight of your dear faces, but I fear we shall not meet on Earth. I am preparing for the end very quietly and calmly. The Lord is wonderfully near, and He will not fail me. I was very restless and excited while there seemed a chance of life, but God has taken away that feeling, and now I just pray for grace to meet the terrible end bravely. The pain will soon be over, and oh the sweetness of the welcome above! My little baby will go with me. I think God will give it to me in heaven and my dear mother will be so glad to see us. I cannot imagine the Savior's welcome. Oh, that will compensate for all these days of suspense. Dear ones, live near to God and cling less closely to Earth. There is no other way by which we can receive that peace from God which passeth understanding. I must keep calm and still these hours. I do not regret coming to China.
>
> On August 15, 1900, soldiers took Lizzie and ten others away from the relative safety of a nearby town and hacked them to death with their swords, tossing the bodies into a pit."[181]

12. What have you learned from Stephen to apply to your life? Your church? Your nation?

13. Write your closing prayer to the Lord. Ask Him to give you strength to be obedient to the call of Christ, no matter what.

*"For if while we were enemies we were reconciled to God through the death of His Son, much more, having been reconciled, we shall be saved by His life."*
**Romans 5:10**

# WEEK 8—DAY 4

Today, as we finish our study on William Tyndale, I pray the story of his life has encouraged, challenged, and taught you in the ways of the Lord. Christians need to learn from more godly examples like Tyndale. Write your prayer to the Lord. Ask Him to give you a passion, as He did for Tyndale, for the purpose to which He has called you.

Let's review what we've studied. We will add more information on Martin Luther and William Tyndale at the end of today's lesson.

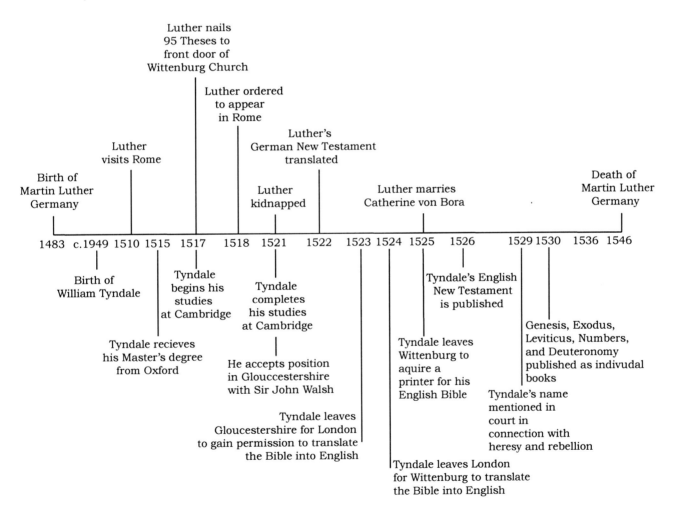

There is so much left to examine in the life of William Tyndale. Read the important and interesting facts listed, before we delve into Tyndale's final days.

## 1529–

- ❖ Sir Thomas More's four-volume work, *Dialogue Concerning Heresies,* attacked both Tyndale and Luther.
- ❖ King Henry VIII began to seek a papal annulment from his first wife, Queen Catherine, in order to marry Anne Boleyn.
- ❖ Pope Clement sidestepped the church's responsibility by signing a treaty stating that with Queen Catherine's willing consent, the annulment would be granted, a request to which Queen Catherine would never agree.

## 1530–

- ❖ Persecution of the reformed church increased. Little or no evidence was needed for an arrest.
- ❖ A man was arrested for believing the church service should be spoken in English rather than Latin.
- ❖ Tyndale wrote *The Practice of Prelates,* which concluded that the marriage between King Henry and Queen Catherine could not be dissolved in the eyes of God.
- ❖ *The Practice of Prelates* was banned in England.
- ❖ King Henry denounced Tyndale's writings, *The Parable of the Wicked Mammon* and *The Obedience of the Christian Man,* demanding all copies of the books be relinquished to the church and burned within fifteen days.
- ❖ "Holy Roman Emperor Charles V ordered all copies of the New Testament in any language to be surrendered and the printing of them stopped. Convicted heretics were regularly condemned to death either by sword, fire, or live burial."[182]
- ❖ In November, King Henry VIII invited Tyndale back to England and offered him several good appointments and a seat on the king's council.

## 1531–

- ❖ Tyndale refused the offer of the king, believing it to be a trap. It was reported that Tyndale would agree to return to England, even if it meant his death, if the English translation of the Bible would be printed and distributed to the public.
- ❖ Tyndale completed *Answer unto Sir T. Mores [sic] Dialogue.*
- ❖ In August Thomas Bilney was burned at the stake for possessing a Tyndale New Testament.
- ❖ In December Richard Bayfield was burned at the stake for possessing a Tyndale New Testament.

## 1532–

- ❖ In July John Frith, a personal advisor and friend of Tyndale's, was burned at the stake for heresy.

Tyndale was attacked from all sides and most of those who were martyred for offenses against the church were friends and colleagues from Tyndale's time at Cambridge. Tyndale's willing pursuit of God's calling on his life was proving dangerous. He made a conscious decision to pursue his passion for translating God's Word over his personal safety.

Tyndale trusted God to care for him in that dangerous environment. He understood these teachings of David, "The days that were ordained for me, when as yet there was not one of them" (**Psalm 139:16**). David, too, had been placed in extremely dangerous situations and knew God was the One who would sustain him or carry him to his eternal home. Both Tyndale and David knew they could not add or subtract one day from their earthly body. Their days had already been determined before time. Therefore, they fearlessly went about the work to which their Lord had called them.

I'm sure Tyndale also knew **2 Corinthians 4:7-12** well. "But we have this treasure in earthen vessels, so that the surpassing greatness of the power will be of God and not from ourselves; we are afflicted in every way, but not crushed; perplexed, but not despairing; persecuted, but not forsaken; struck down, but not destroyed; always carrying about in the body the dying of Jesus, so that the life of Jesus also may be manifested in our body. For we who live are constantly being delivered over to death for Jesus' sake, so that the life of Jesus also may be manifested in our mortal flesh. So death works in us, but life in you."

Tyndale's power was from God and not himself; despite his persecution, Christ was manifested through his work. Tyndale's death to his own flesh was giving the life of Christ to the English-speaking common man.

By 1532 William Tyndale had become an official target of King Henry VIII and the king would use the church to fulfill his purpose. The offer to Tyndale from King Henry for an appointment and a seat on his council was officially rescinded. From that moment on, the king was determined to arrest Tyndale. Tyndale, aware of the king's obsession, was busy refining the English New Testament translation and fervently working on many of the Old Testament books. By this time he had completed "Jonah, Joshua, Judges, Ruth, 1 and 2 Samuel, 1 and 2 Kings, as well as 1 and 2 Chronicles. Perhaps he sensed time was running out."[183]

While the king zealously worked to weaken the power of the church, he still used the English church for his purposes. New laws kept the payments for dispensations, indulgences, and other services in England rather than sending them to Rome. Finally, in May of 1532, the church in England officially broke ties with the Roman Catholic Church. The king's motivation was solely to control all matters, especially the money. However, William Tyndale and his influence were *not* under the king's control; therefore, he employed the assistance of the church officials in England to "handle" Tyndale.

In 1533 Christopher von Endhoven, publisher of Tyndale's work since 1526, was in prison for selling the New Testament, and he remained there until his death. His wife was given the task of overseeing the fourth edition of Tyndale's New Testament. Because Mrs. Von Endhoven did not speak English, she hired a Cambridge graduate, George Joye, to oversee the English translation of the New Testament. Joye greatly overestimated his abilities and Tyndale was embarrassed with this edition. Tyndale hurriedly wrote an eight-page prologue to the Testament explaining many of the serious errors and apologizing for the numerous grammatical errors.

Tyndale's knowledge of Greek had vastly improved since his first translation of the New Testament. This was his motivation for updating the New Testament. In the updated version Tyndale made more than 5,000 changes to make it closer to the original language. This compounded Tyndale's disappointment in the edition Joye oversaw.

Despite the many issues, the revised version of Tyndale's New Testament made its way to England in 1534. The climate in England had changed. Many leaders who had sought to destroy Tyndale had died or been replaced in office. This left Tyndale hopeful that soon the English New Testament could be read openly without fear of persecution. He could not have been more wrong. More than half of the Old Testament remained untranslated but Tyndale was steadfast to finish.

In 1535 an English businessman, Thomas Poyntz, and a few of his friends became staunch supporters of Tyndale. For the first time since Tyndale's childhood, he was living a comfortable life in Antwerp. He had more than enough funds to support himself, purchase resources, and pay assistants. There were even funds to print and distribute the English translations as well as Tyndale's books.

One day Tyndale brought a young Englishman, Henry Phillips, to dinner with Thomas Poyntz. Tyndale also showed Phillips his many manuscripts, books, and other theological secrets. Once Phillips left their company Thomas Poyntz quickly questioned Tyndale about Henry Phillips. Tyndale "answered he was an honest man, handsomely learned and very comfortable [i.e. Lutheran in sympathy]."[184] Assuming Tyndale had met Phillips through a friend; Poyntz dropped the conversation and did not question Tyndale further.

Phillips offered to buy Tyndale's dinner one evening. Phillips put Tyndale in front of him as they came to a narrow passageway, and at the opening two officers apprehended Tyndale. They whisked him off to a castle in Vilford near Antwerp. "The exact date of Tyndale's abduction is not known, but the best estimates place it on or about May 21, 1535."[185] He was held at the castle on charges of heresy.

Henry Phillips was his enemy all along. He was hired by the Roman Catholic officials in England and paid a large sum of money to track down reformers, especially Tyndale. He was also promised greater rewards upon their capture.

Of course Poyntz went to Tyndale's defense. Yet time after time Poyntz's pleas for Tyndale's release were denied. "Though the outcome of most heresy trials was a forgone conclusion, it was still important to the Roman Catholic establishment to maintain the appearance of fairness. In order for their eventual victory to be convincing, they had to give William Tyndale a real chance to defend himself . . . The guilt or innocence of William Tyndale turned not so much on what he had said or done, but on what he had written."[186]

Tyndale chose to defend himself. The reasoning behind the decision is still up for debate. He requested all his theological material to prepare for his defense. Did he really need these to prepare? Or was the real motivation to continue working on the translation of the Old Testament to English? Both could be true.

In early 1536 official charges were presented and the accusers and Tyndale relayed their written defenses back and forth. The main topic was the discussion of salvation. Was salvation by faith through Christ alone? Or were indulgences an integral part of Christianity? What was Tyndale's response to the supremacy of the pope? His accusers were not interested in the answers to these questions, answers based on truth—the Word of God. They wanted written evidence that Tyndale's views were in opposition to the Roman Catholic establishment.

William Tyndale spent over a year and a half imprisoned in Vilford Castle. John Foxe, who wrote in *Foxe Book of Martyrs,* of Tyndale's time there, "Such was the power of his doctrine and the sincerity of his life, that during the time of his imprisonment . . . he converted his keeper, the keeper's daughter, and others of his household. Also the rest that were with Tyndale conversant in the castle, reported of him, that if he were not a good Christian man, they could not tell whom they might take to be one."[187]

In August 1536 those who had hunted Tyndale like ravaging wolves saw their years of labor come to a triumphant end. Tyndale was convicted of heresy, removed from the priesthood, and scheduled for execution.

William Tyndale was publicly executed in early October 1536. John Foxe reported that Tyndale cried "at the stake with a fervent zeal, and a loud voice, 'Lord! Open the king of England's eyes.'"[188]

The Lord answered Tyndale's final prayer within a year of his death. King Henry granted licenses to John "Thomas Matthew" Rogers and Myles Coverdale for complete English translations of the Bible to be printed and distributed in England. The King's objection had been to Tyndale and his failure to yield to the king's dictates. King Henry achieved his end. Tyndale was dead; King Henry remained in control of the Bible, and received credit for giving the people God's Word in their own language.

The Matthew Bible was all of Tyndale's New Testament and the Old Testament portion (fifteen of the thirty-nine books) Tyndale had completed. The Coverdale Bible relied on translating from the Latin (Vulgate) and Martin Luther's German Translation. By 1538 the king demanded that a copy of the English Bible be placed in every church so the public could have access to read God's Word in his or her own language. William Tyndale's life's call was finally accomplished.

The spiritual war was not over for the reformers, in many respects it had just begun. Listed below are other English reformers or colleagues of Tyndale's at Cambridge who suffered persecution and tribulations.

❖ Poyntz, who had sustained Tyndale, was put under house arrest for heresy because of the testimony of Henry Phillips. He escaped and lived the remainder of his life in poverty. His wife and children refused to join him and kept all of his financial investments.

❖ John "Thomas Matthew" Rogers was burned at the stake in 1555 for denying key tenets of the Church of Rome. (The very man who was granted a license from the king to complete the translation of Tyndale's English Bible.)

❖ Hugh Latimer and Nicholas Ridley were burned at the stake on the same day in 1555 by order of Queen Mary for preaching that the death of Christ was the only sacrifice needed to satisfy forgiveness of sin.

"In 2005 Americans purchased some twenty-five million Bibles. . . .The amount spent annually on Bibles has been put at more than half a billion dollars. Research has found ninety-one per cent of American households own at least one Bible—the average household owns four."[189] Of course there are many different translations today, but the marrow or essence of each translation stems from Tyndale's original work. If you have ever read an English Bible you owe a debt to him you can never repay.

## Questions to Ponder

❖ How has William Tyndale's sacrifice made you rethink the value of your English language Bible?

❖ How has the testimony of Tyndale's life impacted you?

❖ How has his life transformed your thinking?

Before we close, read these Scriptures that teach us what the Bible says about the Lord's martyrs.

1.  Read **Hebrews 11:32-38**.

    a.  How were believers martyred in biblical times?


    b.  What was said about these men and women in **Hebrews 11:38**?



2.  Read **Philippians 2:14-18**.

    a.  What was Paul's exhortation (v. 14)? Why?


    b.  How was the generation described?


    c.  What was the job of Paul's readers despite the evil around? Why?


    d.  How did Paul describe his life (v. 17)?


    e.  What did Paul tell believers to do even if his life was poured out as a drink offering?


3.  Read **2 Timothy 4:1-8**.

    a.  How did Paul tell Timothy to behave despite Timothy's possible audience?
        *   
        *   
        *   
        *   
        *   
        *   
        *   
        *   
        *   
        *

b. How did Paul describe his life?

❖

❖

❖

❖

❖

c. What would be the result of Paul's perseverance?

d. What was Paul's exhortation for one who fought the good fight as he did?

4. Reread the text in the above questions and insert your own name where appropriate to personalize Paul's message to Timothy.

In about AD 64 Paul wrote this final letter to Timothy, just before the Roman government beheaded him. Paul was a Roman citizen, and the laws forbid him to be crucified as Christ had been, therefore he was beheaded.

5. Read **Revelation 6:9-11**.

a. Why were these souls under the altar?

b. What was their question?

c. What were they given?

d. What was the answer to the martyr's question?

Today (August 2014) the Islamic State in Iraq and Syria (ISIS) militants are slaughtering untold numbers of men, women, and children. Why? They are martyred because they believe Jesus is the Christ, the Son of the Living God who died for the sins of the world, including the sins of the ISIS militants. Martyrdom is not an issue only relevant in biblical times. It is not an issue only relevant in the 1500s. Martyrdom is an issue very relevant today!

You may never have considered what you would do if you were told to recant your faith or die. The time to ponder such a question is not as it is happening. The time is now. The reality is that most of us will never come close to living the persecuted life of these men and women who gave their lives for Christ's sake. Yet we still need to prayerfully contemplate such a reality.

6.   Finally, we need to have peace in knowing the words of Jesus in **Matthew 10:19-20**. Write them below.

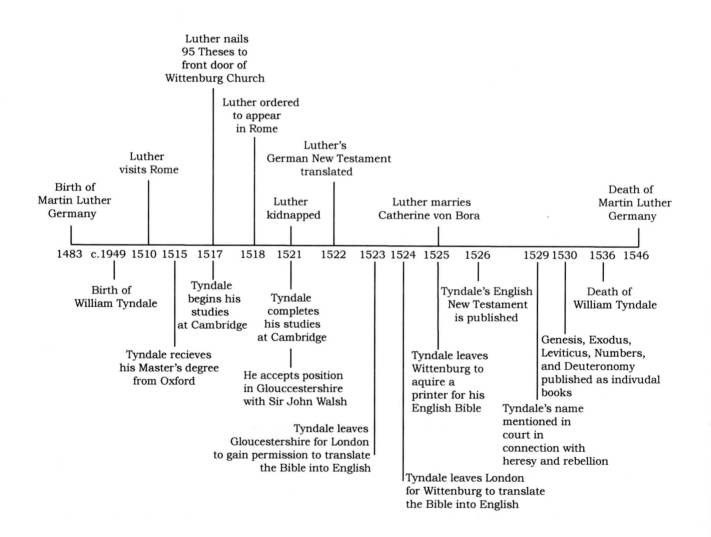

7. Looking at the chart:

   ❖ What have you learned about how God works in and through people's lives?

   ❖ What have you learned about how God works in and through a time period in history?

I strongly encourage you to read a biography on William Tyndale. Listed below are a few you might like.

   ❖ *William Tyndale: Bible Translator and Martyr* by Bruce and Becky Durost Fish.

   ❖ *William Tyndale: A Biography* by David Daniell

   ❖ *Tyndale: The Man Who Gave Us the English Voice* by David Teems

Let's close today with our application questions and prayer.

8. What have you learned today to apply to your life? Your church? Your nation?

9. Close with prayer. Ask the Lord to give you wisdom and understanding about the challenging subject we've studied. Ask Him to equip you for the difficult days in your life.

*"But whenever they persecute you in one city, flee to the next; for truly I say to you, you will not finish going through the cities of Israel until the Son of Man comes."*
***Matthew 10:23***

# WEEK 8—DAY 5

We've had quite an adventure these past weeks. I am both sad and excited to come to the final day of study. You have persevered and been found faithful! This is something to get excited about, yet knowing we have so little time left together is something I don't care to think about, quite frankly.

We have learned belief in Jesus Christ for salvation was the driving force behind the first-century church and should also empower us today. This belief led Peter and John to proclaim to the Sanhedrin, "For we cannot stop speaking about what we have seen and heard" (**Acts 4:20**). We've studied Martin Luther, William Tyndale and William Bradford, men whose belief in Christ impacted their generation and still impact us today. We read how the Maccabees couldn't stand by and allow evil to infiltrate God's people. We've seen the importance of prayer for ourselves and for our lost generation who need us to shine the light of Jesus for their healing. We looked at the need to be bold and humble. We've seen if we want our nation to be impacted for Christ, change begins in our own lives. We've learned the importance of loving the unlovable and have been challenged to never compromise our faith. What immeasurable insight we have gained from God's Word over the last eight weeks.

As always, before we begin today, let us start with prayer. Just as we want the Lord to incline His ears to our prayers, we need to have ears to hear what He says to us. Pray for the Lord to open your ears to His voice and for the willingness to obey.

We've been studying how the Great Awakening influenced the foundation of America. Only a few men changed the course of our lives by setting into motion the American Revolution, and these events are still sending aftershocks into the world today. *Merriam-Webster's Dictionary* defines revolution as, "a fundamental change in political organization; especially: the overthrow or renunciation of one government or ruler and the substitution of another by the governed."[190]

Last week we began looking at the fundamental change our Founding Fathers wanted. David Barton, founder of Wallbuilders, reminds us, "Fifty-six men with no army, no navy, and no military, pledged their lives, their fortunes, and their scared honor to defeat the world's greatest power."[191] Let's review the principles we studied last week from Thomas S. Kidd's book *God of Liberty: A Religious History of the American Revolution.*

> **Principle One:** *The necessity to disestablishment of the state churches.*
>
> **Principle Two:** *God is the creator and guarantor of fundamental human rights.*
>
> **Principle Three:** *Human sinfulness posed a threat to the polity (society).*
>
> **Principle Four:** *A republic would be sustained by virtue.*
>
> **Principle Five:** *The belief that God—or Providence, as deists and others might prefer to deem it—moved in and through nations.*

But wait! What about the issue of excess taxes? Didn't this contribute to the American Revolution? Absolutely, but the colonists' resistance to excess taxes stemmed from their biblical foundation; one could not be separated from the other. Let's look at the Stamp Act as an example of this truth. By 1765, the colonies were entangled in a dispute over the Stamp Act, Parliament's effort to generate more tax revenue from the colonists. Twenty-nine-year-old John Adams was thrust into the limelight when he

> "insisted that the colonists should not be taxed by Parliament because they were not represented there . . . . Adams wrote [in the 'Braintree Instructions'] that the people of Massachusetts should allow "the most clear and explicit assertion and vindication of our rights and liberties to be entered on the public records, we have a clear knowledge and a just sense of them, and, with submission to Divine Providence, that we never can be slaves" . . . Adams warned Americans that the threat posed by British power and its minions was not simply political. It was also religious. In *A Dissertation on the Canon and Feudal Law* (1765) he told colonists that the Stamp Act revealed a conspiracy within the British government to destroy the colonists' precious liberties. . . . He anticipated the British would use not only the power of taxation but the might of the Anglican Church [the Church of England] to subdue the colonists. Such an assertion spoke to the very core of the motives that had led so many of his fellow Americans to the shores of this continent. . . . Adams's estimation of the value of human liberty was explicitly theological: 'Liberty must at all hazards be supported,' he avowed, because all people had 'a right to it, derived from our Maker.'"[192]

Because of continual issues like the Stamp Act, our Founding Fathers felt there was no other choice but to take up arms. Therefore, on July 6, 1775, representatives from the United Colonies of North America met in Philadelphia to discuss the compelling reasons and necessity to revolt against Great Britain. John Dickinson and Thomas Jefferson wrote, in the *"Declaration of the Causes And Necessity of Taking Up Arms"*:

> "If it was possible for men, who exercise their reason to believe, that the divine Author of our existence intended a part of the human race to hold an absolute property in, and an unbounded power over others, marked out by His infinite goodness and wisdom, as the objects of a legal domination never rightfully resistible, however severe and oppressive, the inhabitants of these colonies might at least require from the parliament of Great-Britain some evidence, that this dreadful authority over them, has been granted to that body. But a reverence for our Creator, principles of humanity, and the dictates of common sense, must convince all those who reflect upon the subject, that government was instituted to promote the welfare of mankind, and ought to be administered for the attainment of that end . . . With an humble confidence in the mercies of the supreme and impartial Judge and Ruler of the Universe, we most devoutly implore [H]is divine goodness to protect us happily through this great conflict, to dispose our adversaries to reconciliation on reasonable terms, and thereby to relieve the empire from the calamities of civil war."[193]

1. Before you answer the following questions, reread the above quotation, as it is written in an older style of English and is more difficult to comprehend.

    a. Who did John Dickinson and Thomas Jefferson cite as their authority to take up arms for a civil war against Great Britain?

    b. What was their complaint against Great Britain?

    c. How was God described throughout this document?

    d. For what did they believe government was instituted?

Ralph Waldo Emerson penned the famous phrase, "the shot heard round the world" in a poem. He forever memorialized the beginning battles of the American Revolution. The American colonial militias, a band of 500 men, were outnumbered, but the American War for Independence was now in full swing.

Do John Dickinson and Thomas Jefferson's thoughts line up with God's Word? Let's take a look.

2. Read **Philippians 2:3-5.**

    a. What are we not to do?

    b. Whose interest are we to look after?

       ❖

       ❖

    c.  Whose attitude are believers to emulate?

3.  Read **Galatians 3:28**.

What does this Scripture teach us about what our Lord thinks about people?

4.  Read **Acts 10:34-35**.

    a.  What do we learn about God in Acts 10:34?

    b.  What happens to the man who fears the Lord?

5.  Write out **Acts 17:26**.

Most of you have heard the expression "the elephant in the room." Well, this is what we are going to talk about, the invisible elephant some of you have been thinking about—slavery. How could Thomas Jefferson, who wrote the equality statement of the 18ᵗʰ century, believe this statement if he himself owned slaves?

> "The gap between Jefferson's beliefs and his behavior is indicative of the struggle of the revolutionary Americans to grasp new implications of what they saw as an ancient truth: the common creation of mankind by God. This assertion of this truth became the heart of the case for American independence and for human equality in the newly established nation. But the application of the principle of equality by creation faced tremendous obstacles erected by traditional belief in inequality, monarchy, and slavery. It would take decades—even centuries—for the nations to live up to 'the proposition that all men are created equal,' as Abraham Lincoln put it in the Gettysburg Address. America's Civil War president was speaking at a battlefield cemetery that memorialized how bloody the struggle over equality had become. How could it have been easy for the revolutionary generation, or its descendants, to sort out the meaning of equality, by creation, when a slaveholder proposed it?"[194]

**Acts 17:26**, "He made from one man every nation of mankind to live on all the face of the earth, having determined their appointed times and the boundaries of their habitation" is one verse that was often cited to demonstrate God established equality at creation and was used by Christians to refute slavery. Many "radicals" of the Great Awakening not only believed but also lived out their faith that "all men are created equal." They demonstrated this belief by agreeing that the poor, the uneducated, women, African Americans, and Native Americans would have prominent roles in God's awakening movement across America. The battle for equality for all was a spiritual battle ignited in America during the Great Awakening and lasted over 200 years. God's plan was for all humanity to be treated as the special creation He designed. In His sovereign plan, God chose to use imperfect, sinful man to bring about His desired result. We can choose to point fingers and be disgusted by slavery or we can choose to be like Jesus. **"But when they persisted in asking Him, He straightened up, and said to them, 'He who is without sin among you, let him be the first to throw a stone at her' . . . Straightening up, Jesus said to her, 'Woman, where are they? Did no one condemn you?' She said, 'No one, Lord.' And Jesus said, 'I do not condemn you, either. Go. From now on sin no more'" (John 8:7, 10-11)**.

One thing we can trust is God placed these leaders in their position for that very time. Throughout history God has placed and removed leaders. Time does not allow us to travel through the Bible to study every instance where He created circumstances for one nation to overcome another. Yet, let's look at what God's Word says about His sovereignty over kings and nations.

6. Read **Daniel 2:19-21**. This is Daniel's prayer to the Lord after God revealed the interpretation of Nebuchadnezzar's dream. What did Daniel say about God in reference to kings?

In **Daniel 5**, Daniel was asked to interpret for King Nebuchadnezzar's grandson, Belshazzar. King Nebuchadnezzar had died and Belshazzar had taken the throne of Babylon. Belshazzar was having a great party with many guests when suddenly the "finger of God" began to write on the wall. The words inscribed were, "MENĒ, MENĒ, TEKĒL, UPHARSIN." Belshazzar called upon Daniel to decipher the code. The message from God was clear. Daniel spoke the words to Belshazzar that God had numbered the days of his kingdom and they had come to an end. God had weighed his kingdom and found him to be deficient; therefore, the Lord would divide his kingdom and hand it over to the Medes and the Persians. **(Daniel 5:17-28)**

7. Read **Daniel 5:30-31**.

   What does this tell you about God?

Review what we have learned from Philippians, Acts, Galatians, and Daniel. Think about the reasons John Dickinson and Thomas Jefferson cited for taking up arms and starting the American Revolution. They stated that the British were dominating and oppressing the Colonies without regard for the people, acting outside the boundaries of God's design of government.

8. Did Dickinson and Jefferson believe they were acting in accordance with the will of God?

   Would you agree with them? Why or why not?

Just one short year later after the "Declaration of the Causes And Necessity of Taking Up Arms," all delegates of the thirteen colonies were *unanimous* in their support and signed the Declaration of Independence on July 4, 1776. Our country's Fathers again gave credence to God, our creator, as the reason to form the United States of America. Read the introduction to this famous document.

> "When in the Course of human events it becomes necessary for one people to dissolve the political bands which have connected them with another and to assume among the powers of the earth, the separate and equal station to which the Laws of Nature and of Nature's God entitle them, a decent respect to the opinions of mankind requires that they should declare the causes which impel them to the separation.
>
> We hold these truths to be self-evident, that all men are created equal, that they are endowed by their Creator with certain unalienable Rights, that among these are Life, Liberty and the pursuit of Happiness".

9. What event did our Founding Fathers find necessary?
   - ❖
   - ❖

   a. What did the Founding Fathers believe gave them the power to dissolve the political bands?
      - ❖
      - ❖

   b. What did the writers of the Declaration believe?
      - ❖
      - ❖

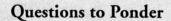

---

**Questions to Ponder**

Are you better equipped to answer the question, "Was America founded on Judeo-Christian values?" Explain.

---

10. Based on what you have studied today, do you believe the actions of our Founding Fathers were based on the compelling belief in their creator, Jesus Christ? Why or Why not?

We have just touched the surface with studying the Great Awakening and the American Revolution. Listed are some historical resources to help you continue as you continue to equip yourself.

   ❖ www.wallbuilders.com—Founded by David Barton in Aledo, Texas. David has spent most of his adult life researching and writing about America's godly heritage. He is a wealth of information.
   ❖ *God of Liberty: A Religious History of the American Revolution* by Thomas S. Kidd
   ❖ *The Founders' Bible* by David Barton

11. What has our Lord shown you today? Write what you gleaned from today's lesson to apply:

12. Write your closing prayer to Him. Thank Him for being a God who is not partial, and who has our best interests in mind. Never forget to ask Him what action you need to take in light of what you learn.

Please don't forget to e-mail or call us at info@wogt.org, (469) 854-3574 and (800) 257-1626. We value your comments and thoughts on *ACTs420NOW* or how any *Words of Grace & Truth* material has impacted your life.

*"You know of Jesus of Nazareth, how God anointed Him with the Holy Spirit and with power, and how He went about doing good, and healing all who were oppressed by the devil; for God was with Him."*
**Acts 10:38**

# ENDNOTES
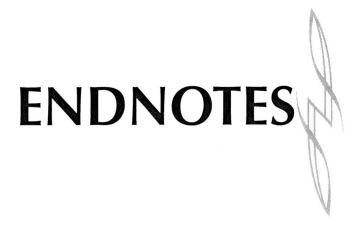

## Introduction

1.  Howard Hendricks, *Teaching to Change Lives: Seven Proven Ways to Make Your Teaching Come Alive* (Colorado Springs: Multnomah Books), 47.

## Week 1

2.  Spiros Zodhiates, *Warren Baker, ed., The Complete Word Study Dictionary: Old Testament* (Chattanooga: AMG Publishers, 1994), 2336.
3.  W.A. Criswell, *The Believer's Bible Study* (Nashville: Thomas Nelson), 1339.
4.  Spiros Zodhiates, *Warren Baker , ed., The Complete Word Study Dictionary: New Testament* (Chattanooga: AMG Publishers, 1993) 907.
5.  Zodhiates, Spiros. *The Complete Word Study Dictionary: New Testament.* Ed. by Warren Baker D.R.E. Chattanooga: AMG Publishers, 1992, Rev. ed. 1993, Ibid., 935.
6.  Charles C. Ryrie, *The Ryrie New American Standard Study Bible, new ed.* (Chicago: Moody Publishers, 1978), 1781.
7.  Merriam-Webster.com, s.v. "Pilgrim," http://www.merriam-webster.com/dictionary/pilgrim.
8.  *Monumental: In Search for America's National Treasure*, DVD, dir. Duane Barnhart (Pyro Pictures, 2012).
9.  Divine Right of Kings. Princeton University. Princeton.edu. Princeton University, s.v. "divine right of kings," www.princeton.edu/~achaney/tmve/wiki100k/docs/Divine_Right_of_Kings.html.

## Week 2

10. The Barna Group, "A Biblical Worldview Has a Radical Effect on a Person's Life," Dec. 1, 2003, http://www.barna.org.
11. Zodhiates, *The Complete Word Study Dictrionary: New Testament*, 485-486.
12. Associated Press, "Americans: My Faith Isn't the Only Way to Heaven, June 24, 2008, foxnews.com, August 31, 2012, http://foxnews.com/story/0,2933,370588,00.html.
13. D.R.W. Wood and I.H. Marshall, New Bible Dictionary, 3rd ed. (Leicester, England, Downer's Grove, ILL.: InterVarsity Press, 1996) 1060.

14. Voice of the Martyrs, "About Our Founders," March 7, 2013, persecution.com, http.//www .persecution. com/public/ourfounders.aspx?clickfrom=c2lkZWJhcg%3D%3D. March 7, 2013.

15. Dmitri Dudko, "About Our Hope" ("O Nashem Upovanti, Russian) (Paris: YMCA Press, 1975), 51.

16. Richard Wurmbrand, *Marx and Satan* (Bartlesville, OK: Living Sacrifice Book Co.) 77, 107-108.

17. Spiros Zodhiates, *The Complete Word Study Dictionary*: New Testament, 1124.

18. Ibid., 75.

19. Ibid., 756.

20. Ibid., 624.

21. Richard Wurmbrand, *Tortured for Christ* (Bartlesville, OK: Living Sacrifice Book Co.), 39-40.

22. Zodhiates, 959-960.

23. Ibid., 66-67.

24. Merriam-Webster.com, s.v. "Propitiate," www.merriam-webster.com/dictionary/propitiate.

25. Zodhiates, 769-771.

26. W.E. Vine, *Vine's Expository Dictionary* of Old and New Testament Words (Nashville: Thomas Nelson, Inc., 1997), 108.

27. Precept Ministries, *The International Inductive Study Bible* (Eugene: Harvest House Publishers, 1993), 1427.

28. Dallas Theological Seminary Faculty, J.F. Walvoord and R.B. Zuck, eds., *The Bible Knowledge Commentary: An Exposition of the Scriptures* (Old Testament) (Wheaton, IL: Victor Books, 1983), Dan. 11:33-35.

29. About.com, s.v. "Martin Luther," "Christianity," March 22, 2012, http.//christianity.about.com/od/ lutherandenomination/a/martinlutherbio_2.htm.

30. Edwin P. Booth, *Martin Luther* (Uhrichsville, OH: Barbour Publishing, Inc.), 26.

31. Ibid., 65.

32. Ibid., 61.

33. Ibid., 77.

34. Internet Christian Library, s.v. "Luther," iclnet.org, http://www.iclnet.org/pub/resources/text/wittenberg/ luther/web/ninetyfive.html.

35. Gary D. Schmidt, *William Bradford: Plymouth's Faithful Pilgrim* (Grand Rapids: Eerdmans Books for Young Readers, Wm. B. Eerdmans Publishing Co., 1999), 4-7.

36. Ibid,. 7.

37. Ibid.

38. Ibid., 8-9.

39. Ibid., 12.

40. Kay Kizer, University of Notre Dame du Lac, accessed Dec. 15, 2012, http://nd.edu/~rbarger/www7/ puritans.html.

41. Gary D. Schmidt, *William Bradford: Plymouth's Faithful Pilgrim*, 21.

42. Ibid., 26.

43. Ibid., 36.

## Week 3

44. Craig Parshall, "National Religious Broadcasters to Propose Solution to New Media," National Religious Broadcasters, Sep. 28, 2012, http://nrb.org/news_room/press_center/national-religious-broadcasters-to-propose-solution-to-new-media/.

45. Charles C. Ryrie, *The Ryrie New American Standard Study Bible*, 799.

46. John Foxe, *Foxe: Voices of the Martyrs* (Alachua, FL: Bridge-Logos, 2007), 43.

47. Edwin P. Booth, *Martin Luther: The Great Reformer*, 86.

48. University of Missouri, Kansas City, School of Law, s.v. "Martin Luther trial," Dec. 21, 2012, http://law2.umkc.edu/faculty/projects/ftrials/luther/lutherindulgences.html.

49. Ibid.

50. Ibid., quoting Roland H. Bainton, *Here I Stand: A Life of Martin Luther* (Peabody, MA: Hendrickson Publishers Marketing, LLC), 60-61.

51. Edwin P. Booth, *Martin Luther: The Great Reformer*, 86.

52. BrainyQuote.com, s.v. "Martin Luther," http://www.brainyquote.com/quotes/authors/m/martin_luther.html.

53. Edwin P. Booth, *Martin Luther: The Great Reformer*, 126.

54. Philip Schaff, *History of the Christian Church* (New York: Charles Scribner's Sons, 1910), 5.

55. Gary D. Schmidt, *William Bradford: Plymouth's Faithful Pilgrim*, 30.

56. *Monumental: In Search for America's National Treasure*, DVD.

57. Gary D. Schmidt, *William Bradford: Plymouth's Faithful Pilgrim*, 31.

58. Ibid., 31-33.

59. Ibid., 35.

60. Ibid., 36-39.

61. Ibid., 40-41.

62. A. Knowles, *The Bible Guide* (Minneapolis: Augsburg, 2001), 446.

63. A. Judge, *"Nero,"* in *New Bible Dictionary,* D.R. Wood, I.H. Marshall, A.R. Millard, J.I. Packer & D.J. Wiseman, eds. (Leicester, England, Downer's Grove, IL: InterVarsity Press, 1996), 816.

64. *Monumental: In Search for America's National Treasure*, DVD.

## Week 4

65. Mark Ellis, "Three Christians Arrested by Dearborn, Michigan Police During Muslim Outreach," *The Persecution Times*, June 19, 2010, http://freerepublic.com/focus/f-news/2538820/posts.

66. Bob Unruh, "City Faces More Penalties for Arresting Christians," *World Net Daily*, Feb. 8. 2012, http://www.wnd.com/2012/02/city-faces-more-penalties-for-arresting-christians.

67. Ken Klukowski, "Pentagon Confirms Will Court Martial Soldiers Who Share Christian Faith," www.breitbart.com, May 1, 2013, http://www.breitbart.com/Big-Peace/2013/05/01/Breaking-Pentagon-Confirms-Will-Court-Martial-Soldiers-Who-Share-Christian-Faith.

68. Morgan Lee, "So Help Me God Now Optional in US Air Force Academy Oath," Christianpost.com, Oct. 26, 2013, http://www.christianpost.com/news/so-help-me-god-now-optional-in-us-air-force-academy-oath-107506/

69. Zaimov Stoyan, "ACLJ Challenges 'Anti-Christian Crusade' Removing References to God in US Military," Christianpost.com, Oct. 28. 2013, http://www.christianpost.com/news/aclj-challenges-anti-christian-crusade-removing-references-to-god-in-us-military-107630/

70. W.E. Vine, *Vine's Expository Dictionary of Old and New Testament Words*, 108.

71. Spiros Zodhiates, *The Complete Word Study Dictionary: New Testament*, 925.

72. Ibid.

73. Ibid., 916

74. David Daniell, *William Tyndale: A Biography (New Haven, London: Yale University Press, 1994), 9.*

75. David Teems, *Tyndale: The Man Who Gave God an English Voice* (Nashville: Thomas Nelson), xxii.

76. David Daniell, *Willaim Tyndale: A Biography*, 3.

77. David Teems, *Tyndale: The Man Who Gave God an English Voice*, xxii.

78. Greatsite.com, s.v. "William Tyndale, English Bible History," http://www.greatsite.com/timeline-english-bible-history/william-tyndale.html.

79. *Encyclopaedia Judaica*, s.v. "cupbearer," Jewishvirtuallibrary.org, http://www.jewishvirtuallibrary.org/jsource/judaica/ejud_0002_0005_0_04762.html.

80. Bruce and Becky Durost Fish, *William Tyndale: Bible Translator and Martyr* (Uhrichsville: Barbour Publishing, Inc., 2000), 55-56.

81. Ibid., 31-32.

82. Biography.com, s.v. "King Henry VII," http://www.biography.com/people/henry-viii-9335322#catherine-of-aragon-and-princess-mary&awesm=~oBacFIqUx1bT7F

83. Gary D. Schmidt, *William Bradford: Plymouth's Faithful Pilgrim*, 43.

84. Ibid.

85. Ibid., 44.

86. Merriam-Webster.com, s.v. "Providence," http://www.merriam-webster.com/dictionary/providence.

87. William Bradford, *Of Plymouth Plantation* (Mineola: Dover Publications, Inc., 2006), 32.

88. Gary D. Schmidt, *William Bradford: Plymouth's Faithful Pilgrim*, 65.

89. Ancestry.com, s. v. "Upper Level Compact Study of the Mayflower Compact,"

90. Gary D. Schmidt, *William Bradford: Plymouth's Faithful Pilgrim*, 100.

91. Ibid., 182.

92. Ibid., 186.

## Week 5

93. R. Laird Harris, Gleason L. Archer Jr., Bruce K. Waltke, *Theological Workbook of the Old Testament* (Chicago: The Moody Bible Institute, 1981), 445.

94. Ibid.

95. Spiros Zodhiates and Warren Baker, *The Complete Word Study Old Testament: Hebrew and Chaldee Dictionary* (Chattanooga: AMG Publishers, 1994), 25.

96. Harris, Archer and Waltke, *Theological Workbook of the Old Testament*, 445.

97. Spiros Zodhiates and Warren Baker, *The Complete Word Study Old Testament*, 2355.

98. Ibid., 23.

99. Ibid., 2371.

100. Bruce and Becky Durost Fish, *Willaim Tyndale: Bible Translator and Martyr*, 48-49.

101. Ibid., 51.

102. Ibid., 51-54.

103. Ibid., 54.

104. Ibid., 55-59.

105. Ibid., 57.

106. Census.gov, s.v. "Colonial and Pre-Federal Statistics," http://www2.census.gov/prod2/statcomp/documents/CT1970p2-13.pdf.

107. Thomas S. Kidd, *The Great Awakening: A Brief History with Documents* (Boston: Bedford/St. Martin's, 2008), 4.

108. Richard Owen Roberts, *Revival* (Wheaton: Richard Owen Roberts Publishing, 1997), 19.

109. Jonathan Edwards, "A Faithful Narrative of the Surprising Work of God" (London: Dr. Watts and Dr. Guyse, publishers, 1737).

## Week 6

110. W.A. Criswell, *The Believer's Bible Study* (Nashville: Thomas Nelson, 1991), 1560.

111. Ibid., 929.

112. Harris, Archer, Waltke, *Theological Workbook of the Old Testament* (Chicago: The Moody Bible Institute, 1981), 857.

113. Spiros Zodhiates and Warren Baker, *The Complete Word Study: Old Testament*, 776.

114. Spiros Zodhiates, *The Complete Word Study Dictionary: New Testament*, 26.

115. Bruce and Becky Durost Fish, *William Tyndale: Bible Translator and Martyr*, 72.

116. Erik Stanley, "What is Pulpit Freedom Sunday All About?", Townhall.com, Sept. 14, 2011, http://townhall.com/columnists/erikstanley/2011/09/14/what_is_pulpit_freedom_sunday_all_about/page/full.

117. Bruce and Becky Fish, *William Tyndale: Bible Translator and Martyr*, 65-67.

118. Ibid., 68.

119. Ibid., 75-76.

120. Ibid., 76-78.

121. Ibid., 87.

122. Ibid., 94-95.

123. Ibid., 97-101.

124. Ibid., 102.

125. Thomas S. Kidd, *The Great Awakening: A Brief History with Documents*, 9.

126. Ibid., 60-63.

127. Ibid., 13.

128. Ibid., 13.

129. Ibid., 78.

130. Ibid., 20-21.

131. Ibid., 18-19.

## Week 7

132. Pew Research Center, "A Report on the Size and Distribution of the World's Christian Population," Pewforum.org, Dec. 19, 2011, http://www.pewforum.org/2011/12/19/global-christianity-exec.

133. Open Doors, USA, s.v. "Persecution," opendoorsusa.org, Oct. 16, 2013, http://www.opendoorsusa.org/landing-pages/christian2/persecution/christian-persecution-a.html?utm_expid=3981988-15.EOUf-EpYQ-i7Q_5dCaskrw.1&gclid=CNH7-J7xm7oCFXBo7AodZ0wAiw&utm_referrer=http%3A%2F%2Fwww.

google.com%2Faclk%3Fsa%3Dl%26ai%3DCM6eYes1eUuHEIMmHyQHQxIHoCKv9hswGq9y MyHej7Z6cuwEIABACKAJQ-fGs3fj%26sig%3DAOD64_3Tt7XMVmUDTx9lyvOirlU5ZtTTE A%26rct%3Dj%26frm%3D1%26q%3Dhow%2Bmany%2Bchristians%2Bare%2Bpersecuted%2 Beach%2Byear%26ved%3D0CDMQ0Qw%26adurl%3Dhttp%3A%2F%2Fwww.opendoorsusa. org%2Flanding-pages%2Fchristian%2Fpersecution%2Fchristian-persecution-a.html.

134. Mary Fairchild, Christianity Today, "General Statistics and Facts of Christianity," about.com, Oct. 18, 2013, http://christianity.about.com/od/denominations/p/christiantoday.htm.

135. Steven Ger, *The Book of Acts: Witnesses to the World* (Chattanooga: AMG Publishers, 2005), 227-232.

136. Ibid., 229.

137. R. J. Utley, *Luke the Historian: The book of Acts, Study Guide Commentary Series*, vol. 3B (Marshall, TX: Bible Lessons International, 2003), 195.

138. Ibid., 196.

139. Spiros Zodhiates, *The Complete Word Study Dictionary: New Testament*, 73.

140. Spiros Zodhiates, *The Complete Word Study Dictionary: Old Testament*, 2311.

141. Spiros Zodhiates, *The Complete Word Study Dictionary: New Testament*, 2311.

142. R. J. Utley, *Luke the Historian: The Book of Acts*, 196.

143. Raymond Ibrahim, "Top Muslim Declares All Christians Infidels," Frontpage Magazine, Nov. 1, 2011, http://frontpagemag.com/2011/raymond-ibrahim/top-muslim-declares-all-christians-%E2%80%98infidels%E2%80%99/.

144. Spiros Zodhiates, *The Complete Word Study Dictionary: New Testament*, 66-67.

145. Ibid., 24.

146. Ibid., 921.

147. Ibid., 925.

148. Ibid., 905.

149. Ibid., 907.

150. Clausenbooks.com, s.v. "The Chronological History of the Bible—16th Century," rev. March 9, 2014, http: [add url].

151. Bruce and Becky Durost Fish, William Tyndale: Bible Translator and Martyr, 104-105.

152. Ibid., 110 -115.

153. Ibid., 131.

154. Ibid., 131-132.

155. Ibid., 135 -138.

156. Kevin Bennardo, "Uneasy Allies: British and Colonial Interaction During the French and Indian War," Earlyamerica.com, www.earlyamerica.com/review/2005_summer_fall/redcoats.html.

157. Ibid.

158. Loc.gov, s.v. "Religion as Cause of the Revolution," www.loc.gov/exhibits/religion/rel03.html#obj081.

159. Thomas S. Kidd, *God of Liberty: A Religious History of the American Revolution* (New York: Basic Books), 5-6.

160. Ibid., 6.

161. Ibid., 6.

162. Ibid., 7.

163. Ibid., 8.

164. Ibid., 8.

165. Oxforddictionaries.com, s.v. "Deism," http://www.oxforddictionaries.com/us/definition/english/specific.

166. Archives.gov, s.v. "Declaration of Independence," http://www.archives.gov/exhibits/charters/declaration_transcript.html.

167. Thomas S. Kidd, *God of Liberty: A Religious History of the American Revolution*, 7.

168. FoundingFatherquotes.com, s.v. "Samuel Adams," http://www.foundingfatherquotes.com/father/id/2#section=quotes.

169. FoundingFatherquotes.com, s.v. "George Washington," http://www.foundingfatherquotes.com/father/id/5/s/15#section=quotes.

## Week 8

170. John Foxe, *Foxe: Voices of the Martyrs* (Alachua, FL: Bridge-Logos, 2007), 314-315.

171. Ibid.

172. Seven Ger, *The Book of Acts: Witnesses to the World*, 96.

173. Ibid., 95-96.

174. John Foxe, *Foxe: Voices of the Martyrs*, 82.

175. Steven Ger, *The Book of Acts: Witnesses to the World*, 100.

176. Ibid., 101

177. Ibid., 103-104.

178. Spiros Zodhiates, *The Complete Word Study Dictionary: New Testament*, 896-897.

179. Steven Ger, *The Book of Acts: Witnesses to the World*, 105-106.

180. Spiros Zodhiates, *The Complete Word Study Dictionary: New Testament*, 2312.

181. John Foxe, *Foxe: Voices of the Martyrs*, 216-217.

182. Bruce and Becky Durost Fish, *William Tyndale: Bible Translator and Martyr*, 137.

183. Ibid., 153.

184. Ibid., 168.

185. Ibid., 172.

186. Ibid., 186.

187. Ibid., 194.

188. Ibid., 198.

189. Daniel Rodish, "The Good Book Business," *The New Yorker*, Dec. 18, 2006, http://www.newyorker.com/magazine/2006/12/18/the-good-book-business.

190. Merriam-Webster Dictionary, s.v. "Revolution," www.merriam-webster.com/dictionary/revolution.

191. David Barton, *The Spirit of the American Revolution*, mp3 (Aledo, TX: Wallbuilders, LLC.)

192. Ibid., 11-12.

193. Theamericanrevolution.org, "Declaration of the Causes and Necessity of Taking Up Arms," http://www.theamericanrevolution.org/DocumentDetail.aspx?document=19.

194. Thomas S. Kidd, *God of Liberty: A Religious History of the American Revolution*, 131-132.

# Contact Information

To order additional copies of this book, please visit
www.wogt.org or www.redemption-press.com
Also available on Amazon.com and BarnesandNoble.com
Or by calling Words of Grace & Truth at 1-800-257-1626
Or by calling toll free 1-844-2REDEEM.

CPSIA information can be obtained
at www.ICGtesting.com
Printed in the USA
FSOW02n0613301215
14885FS